26 April 2025

For Kevin Bigelman,

With great respect
and appreciation.

Robert F. Foley
Lieutenant General
U S Army Retired

"For a time and culture with values often confused if not chaotic, this lively autobiographical portrait of a true patriot strong in faith and family, is sure to inspire, reassure and encourage readers of every persuasion!"
—His Eminence Edwin Cardinal O'Brien, Grand Master, Equestrian Order of the Knights of the Holy Sepulchre.

"*Standing Tall* tells the extraordinary life story of an American hero, Lieutenant General Robert Foley. In this memoir, General Foley shares how he became a warrior, from his time as a new cadet to his experience commanding men in combat. Written by one of the few Americans in history to receive our nation's highest military honor, this book contains battle-tested truths about what it takes to be a leader."
—Senator Tom Cotton, US Senator for Arkansas and author of *Sacred Duty: A Soldier's Tour at Arlington National Cemetery.*

"Beautifully written. A concise, entertaining and poignant memoir from a true American hero."
—Jeff Shaara, author of *Gone for Soldiers: A Novel of the Mexican War* and recipient of the 2017 Medal of Honor Foundation Bob Hope award for Excellence in Entertainment.

"Lieutenant General (R) Bob Foley's story is about how humility made him one of the most popular and effective leaders in the Army—truly a rare combination."
—General Dennis J. Reimer, US Army Retired, former Army Chief of Staff, Chairman of the Board for American Armed Forces Mutual Aid Association.

"Bob Foley presents a compelling narrative of a Soldier's life that transcends the test of time."
—General Robert W. RisCassi, US Army Retired, former Army Vice Chief of Staff.

"*Standing Tall* is an excellent memoir by an outstanding soldier and leader. A must read for all who are committed to the defense of the nation."
—General George Joulwan, US Army Retired, former Supreme Allied Commander Europe and author of *Watchman at the Gates: A Soldier's Journey from Berlin to Bosnia.*

"*Standing Tall* is a terrific book following a true American hero's journey during a stellar career in the U.S. Army. Lieutenant General (Retired) Bob Foley has written a must read for anyone interested in learning leadership lessons during the toughest situations imaginable."
—General Robert B. Brown, US Army Retired, former Commanding General, US Army Pacific, President & Chief Executive Officer, Association of the US Army.

"General Foley's book presents a marvelous description of character-focused leadership, of both its development and practice during a full career of service to our country. The story is superbly told in succinct, clear, and memorable prose."
—Lieutenant General Dave R. Palmer, US Army Retired, former Superintendent of the US Military Academy and author of *George Washington and Benedict Arnold: A Tale of Two Patriots*

"One of America's most heroic soldiers, General Robert Foley has written a practical guide to values-based leadership woven from the rich tapestry of his exemplary life of selfless service and battlefield courage. This is one of the finest contemporary reads available on a life of duty, honor, and country."
—Lieutenant General David H. Huntoon, US Army Retired, former Superintendent of the US Military Academy and Commandant of the Army War College.

"Bob Foley has been Standing Tall his entire life. I was privileged to serve alongside him and saw his devotion to Nation and Soldiers firsthand. A Warrior, a gentleman, a friend. This book chronicles it all-a must read."
—Lieutenant General Keith Kellogg, US Army Retired, former National Security Advisor to President Trump and Vice President Pence; author of *War by Other Means: A General in the Trump White House.*

"Everybody benefits from having an idol. Bob Foley is mine. I have known him for more than half a century, and he never ceases to teach me things that I need to know. His intellect, his insight and—almost as important as anything else—his humor are all on full display in *Standing Tall*. This is fascinating and essential reading for everyone."
—Colonel Jack Jacobs, US Army Retired, Vietnam War Medal of Honor recipient and author of *If Not Now, When?*

"*Standing Tall* is an awesome and amazing story of a humble American war hero, who grew up in middle America, endured the discipline of a West Point education and amidst the harshness and challenges of Vietnam, exhibited the ultimate expression of leadership, when he personally assaulted enemy bunkers. A book to inspire young people, to uplift military and veterans and to motivate any reader to reflect a caring attitude to all."
—The Honorable Allen Clark, author of *Wounded Soldier, Healing Warrior: A Personal Story of a Vietnam Veteran who lost both legs but Found His Soul.*

# STANDING TALL

# STANDING TALL

Leadership Lessons in the Life of a Soldier

ROBERT F. FOLEY
Lieutenant General
U.S. Army Retired

CASEMATE
*Philadelphia & Oxford*

AN AUSA BOOK
Association of the United States Army
2425 Wilson Boulevard, Arlington, Virginia, 22201, USA

Published in the United States of America and Great Britain in 2022 by
CASEMATE PUBLISHERS
1950 Lawrence Road, Havertown, PA 19083, USA
and
The Old Music Hall, 106–108 Cowley Road, Oxford OX4 1JE, UK

Hardback Edition: ISBN 978-1-63624-224-8
Digital Edition: ISBN 978-1-63624-225-5

A CIP record for this book is available from the British Library

Printed and bound in the United States of America by Integrated Books International

Typeset in India by Lapiz Digital Services, Chennai.

For a complete list of Casemate titles, please contact:

CASEMATE PUBLISHERS (US)
Telephone (610) 853-9131
Fax (610) 853-9146
Email: casemate@casematepublishers.com
www.casematepublishers.com

CASEMATE PUBLISHERS (UK)
Telephone (01865) 241249
Email: casemate-uk@casematepublishers.co.uk
www.casematepublishers.co.uk

# Contents

# Author's Note

Before taking command of a mechanized infantry battalion in Germany, I sought advice from former Sergeant Major of the Army, Julius W. Gates when he was the command sergeant major of the 3rd Infantry Division. Among other things, he told me to "Be visible and be accessible"—guidance which has served me well throughout my military career.

Soldiers need to know they are valued and understood. They appreciate it when you join them for lunch in the dining facility at Schofield Barracks, sit in a muddy foxhole with them on a rainy night in Vietnam, run by their side on a misty early morning in Germany, or present them a coin while they are performing maintenance beneath a 5-ton bridge truck on a cold winter day in Korea.

They want to be part of a unit with *esprit de corps* and discipline. The history and nickname of an outfit linked together with strong leadership can generate an enduring spirit. I joined the 27th Infantry Regiment (Wolfhounds) as a second lieutenant in Hawaii, commanded Alpha Company, 2nd Battalion, 27th Infantry, as a captain in Vietnam, and served as the 27th Infantry honorary colonel in the grade of lieutenant general for 20 years.

I found listening to be a lost art. Everyone has thoughts and opinions valuable to the organization, but leaders need to carve out time, designate the proper venue, and place themselves in the receive mode. Conversely, leaders need to exhibit command presence by standing before their soldiers and speaking about organizational values and expectations. And it's essential to follow verbal guidance with written directives to ensure there is no misunderstanding of commander's intent.

The emphasis on effective military writing has also been lost over time. As Commanding General of Fifth Army in 1998, I had to rely on monthly email reports sent by commanders of 11 readiness groups strategically located in 22 states west of the Mississippi River. The first reports I received read like chat room conversations. At the next face-to-face meeting, I wasted no time imposing guidelines for clear, concise written communications and I provided each commander with a copy of *The Elements of Style* by William Strunk, Jr., and E. B. White.

In his book, *The Founding Fathers on Leadership*, Donald T. Phillips declared that "The mark of great leaders, whether they're founding a nation or running a business, is that they have an ability to delegate and trust people." Micromanagement simply doesn't work.

When he was the Army chief of staff in 1985, General John A. Wickham, Jr. authored a pamphlet entitled *Guideposts for a Proud and Ready Army*. In it, he stated that, "the strength of character, in our personal and professional lives, which we and our country seek in time of war must be fostered in times of peace." The courage and determination to fight and win our nation's wars will not automatically show up on the battlefield. Institutional values must be continually integrated into the unit ethos by the officer and NCO team at each level of command, from platoon leader and platoon sergeant to Army chief of staff and sergeant major of the Army.

The most dangerous threat in combat is not the enemy—it's complacency. Stop everything when you hear the terms "routine mission" or "all is going well." Continuous threat analysis is vital. A patrol that leaves at the same time at night, using the same path, and returns on the same route at the same time subjects the patrol and the parent unit to the risk of ambush and infiltration. The same is true for commercial enterprises that are competing in the marketplace every day—embracing new ideas and securing proprietary technology is key to corporate longevity.

Aristotle said that character is a habit—the daily choice of right over wrong. Values-based decision-making is vital, yet becomes more difficult with greater responsibilities involving more complex issues. Nonetheless, it remains a straightforward process which begins with recognizing the existence of a dilemma followed by determining appropriate courses of action and possessing the moral courage to do the right thing.

I regret that many of the leadership challenges I faced were not dealt with in the right way, but I learned from my mistakes and have concluded that nothing is perfect, life's not fair, and there is nothing to be gained by worrying about things over which you have no control. I have concentrated, instead, on being strong in faith and active in good works.

And for heaven's sake—lighten up. Injecting a sense of humor into everyday events has a way of striking the right balance in maintaining a positive command climate. There are stressful times in the profession of arms but plenty of humorous situations occur. Leverage those amusing times to create a relaxed but productive atmosphere.

CHAPTER I

# Early Years

I entered this world on May 30, 1941, at Newton-Wellesley Hospital with all the clamor of a newborn baby. Adding to the excitement, a nurse in the delivery room took one look at the size of my feet and declared I was going to be a Boston police officer—a flatfoot. According to my mother, my feet increased one size every year beginning at age eight. Fortunately, after I turned 17, my shoe size remained at 16.

Blessed with loving parents, William Frederick Foley and Mildred Jesse (McCabe) Foley, I had a happy childhood. We lived in the downstairs unit of a two-family duplex located in Auburndale, Massachusetts, a small residential community 20 miles west of Boston. My brother Bill, nine years older than me, has been my lifelong mentor and confidante. We shared bunk beds in a tiny bedroom furnished with a cedarwood chest and a small closet crammed with all our clothes.

My father was the family breadwinner—an honest, hardworking, well-respected gentleman who was liked by everyone. He left high school in the 10th grade to work at a soda fountain in Boston. This entailed a 10-minute walk to downtown Auburndale and a 40-minute train ride to the South Boston station. After a few years, he got a job at a James H. McManus restaurant closer to home, eventually became the manager, and later a traveling manager opening new restaurants in the greater Boston metropolitan area. My mother, brother, and I learned the meaning of the family business after Dad acquired the franchise for a McManus luncheonette in Belmont—a 30-minute drive from Auburndale. Beginning in the 5th grade, I walked to the corner of Ash Street and Commonwealth Avenue after school and took two buses and a streetcar to get to the restaurant. I washed dishes and ran errands until it was time to go home.

My mother was the family matriarch and central figure in the upbringing of my brother and me. One of four siblings whose father was a carpenter, Mom dropped out of school in the 9th grade to work as a seamstress. She wanted me to finish high school, learn a trade, and land a job like my father's or like that of the exhausted-looking, grease-covered gentleman who ambled across the street from his gas station every morning for a cup of coffee at Dad's luncheonette.

Growing up in Auburndale was a genuine Norman Rockwell experience. Summer was my favorite season. I rode my bike to the Charles River to go fishing, swam at the Riverside Recreation Center, and ran errands to the "little store" for milk, bread, and an occasional popsicle. I looked forward to celebrations like the Fourth of July costume parade on Newell Road and the Boston Marathon featuring Clarence DeMar, who won seven times, running his last marathon at age 65. I also enjoyed the Halloween goblin gauntlet in the Burr Elementary School basement and the Thanksgiving Newton-Waltham football game followed by a huge turkey dinner. The New England winters were long and cold, but I had fun building forts for snowball fights, playing hockey, and leaping for joy after hearing the no-school announcements. As part of my winter household chores, I got dressed early in the morning, descended the back stairs to the basement, placed old newspapers on a grill at the bottom of the furnace, shoveled in coal, and lit the newspapers. On trash day, I scooped the ashes into a sturdy metal bucket and lugged it out to the sidewalk.

In the 7th and 8th grades, I delivered the *Boston Globe*, the *Boston Herald Traveler*, and the *Christian Science Monitor* to homes in surrounding neighborhoods. On weekday afternoons, I rode my bike to the Auburndale train station, folded and organized the newspapers, placed them in a large canvas bag, and loaded the bag into the metal basket on my handlebars. Each paper had a special fold so I could tell the difference when flinging them to the customer's front porch as I rode by. If a fold came loose and the newspaper fell apart in flight, I put it together and carried it to the front door. For houses with a "Beware of the Dog" sign, I slowed down to ensure my aim was perfect. Although delivering the papers in good weather elicited a sense of accomplishment, slogging through the snow and slush during the winter was a different story. I don't remember how much I was paid, but I know my mother enjoyed receiving the cash in the envelope I gave her every week.

My life was not all work and no play. On lazy summer days, I drank ice-cold lemonade and played Monopoly with my friends for hours on the screened-in porch adjacent to our bedroom. In the evening, my father gathered the next-door neighbors in our backyard to follow the Boston Red Sox or Boston Braves baseball games on our Zenith radio. And I ran around capturing fireflies in a quart-size glass jar.

I loved Norumbega Park—a unique amusement area located within walking distance from our home. It covered 300 acres of woods, trails, and gardens with merry-go-round, caterpillar, and seaplane rides. It also had a penny arcade, canoes for rent, and booths for throwing baseballs or flipping small wooden hoops at stationary targets to win a prize. It had the largest zoo in New England, a ballroom adorned with totem poles, a theater, and a multi-tiered, artistic fountain. At night, we ate cotton candy, watched Charlie Chaplain silent movies, and sang songs by watching the bouncing ball as it hit the lyrics projected on a large outdoor screen.

My favorite pastime was exploring the bog—a marshy area where we caught frogs and turtles, collected cattails, and dug up worms when we went fishing in the Charles River. We liked to jump across the gaps between dirt stumps, daring one another to make it without falling in the water. At times, we were unsuccessful, which led to a quick trip home to change clothes. One summer day, Billy Denty and I decided to construct a fort on a piece of dry land. Using a small saw and a hatchet, we cut branches, put stakes in the ground, and rigged sides to the fort. I was continually wiping the sweat off my face and was horrified when I woke up the next morning and looked in the bathroom mirror. My face was red and swollen and my eyes and mouth were almost shut. When my mother saw me, she put her hands to her face and cried out, "Jesus, Mary, and Joseph." Our family doctor knew immediately that I had a severe case of poison sumac, which would take several weeks to clear up. Although I spread calamine lotion over the affected areas, my skin was sore and itchy. I drank Kool-Aid and soup through a straw for 10 days until the swelling went down. Complete recovery took all summer and left me with tiny scars on both sides of my face that were visible through my teenage years.

Hockey was my favorite sport—heavily influenced by my brother, who played as a defenseman on the Newton High School hockey team and by the Boston Bruins, one of the best teams in the National Hockey League. At the first sign of wintry weather, we grabbed our skates, sticks, and pads and raced down to Ware's Cove on the Charles River. When the ice was thick enough, the City of Newton Recreation Department built a rink with wooden sideboards on the ice and maintained a warming cabin with a large coal stove.

At Warren Junior High School in West Newton, I attended vocational school in the 7th and 8th grades. I took classes in woodworking, printing, and metal crafts in addition to basic math and English. The school was in a tough neighborhood. Fights between students using wooden rulers edged with sharp copper strips were not uncommon occurrences. I succumbed to this endemic culture by hanging out with boys wearing white T-shirts with sleeves rolled up to our shoulders, blue jeans, a black belt with a sharpened buckle, leather jackets, and boots. My parents worried that I might get arrested someday if they didn't get me out of that environment.

In the summer of 1955, we moved to Belmont. At the beginning of 9th grade, I knew that life would be different. I was enrolled in standard college preparatory classes. The students were friendly and the teachers helpful. The boys had crew cuts and concentrated on studies and sports. Conspicuous with my hair combed back like John Travolta in the movie *Grease*, I went straight to the barber shop on the first day of school and got a crew cut.

When I tried out for the junior high school hockey team, I wore my brother's size 12 skates, which did not accommodate my size 13 feet. On the day my mother and I went to buy new skates, we learned that size 13 and up had to be custom made at a cost of $200 ($1,800 today). My hockey days were over. Because I was the tallest lad in 9th grade, my friends encouraged me to play basketball. Coach Ruprecht selected me to be on the team, but the transition was humbling. I was the only one who shot layups with two hands.

One Saturday afternoon while shooting baskets with my friends, Billy Callahan and Paul Sullivan, they announced that it was time for confession. I quickly proclaimed that I had to go home. For years, I had been making excuses because I had never been to confession. But this time was different. I strode directly to the rectory at Our Lady of Mercy Catholic Church and rang the doorbell. When Monsignor Griffin invited me in, I explained that I had been baptized at Corpus Christi Church in Auburndale but had never received my First Holy Communion or Confirmation. He called my parents and with their approval, I was enrolled in Sunday School. At 6 foot 5 inches, I towered over the elementary school children in catechism class. But after receiving my First Holy Communion and Confirmation, I experienced great peace of mind and looked forward to confession every Saturday and receiving communion at Mass on Sunday.

In the summer after 9th grade, I shoveled out a dirt basketball court behind our house and received help from the landlord in erecting a hoop with a plywood backboard on the garage roof. It wasn't ideal but in good weather I shot baskets for hours without interruption and it paid off. I made the junior varsity (JV) basketball team as a sophomore. In the restaurant, I progressed from washing dishes to making sodas, sundaes, milkshakes, and ice-cream cones as well as cooking hamburgers, hot dogs, and waiting on customers. I normally put in three nights a week and worked all day Sunday.

In the summer between the 10th and 11th grades, I went to a YMCA Caddie Camp on Cape Cod run by Coach T. Meldon Wenner, the Belmont High School varsity basketball coach. I was surprised when my parents allowed me to be gone all summer, but Coach Wenner convinced them it would be a good experience for me. In addition, the caddie fees amounted to roughly $500 by the end of the summer. I caddied in the morning, practiced basketball in the afternoon, and played in games three nights a week. The summer experience was beyond helpful. As a junior, I became the starting center for the Belmont High basketball team.

In an article from the *Belmont Herald*, I was described as:

> Bobby "Stretch" Foley, 6'6". The surprise of the year, this fellow has been transformed from a fair JV player last year through one summer of hard work. Possessed with the equipment needed for real greatness, size, speed and a nice shooting touch, Bob has averaged over sixteen points a game in the league. In addition, he sweeps the boards every game and is tough to score against. His ability to dunk the ball has delighted the fans.[1]

We won the state championship my junior year and lost to Charlestown in the final game of the state championship in my senior year.

Recruited by 15 colleges, I made campus visits to the Citadel, Providence, and Holy Cross before Jack Riley, the West Point hockey coach, read an article in the *Boston Globe* about a state championship game in which I scored 44 points and collected 28 rebounds.[2]

He gave the newspaper clipping to George Hunter, the West Point head basketball coach, who invited my parents and me to visit the academy. I was not at all interested in a military school, but my father and mother wanted to see the campus because they

# FOLEY NETS 44

_March 2, 1959._

## Belmont Ace Sets Mark: Matignon, Durfee Win

### By ERNEST DALTON

Most of the 7,139 fans at the Garden last night were there to see the late evening Class A games of the Tech Tourney and missed a tremendous show put on by 6 ft. 7 in. Bob Foley of Belmont.

As Belmont beat Methuen, 76 to 64, in a B-quarterfinal, the hefty 17-year-old center scored 44 points—both a Class B and All Tech Tourney record—and bagged an amazing total of 23 rebounds.

He also helped Belmont set a new foul-point record, of 36, and equalled the individual foul shooting mark, 16 out of 20 from the line.

In the other B quarter final, Natick defeated Winthrop, 66 to 60, the third straight year it has beaten that team at Tech, and now meets Belmont for the third time—but this time in the semifinal round. The past two years, they met in the final, Natick winning in 1957, Belmont last year.

Newspaper clipping from the _Boston Globe_.

enjoyed watching the TV series _The West Point Story_ with Steve McQueen, Robert Vaughn, and Clint Eastwood. After we drove to West Point, I walked the grounds of this historic institution, had discussions with Coach Hunter and members of the Army basketball team, and met with All-American football players Pete Dawkins and Bob Anderson. I came away impressed with West Point's history, tradition, and institutional values. After returning home and reflecting on the last passage of Robert Frost's poem "The Road Not Taken," I was positive I wanted to be a cadet at the United States Military Academy.

> Two roads diverged in a wood, and I—
> I took the one less traveled by,
> And that has made all the difference.[3]

## CHAPTER 2

# New Cadet Barracks

The possibility of attending West Point was exciting. I did, however, harbor misgivings about my chances for admission. First, I did not have exceptional grades in high school. Second, I encountered a problem during the physical entrance exam. When I couldn't see any numbers or letters in the "hidden digit" eye charts, a test official pulled me out of line and led me to a back office. I sat at a desk and followed his instructions to arrange tiny balls of yarn according to the five primary colors. Although I did pass this modified test, I worried about the effect my colorblindness would have on getting accepted. Happily, two weeks later, I received a telegram confirming my appointment.

I reported to the academy in-processing station on Reception Day (R-Day) wearing summer civilian clothing and a comfortable pair of black leather shoes. I didn't ask many questions about induction into the United States Corps of Cadets, but I suspected that a six-week training program commonly referred to as "Beast Barracks" was not going to be recreational in nature. The objective, as stated in the Memorandum of Instruction issued by the Department of Tactics was, "To receive, process and equip new cadets; to train new cadets in basic military subjects; to instruct new cadets in the facets of cadet life and in the concepts of Duty and Honor."[1]

In his book *West Point Today*, first published in 1937, Kendall Banning said:

> Every new arrival, without discrimination, is dumped unceremoniously into the hopper of the West Point machine that four years later grinds him out as the finished product. Those four years are, without much doubt, the toughest four years to be found in any educational institution in the world. Tough not only in the academic requirements but more particularly in the uncompromising and unceasing discipline.[2]

On R-Day the upper class cadre taught us three practical responses—"Yes sir; no sir; and no excuse sir." They introduced us to bracing—pulling your chin into your neck as part of maintaining a straight posture. Bracing was required except in designated areas such as cadet rooms, the latrine, the athletic field, and the classroom, where we could "Fall out"—return to a more relaxed position. This plebe year convention remained in effect for one year from R-Day in July 1959 until recognition by upper class cadets at the graduation parade in June 1960.

The cadet cadre marched us to cadet supply several times during the first few days to pick up uniforms and military items including fatigues, socks, boots, shoes, belts, underwear, shower clogs, hats, rifle, and bayonet. Unfortunately, cadet supply did not have size 16 boots, shoes, running shoes, or shower clogs. This made each day extraordinarily more difficult for me due to the disparate footwear required for each activity, as indicated on the schedule for July 8—the second day of new cadet training.

> Reveille (0600) – T-shirt with shorts and sneakers.
> Breakfast (0630–0730) – Gray trousers, undershirt with dress shoes.
> Issue Point (0745–0835) – Army fatigues with combat boots.
> Dismounted Drill (0850–0940) – Army fatigues with combat boots.
> Issue Point and Mark Clothing (0955–1050) – Gray trousers with undershirt and dress shoes.
> Room Arrangement (1100–1150) – Gray trousers with undershirt and dress shoes.
> Lunch (1210–1245) – Army fatigues with dress shoes.
> Dismounted Drill (1320–1410) – Army fatigues and combat boots.
> Swim Test (1420–1515) – Gym Alpha (T-shirt) with swim trunks and sneakers.
> Swim Test (1530–1630) – Gym Alpha (T-shirt) with swim trunks and sneakers.
> Fire and Air Raid Drill (1700–1800) – Khaki shirt and trousers with dress shoes.
> Supper (1815–1850) – Khaki shirt and trousers with dress shoes.
> Chaplain's Orientation (1915–2030) – Khaki shirt with trousers and dress shoes.
> Shower and Foot Inspection (2030–2130) – Beach Robe and shower clogs with soap dish and towel.
> Taps/Lights out (2200)[3]

I had one pair of civilian dress shoes for all formations. After physical training in the morning, my classmates jumped out of their running gear and put on spit-shined dress shoes for breakfast formation while I spent every minute washing mud and grass off my civilian shoes. Despite my best efforts at cleaning and polishing, my shoes had no shine and revealed white stains from the sweat. The corrections made by upper class cadets as they walked up and down the ranks comparing my shoes with those of my classmates were painful. I can hear the echoes of cadre members screaming subtle encouragement like, "Mister, those are the grossest shoes I have ever seen. Get your neck in."

Fortunately, my squad leader, Cadet Corporal Bob Strauss, a member of the Army basketball team, placed the issue squarely in the hands of the cadet chain of command, which included the cadet platoon leader and cadet company commander. The problem went directly to the company tactical officer, who was a regular U.S. Army officer holding the rank of captain or major with six years or more of active-duty service. The company tactical officer's primary responsibility was to supervise the upper class cadre in training and caring for new cadets. When situations arose that the cadet chain of command was unable to resolve, company tactical officers were the link to obtaining assistance from appropriate academy officials, including taking issues directly to the commandant of cadets. My case was more complicated as it involved the Army supply system external to West Point. Three days after R-Day, I was told that a high-ranking officer would assess my predicament. The inspecting officer turned out to be Brigadier General John L. Throckmorton, the commandant of cadets. When he asked me why I was wearing civilian shoes while everyone else was in combat boots. I said, "Sir, because of the size of my feet, I have not yet been issued my full complement of footwear." Three days later, I went to cadet supply, where I picked up size 16 boots, dress shoes, running shoes, and extra-large shower clogs that were shipped to the academy on a priority basis from Fort Bragg, North Carolina. I had to manage this frustrating situation for seven interminable days but receiving my authorized footwear gave me a huge psychological lift. I am profoundly grateful to General Throckmorton for his prompt intervention.

During Beast Barracks, I had three excellent roommates—Gordon Arbogast, Charles "Buz" Rolfe, and John Oliver. Gordon came to the academy directly from high school in New York City. After graduating from West Point, he served in Vietnam, obtained a PhD in industrial management, retired as a full colonel with 27 years of service, and became a professor at Jacksonville University. Buz was commissioned in air defense artillery, served in Vietnam, and became president and CEO of a community bank in Dallas. John Oliver spent three years at Vanderbilt before receiving his appointment. I asked him why he chose to become a plebe at West Point when he was about to enter his senior year at Vanderbilt. He said, "Because I wanted to be a West Point graduate." John received a commission in air defense artillery, served in Vietnam, and held several corporate executive positions before retiring in Dallas.

We ate family style in the cadet mess hall, where the daily menu averaged 3,200 calories per cadet and was increased to 6,000 calories for intercollegiate athletes.[4] Prior to each meal, we stood in formation on the concrete apron in front of Washington Hall while the cadet cadre obtained accountability reports. After marching to the mess hall, we double-timed to assigned 10-person tables, stood at attention behind our chairs, and waited for the command "Take seats." We sat on the first 4 inches of our chairs, passed food around the table on metal trays, and remained at attention until given the command "Eat." Under the supervision of two cadre members at the table, we ate meals with military precision by taking the food from our plates with fork or spoon while looking straight ahead, raising it up to chin level and bringing the food directly into our mouths. The cadre found meals a convenient time to check our proficiency with the customs, traditions, chants, and songs we were required to memorize from our *Bugle Notes* handbook. Failure to repeat new cadet knowledge normally resulted in the command of "Sit up"—stop eating until given permission.

On Saturday afternoons, we were granted two hours of relaxation and a chance to visit the "Boodlers"—a campus snack bar where we could spend a grand total of 40 cents. Routinely, I purchased a pint of ice cream and three candy bars. These two hours proved to be the only opportunity we had to gather in our room, discuss the week's activities, and enjoy a little camaraderie.

The evening shower formation was designed for us to be cleansed from the day's activities and get inspected by the cadre for blisters and athlete's foot. We reported to the sinks (the basement area where shower stalls were located) wearing a beach robe and shower clogs. We held a soap dish clutched tightly in our left hand with a towel folded over the forearm extended at a 90-degree angle to our bodies. (For the first seven days, I wore my civilian black shoes since I had no other footwear). The command "Thirty seconds in the showers" was followed closely by "Out of the showers." After drying off, we put on our beach robe and stepped up on a bench so a cadre member could conduct the foot inspection. In a loud voice, each new cadet said, "Sir. I have taken a shower, brushed my teeth, consumed three meals, and had a bowel movement in the last 24 hours." One evening, I was standing behind my classmate, a 6-foot 5-inch, 250-pound candidate for lineman on the Army football team. When he stepped up on the bench, I was looking straight at his rear end. He yelled out, "Sir, I have taken a shower, brushed my teeth, consumed three meals, and have not had a bowel movement in eight days." As my brain registered this alarming bit of news, I made a sharp military sidestep to the right. In a split second, I heard a loud voice say, "Mr. Foley, what are you doing?" Remembering instructions from the rifle range that day, I said, "Sir, I am getting out of the line of fire." The spontaneous laughter from my classmates and the stern-faced cadre fractured the military decorum of the shower formation and sent me to the end of the line.

Because Beast Barracks went by quickly, I didn't give much thought to the other colleges that had offered me basketball scholarships. But one hot day in July, my mind wandered while taking a break from marching on the Plain (the main parade field). After drinking from my canteen and wiping the sweat off my face, I looked at the blue sky with the Hudson River in the background. I thought about what I might have been doing that summer if I had selected Holy Cross or some other school—probably soaking up the sun on a Cape Cod beach. This fleeting moment was abruptly interrupted by the sound of my squad leader's voice loudly exclaiming, "Attention, Right shoulder, Arms." I never thought about it again.

Our last major event in Beast Barracks was the Plebe Hike—a 12-mile march to Lake Frederick for a week of field training and camping in two-man pup tents. On the final day, we marched proudly back to West Point behind a jeep displaying a sign with our class motto, "Quality '63." This maxim evolved from a lecture given by the superintendent, Major General Garrison H. Davidson. He said, "If you learn no other word while you are members of the Corps of Cadets, I hope the word will be 'quality'. You will find that we pursue quality in everything we do here regardless of how big or how small."[5]

## CHAPTER 3

# Plebe Year

In 1959, the Military Academy had an authorized strength of 2,400 cadets organized into two regiments, each with 12 companies. Every company consisted of cadets from all four classes—firsties (first classmen or seniors), cows (second classmen or juniors), yearlings (third classmen or sophomores), and plebes (fourth classmen or freshmen). The cadet chain of command provided upper class leadership from squad leader to company commander.

After the completion of summer training at West Point and other Army installations in the United States and overseas, cadets returned to the academy for Reorganization Week. The New Cadet Barracks battalion was dissolved. New cadets became plebes and were assigned to regular lettered companies along with returning upper class cadets in preparation for the academic year. I was assigned to Company A1, which comprised the tallest cadets in First Regiment, while Company M1 contained the shortest. The opposite was true for the 2nd Regiment. Company A2 comprised the shortest cadets and Company M2 contained the tallest. A1 through M1 companies were sized with a gradual decrease in height, while A2 through M2 were sized with a gradual increase in height. When both regiments stood side by side on the parade field, which was shaped with a slight elevation in the center, the Corps of Cadets gave the appearance of even height all along the line.

The Corps of Cadets was organized by height for the first time in 1853 when Captain Robert E. Lee was superintendent.[1] But beginning in 1959, plebes were integrated into regular lettered companies with an equitable height spread as well as equality in scholastic, physical, and leadership ability.[2]

My first semester plebe year roommate was Gordon Arbogast, who was also my teammate on the Army basketball team. For second semester, plebes had to switch roommates. Gordon was assigned to another room and Jack O'Donnell moved in with me. Jack was from Idaho, a member of the Army football team and the Company A1 Honor Representative during our firstie year. He served as an artillery battery commander in Vietnam and later as a company tactical officer and special assistant to the commandant of cadets for honor. His daughter, Carolyn, is a West Point graduate, Class of 1993.

Plebes were assigned duties including mail and newspaper carrier, laundry and dry-cleaning carrier, and minute caller. When I was the mail and newspaper carrier, I woke up early, shaved, put on the proper uniform, and watched for the delivery truck to arrive in central area. As soon as I saw the truck tail lights in the sally port, I ran down the stairs from my fourth-floor room and sprinted across central area. Each bundle of newspapers was bound with a rope and marked with a slip of paper indicating the company designation. My job was to bring the A1 newspapers to the company orderly room, organize them by floor, and double-time up and down the stairs until I had placed a newspaper under the closed door of each room before reveille formation.

One morning, I couldn't find the Company A1 bundle in the sally port. I ran back to the company area to see if someone else had picked it up and quickly returned to the sally port, where I found one stack of newspapers with no rope and no company designation. I was reluctant to take an unmarked pile that might belong to another company, thinking it could be a violation of the cadet honor code—"A cadet does not lie, cheat or steal nor tolerate those who do." Assuming that all newspapers had been picked up, however, I grabbed the last batch and delivered them—completing my rounds just as the minute callers were making their final announcement. Preoccupied with meal formations and morning classes, I didn't think about it again until that afternoon. Deciding I might have violated the cadet honor code, I reported the incident to the company honor representative, who told me that I did not commit an honor violation. But, he added, in the future, I should bring a problem like that to my squad leader before acting on my own. I immediately felt enormous relief.

In addition to a rigorous academic schedule, West Point cadets were faced with demanding physical, athletic, and military requirements. As plebes, we had to meet the minimum standard for swimming, wrestling, boxing, and gymnastics. All cadets were tested annually on the Army Physical Fitness Test and had to participate in intramural, club, or intercollegiate athletics throughout the academic year. We were formally evaluated several times over the four years in military aptitude and leadership and were required to embrace the precepts for living in a moral-ethical climate. Strict adherence to the cadet honor code was a way of life involving the inculcation of honorable living every day.

My major concern was maintaining academic proficiency. I studied hard but had trouble keeping up. The caption under my photograph in the 1963 yearbook accurately reflected my plight, "Bob always managed to come out on top in his battle with the academic department, if only by a slight margin at times."

Oddly enough, at Burr Elementary School, I had an insatiable love for reading and was a regular visitor to the Auburndale Public Library. In the 4th grade, however, my mother made it clear that reading was a sign of laziness. I began hiding my library books, but she caught me reading early one Saturday morning while sitting in my father's armchair. She was so upset that she made me return the books and turn in my library card. From that point on, my Saturday routine of reading and playing with friends was altered considerably as I learned new chores, such as wiping the furniture with homemade polish and cleaning the rugs. Doing the laundry was a major production. I rolled the washing machine to the kitchen sink, hooked up a hose, filled the tub with hot water, washed the clothes, drained the water through a spigot into a bucket and emptied it into the ground in the back yard. After filling the tub with cold water for the rinse cycle, I pulled the clothes through wooden rollers operated by a hand crank. I carried the wet clothes to an outdoor clothesline in the same wicker basket used to bring me home when I was born. Hanging clothes on a warm summer day was an unremarkable task as compared to attaching frozen bedsheets on to a stiff line with wet, cold hands in the middle of winter. Since I spilled water on the kitchen floor during the clothes-wringing process, my last chore was to mop the floor.

There is no question that my mother instilled in me a strong work ethic. I am also convinced that my mother's disdain for reading as well as her general indifference toward education had a debilitating effect on my scholastic development. Julie and I have always been delighted to see our children reading and receiving top grades in school. My mother, on the other hand, was thrilled when I brought home a wooden desk that I made in woodworking shop at the junior high vocational school.

Second semester at West Point began with "gloom period"—an appellation given to the characteristically cold weather in January and February. In addition to algebra, geometry, calculus, English, and Spanish, my schedule included map reading, physical development, and basic military training.[3] We benefited from small-group instruction—a policy that goes back 200 years to when Sylvanus Thayer was superintendent. He demanded that standards of mental discipline and scholarship be implemented by limiting the classroom sections to 10 to 14 cadets.[4] Individual proficiency in each subject was determined by the instructors when they announced "Stagger desks" for a spot quiz or "Take boards" for writing solutions to problems on the blackboard.

Because of my poor grades during first semester of plebe year, I felt a need to seek divine guidance—a sentiment that I discussed with my classmates Bill Sipos and John Ahern. We agreed to attend daily Mass, but never anticipated the bitterly cold wind that blew up the Hudson River as we trudged off to the Catholic chapel in the morning. We remained good friends all four years but had different views on which branch of the service to select after graduation. John went into the Marine Corps and after a tour of duty in Vietnam, he began a wealth management career in the civilian sector. Bill went into the Air Force, got married, and was assigned as a forward air controller in Vietnam flying a Cessna L-19/O-1 Birddog (single engine observation aircraft). It was a sad day on April 6, 1967, when news arrived that Bill had been killed in action.

One pleasant break from the stress of plebe year was basketball. I was having a great freshman year, averaging 17 points and 11 rebounds per game. Against Manhattan, I had 36 points. Coach Hunter was so excited about my potential that he included me in the varsity practice one day to role play an opponent's star guard. He explained the type of shots and moves I should make to see if I could score on the varsity. After I made three straight jump shots, he stopped the practice to explain what the varsity players could expect from the other team.

When basketball season was over, I joined the Army track team as a high jumper. At practice one day, I jumped over the cross bar and landed with the spikes of my left track shoe stuck in the wooden siding of the sawdust pit. I knew from the pain in my foot that I had a serious injury. Because I couldn't put any weight on my leg, I was evacuated by ambulance to the hospital. I had torn ligaments in my ankle and the doctors decided to place my foot in a plaster cast, allowing the ankle to heal naturally as opposed to making a surgical repair. Because I was hospitalized for two weeks, I ended up considerably behind in my studies.

At the end of spring semester, I received passing grades in all subjects except Spanish and English. As a result, I had to take term end exams (TEEs) in both subjects. Failing just one TEE meant automatic dismissal. I will never forget the first essay question on the English exam—"How is an inductively derived generalization used in connection with a deductive argument?" Fortunately, I remembered enough logic instruction to respond satisfactorily. I passed both TEEs and will forever be grateful to Al LaVoy and Mike Bowers, two of my Company A1 classmates, for their tutoring assistance. They not only helped me through plebe year, but they gave me academic support for the next three years any time I asked for it. Al received a commission in the Air Force, served two tours as a fighter pilot during the Vietnam War, and became a commercial airline pilot. Mike rose to the rank of major general in the Georgia Air National Guard, received a Juris Doctor degree from the University of Georgia, and served for 16 years as the Georgia state attorney general.

Right after graduation parade, the plebes in Company A1 were formally recognized. From that day forward, we were on a first-name basis with upper classmen. We were no longer called "mister" and were officially designated as yearlings headed for three weeks of leave before reporting to Camp Buckner for summer training.

## CHAPTER 4

# Keeping the Faith

Since my ankle was still on the mend when I reported to Camp Buckner, I took a shuttle bus to the West Point hospital twice a week for physical therapy (PT). One day, I waited for transportation back to camp, but no buses showed up. The hospital staff told me the next bus would depart at 4:00 p.m. With a few hours to wait, I went by the gym to shoot some baskets. I wish I had questioned the wisdom of this notion but getting my hands on a basketball clouded my thinking. After taking the 4:00 p.m. shuttle to Camp Buckner, I was told by a cadet cadre member to report to Major Richard G. Trefry, the company tactical officer.

Major Trefry told me that I had exercised poor judgment by staying all day on main post for PT when I was only authorized a one-hour session. He said it was my duty to seek the cadet chain of command for guidance on transportation instead of asking hospital personnel. I was awarded 22 demerits, 44 punishment tours (marching in central area with my rifle), and two months' confinement. I was upset with myself and embarrassed at this development, but I learned a valuable lesson about duty—the first word in the West Point motto: Duty, Honor, Country. Major Trefry had a distinguished military career, rising to the rank of lieutenant general and has been an unprecedented Army icon due to his knowledge and experience in "How the Army Runs." I served with him on the Army Emergency Relief Board of Managers for 11 years and hold him in the highest esteem for his outstanding leadership and many years of dedicated service.

Yearling year commenced with a challenging academic schedule—calculus, physics, chemistry, Spanish, psychology, graphics, athletic skills, and military heritage.[1] My roommate, Dick Higgins from Melrose, Massachusetts, was a member of the Army hockey team. Our schedules for practice and study time matched perfectly and he was an excellent student who readily helped me with my studies. After graduation, Dick spent five years on active duty as an artillery officer, received an MBA from Harvard, and became an arbitrator. He lived in Londonderry, New Hampshire with his wife, Debra, until his untimely death due to pancreatic cancer on May 4, 2013.

I looked forward to the 1960–61 basketball season, but my ankle required heavy taping. I couldn't leap for rebounds, cut to the basket, or move with the quickness and strength which had been such a major part of my game. Our first opponent was St. John's University—a contest held at Madison Square Garden. I played against LeRoy Ellis, a 6-foot 10-inch center who averaged 16.5 rebounds a game, was voted most valuable player in the New York metropolitan area, and was selected eighth in the draft by the Los Angeles Lakers.[2] I did not play well, got into foul trouble, and sat on the bench most of the time. We lost 69 to 49.

The following Friday, we played Pittsburgh. I was slow in embracing the tempo of the game but scored 16 points and we won 84 to 80. The next day, we flew to Ohio State—an undefeated team featuring two All-Americans—Jerry Lucas and John Havlicek. I scored 18 points against the 6-foot 8-inch, 250-pound Lucas before fouling out but they beat us by the overwhelming score of 103 to 54. I continued to struggle with my shooting touch and halfway through the season I was dropped from the starting five. I finished with limited playing time but was determined to come back the following year with renewed confidence and stamina.

During the summer of 1961 I served as a squad leader during New Cadet Barracks, took three weeks of leave and returned to West Point for cow year. I was excited about basketball and determined to get a head start on academics. My grades for the first two weeks of September were outstanding but I had persistent headaches. I decided to go on sick call and was diagnosed with infectious mononucleosis. I was admitted to the hospital, had a constant fever, and was sleeping 16 hours a day. When my temperature spiked to 105 degrees and remained there for 48 hours, the doctors called my parents, who immediately drove to West Point. Upon arrival, they found my bed surrounded by doctors, nurses, and Coach Hunter. Due to the seriousness of my illness, Father McCormick, the Catholic chaplain, administered Extreme Unction (the last rites).

Fortunately, my temperature returned to normal. One day 10 years later, when I was a company tactical officer, my wife Julie went to a well-baby appointment with our son Mark at the West Point hospital. The same nurse who had been at my bedside when I had mononucleosis asked her if she was married to former cadet Bob Foley. Julie said "Yes, do you know him?" The nurse said, "Well, I remember that we almost lost him."

During my time in the ward, I became friendly with a cheerful Red Cross volunteer. The head nurse said she was surprised that I was so relaxed speaking with the wife of the academy superintendent, Major General William C. Westmoreland. When Mrs. Westmoreland arrived the next day, I jumped up and stood at attention by my bed. She smiled and said, "Oh-oh, looks like someone told you about me." This would not be the last time I would see General Westmoreland or his wife. I was invited to dinner at the superintendent's quarters along with the other intercollegiate team captains just before graduation in May 1963 and I ran into General Westmoreland when he was commanding general of U.S. Military Assistance Command Vietnam welcoming the 27th Infantry (Wolfhounds) as we disembarked from landing craft at Vung Tau, Vietnam in January 1966.

After recovering enough to live in the barracks, I was restricted from engaging in any strenuous physical activity for 30 days. This included basketball. Because I had been hospitalized for so long and missed so much classroom instruction, academy officials suggested I go home to recuperate and return for my junior year with the Class of 1964. I rejected this proposal and studied with a renewed commitment to obtain the best grades possible. I could not go full speed in basketball until after the Christmas holidays and due to my prolonged absence, the team had a new chemistry. This put me on the bench for most of the season. However, I received a great honor when my teammates voted for me to be captain of the 1962–63 Army basketball team.

During the summer of 1962, I was assigned as an assistant platoon leader in a mechanized infantry company with the 3rd Infantry Division in Germany. The purpose of this program was to familiarize cadets with the tactical leadership challenges faced by junior officers. One rainy night, I was leading a patrol through a densely wooded area when I was notified that the 81mm mortar section would be firing illumination rounds overhead as we continued toward the objective. From classes at West Point I remembered that the flare from the illumination round ejects with a parachute and floats in the air while the expended metal canister falls to the ground. I told my platoon sergeant that I thought the overhead firing was a safety hazard and ordered our soldiers to take cover under trees with thick branches until the firing ceased. We heard some of the canisters falling around us but none of our soldiers were hit.

After a month of training, I met George Pappas, my Company A1 classmate, at Rhein-Main Air Base and flew space-available on a cargo aircraft to Athens. We stayed with George's relatives, explored the Parthenon and Acropolis, ate delicious Greek dishes, and relaxed at the beach. After graduation, George became an Airborne Ranger Infantry officer who served two tours of duty in Vietnam before his transition to a business career culminating as chief operating officer of Cingular Interactive.

When we returned to Germany, George took a space-available flight to the east coast. With 10 days of leave left, I took a train to Hamburg then a ferry to Copenhagen and registered at a student hostel. On my limited budget, I could only afford a cot in the men's quarters, which came with communal bathroom, sinks, and showers. But I had no complaints with the accommodations as I was able to walk around a beautiful city filled with courteous and friendly Danish citizens. At the Tuborg and Carlsberg breweries, I discovered a free lunch of open sandwiches and beer available as part of the factory tour. On my last day, I realized I didn't have enough money to purchase a ticket for the ferry from Copenhagen to Hamburg. Luckily, two college students offered to purchase my ferry ticket in exchange for taking photos of the voyage and sending copies to their home address. I agreed and made it to Frankfurt, took a space-available flight to McGuire Air Force Base, caught a bus to Boston, and arrived home enormously hungry. Money problems aside, I enjoyed Denmark and its people so much that I vowed to return while on my 60 days of leave after graduation.

Returning for senior year, Dick Higgins and I landed a corner room on the bottom floor of Pershing Barracks. Although I took great pride in being captain of the Army basketball team, we had a disappointing record of eight wins and 11 losses. I never played up to my expectations, but I was selected to play for the Eastern College All-Stars in the B'nai B'rith Annual basketball game against the Philadelphia College All-Stars.

Several weeks before graduation, General and Mrs. Westmoreland invited the captains of intercollegiate athletic teams to their quarters for dinner. Because the superintendent entertained constantly, he was authorized enlisted aides to assist with cooking, cleaning, and general maintenance of their historic quarters. We sat at a long table in a large dining room with General Westmoreland and his wife seated at opposite ends of the table. Remembering me from my time in the hospital, Mrs. Westmoreland seated me to her left. Just after we sat down, three enlisted aides burst out of the kitchen. She quickly said, "No, not yet." A few minutes later, the aides came charging out of the kitchen again. Waving them back, she looked under the table and saw my big feet resting near a hidden buzzer in the carpet that was used to alert the kitchen staff when to bring the next course. I apologized to Mrs. Westmoreland, who told me not to worry but I kept those big feet under my chair for the remainder of dinner.

As graduation day approached, we began paying special attention to our future as commissioned officers. Branch selection is a big deal as it determines career field and type of assignment. Since yearling training at Camp Buckner, I had my sights set on being an Airborne Ranger Infantry officer. We had to submit a list of five branches by preference and I requested Infantry, Armor, Artillery, Engineer, and Signal Corps in that order. Unfortunately, branch selection was based upon academic standing. Since I was ranked 497 out of 504, there were 496 cadets selecting branches ahead of me. The only branch available when my number came up was Signal Corps. I was bitterly disappointed and tried to get it changed but was told branch designation was final.

As I was crossing central area a few days later, Brigadier General Richard G. Stilwell, our commandant of cadets, came up behind me and said, "Why so glum, Bob? You're about to graduate." He was a great supporter of Army basketball and had many kind words for me during the season. I told him I had been branched Signal Corps when I desperately wanted Infantry. He told me to keep the faith as one never knows what doors might open. Two days later, I received notification that my branch had been officially changed from Signal Corps to Infantry and I would be attending Airborne and Ranger schools. I was also granted my first choice of assignment—with the 25th Infantry Division at Schofield Barracks, Hawaii.

I graduated from West Point with enduring gratitude for the support of two commandants—Brigadier General Throckmorton, who had arranged for me to receive standard military footwear one week after the beginning of Beast Barracks, and Brigadier General Stilwell, who had arranged for me to become an infantry officer one week before graduation. Generals Throckmorton and Stilwell clearly understood the importance of developing leaders of character both individually and collectively. They were present at cadet venues observing and evaluating group performances as well as making themselves accessible to individual cadets. Not only could they make policy in the aggregate, but they could also make on-the-spot decisions affecting singular cadet issues. These leadership lessons were put to good use when I became the 63rd commandant of cadets.

## CHAPTER 5

# Wolfhounds

After a few days with Mom and Dad in Belmont, I took a bus to McGuire Air Force Base in New Jersey. When I learned there were no space-available flights to Frankfurt that week, I joined my classmate, Bill Whitehead, on a flight to Torrejón Air Base in Spain.

Although returning to Denmark was my primary objective, I was captivated by the sights, sounds, and nightlife in Madrid. At lunch one day, I met three Penn State graduates who told me they were driving to Venice in a new Volkswagen and asked if I wanted to join them to share expenses. Garth, the owner of the Volkswagen, agreed to drop me off at the ferry landing in Hamburg on the way to Bremerhaven to ship his car. Thinking this a fun way to eventually get to Copenhagen, I accepted their offer. We stopped in Barcelona, continued along the Mediterranean coastline, spent time in Rome, and arrived in Venice eight days later. After a few days of sightseeing in Venice, Garth and I headed north. When we finally reached Germany, I realized I could not vacation in Denmark, return to Frankfurt, catch a space-available flight to the United States, and be back in time for the weddings of my classmates George Pappas, Dick Higgins, and Jack O'Donnell. In addition, a second lieutenant's monthly salary of $222.30 ($7.41 per day) did not go far traveling through Europe. Even with the advice contained in Arthur Frommer's book, *Europe on Five Dollars a Day*, I was just getting by. Disappointed, I went straight to Rhein-Main Air Base in Frankfurt and took the next space-available flight to New Jersey.

In August, I headed for Fort Benning to begin the Infantry Officer Basic Course. On my first patrol I was designated "point man"—the one who scouts ahead to alert everyone of any obstacles or enemy sightings. Apparently, my fellow lieutenants thought I did a good job because they selected me to be on point for the remaining Basic Course patrols and for every patrol in Ranger School. Earning a Ranger Tab was not easy. The course was designed to test our endurance and leadership ability under exacting conditions. We conducted rigorous physical conditioning sessions, climbed up and down steep mountains in North Georgia, and negotiated snake-infested swamps in Florida. Because patrols were conducted predominantly at night, our biggest challenge was staying awake. Nevertheless, by the end of the course, I had developed remarkable confidence in navigating unfamiliar terrain using a map and compass in all types of weather—a proficiency that would prove to be indispensable as a rifle company commander in Vietnam.

In addition to patrol leader evaluations, I received five excellent spot reports from the officer and NCO lane graders, including one for jumping into a stream on a cold December morning to look for a shallow crossing site. After wading in freezing water up to my chest, I found a place where I thought the patrol could cross in water up to their knees. The one anomaly was the undulant nature of the stream floor. As my classmate and patrol leader, Carl E. "Chick" Chickedantz, led the patrol to the stream bank, it occurred to me that Chick was about 5 feet 6 inches in height. Before I could say anything, he stepped off the bank and disappeared. All I could see floating in the water was the luminescent name tag on the back of his Ranger cap. When he popped up, I could not find any consoling words except "Sorry Chick" as I handed him his cap.

When President Kennedy was assassinated on November 22, 1963, operations at the Ranger School ceased for a 24-hour period of mourning. We spent the day catching up on much-needed sleep. Late in the afternoon, one of the Ranger students in our cabin came across two six-packs of beer. The consumption of alcoholic beverages was strictly forbidden but several of us indulged. Unfortunately, the company tactical officer found out and ordered us to report to his office, where we received a stern lecture. We were lucky not to have been dismissed. This incident, however, did prevent me from competing for Honor Ranger—a title awarded to the Ranger student who had the best scores on individual evaluations and spot reports. I had no thoughts of grandeur in this regard until my company tactical officer pulled me aside the day before graduation. He told me that I was one of three considered for Honor Ranger, but the beer-drinking incident had eliminated me from competition. It was no surprise that the Honor Ranger award went to my good friend and classmate, Bill Boice, a highly regarded member of the Class of 1963. He was captain of the Army baseball team, retired as a major general, and is our class president.

After graduation from Ranger School, I went home for Christmas and returned to Fort Benning for three weeks of Airborne School. My roommate was Peter M. (Pete) Bentson, a classmate and an all-around great guy who, sadly, was killed in action in Vietnam on July 9, 1972. Airborne School began with ground week, which included aircraft orientation, push-ups, and the airborne shuffle. Tower week involved practice landing falls from a 34-foot tower and practice jumps from a 250-foot tower. In the last week, we made five parachute jumps from a U.S. Air Force C-130 aircraft.

In February, I drove across country, shipped my car from the port of Los Angeles, and flew to Hawaii. Because my unit was deployed on an exercise to the Big Island of Hawaii, the battalion adjutant picked me up at the Honolulu airport. The next day, I hopped on a World War II-era Landing Ship, Tank headed for Hilo, and traveled inland by convoy to the Pōhakuloa Training Area—located on a high plateau between the Mauna Loa and Mauna Kea volcanic areas. I was assigned as platoon leader of Second Platoon, Bravo Company, 2nd Battalion, 27th Infantry. Nicknamed the Wolfhounds, the 27th Infantry Regiment was first organized in 1901 and served in the Philippine-American War, the Siberian Intervention, the Pacific Theater in World War II, and the wars in Korea, Vietnam, Iraq, and Afghanistan. When the 27th Infantry was deployed to Siberia in 1918 during the Russian Civil War, the Bolsheviks compared the American soldiers to the Russian borzoi dogs used in hunting wolves due to their tenacious pursuit of the enemy.[1] The 27th Infantry unit crest is engraved with the outline of a Wolfhound and the motto in Latin—*Nec aspera terrent*—"No fear on earth."

Sergeant First Class James Burroughs was my first platoon sergeant and an outstanding non-commissioned officer (NCO). When I asked him what I had to do to be a good officer, he said, "Lieutenant, you have to do two things—accomplish the mission and take care of the troops." He explained how the Army would ensure I became tactically and technically proficient, but he said, "We don't spend near enough time on this business of caring." He explained that caring meant leading by example, possessing moral courage, and carving out time for listening to soldiers—invaluable tenets I have never forgotten. Good leaders make it a habit to get out of the command bunker, walk around the unit area, and be accessible—in the chow line, on the rifle range, in the mess hall, or in the barracks. For many years, I've had a framed silhouette in my office of a 2nd Infantry Division soldier standing on a hilltop in Korea with an M-1 Garand rifle slung over his shoulder. The caption reads, "What have you done for Private First Class Warrior today?"

Another terrific mentor of mine was Captain Malcolm J. (Mack) Howard, West Point Class of 1962, who shared with me his thoughts on small-unit tactical decision-making, leadership principles, and officer/non-commissioned officer relationships. Mack was awarded a Silver Star, two Bronze Stars, a Purple Heart, and two Air Medals as a rifle company commander in Vietnam.

When the battalion returned from the Big Island of Hawaii to Schofield Barracks on Oahu, we commenced preparation for the Annual General Inspection—a comprehensive review of personnel, training, supply, and maintenance readiness. As the company training officer, I was responsible for updating training records, field manuals, and regulations. In reviewing daily distribution, I came across a set of orders indicating that I had qualified expert with my rifle. Since I hadn't been to the rifle range, I immediately grabbed the orders, which included the names of about 20 other officers and NCOs, and walked to battalion headquarters. I showed the orders to the battalion adjutant, explaining that I had not qualified expert with my rifle, and requested that my name be removed from the list. I was told not to worry because any discrepancies would be corrected after the inspection. I persisted until I met with Major Feek, the battalion executive officer, who thanked me for bringing the issue to his attention. That afternoon, I was told all officers and NCOs listed on the orders would be conducting rifle qualification on Saturday and Sunday for the next two weekends. A few days later, while speaking with a group of junior officers in Quad D (the Wolfhound Barracks area), a captain looked at me and said, "So, you're the rat." He was upset because he had to be on the rifle range for two weekends instead of playing golf with his buddies. Although his denigrating accusation bothered me, especially since I was a brand-new second lieutenant, I would not have done anything different than what I did.

Two of my good friends, Ed Meyers, and Bob Corboy, lived across the hall from me in the Bachelor Officer Quarters (BOQ). They attended Reserve Officers' Training Corps (ROTC) at the University of Santa Clara. Ed received his commission in the infantry and after his Army service, had a long career on Wall Street. Bob served in Korea and has been with New York Life Insurance in Honolulu for 50-plus years. We could not believe our good fortune at being bachelor second lieutenants, swimming and surfing at Waikiki Beach every weekend. On Sunday evenings, we habitually gathered in the Barefoot Bar at the Fort DeRussy Officer's Club to have a few Mai Tais and tell war stories. One time, I was advising First Lieutenant Charlie "B-man" Baroody on how to meet some of the ladies when a lovely coed came in. She stood in the doorway, looked around, and headed straight toward us. I said, "B-man, now's your chance." He swiveled around on his bar stool and said, "Welcome to the islands, baby." Without missing a step, she said, "Don't discourage me buddy," and kept on walking. Charlie turned back to the bar uttering a few choice words while we fell off our chairs with laughter.

In the fall of 1964, just six months into my tour of duty in Hawaii, I was busy with unit sports—company flag football followed by battalion and brigade basketball. As a member of the 2nd Brigade basketball team, I was authorized special duty—training with my infantry company from 8:00 a.m. to noon and spending the remainder of the day playing basketball. This was great fun until one day, it came to me that I'd made a big mistake. I was supposed to be leading a platoon and training with my soldiers on a full-time basis. I tried to quit basketball but made no headway until I met with my battalion commander, Lieutenant Colonel John E. Culin. He went to see the division commander, Major General Fred C. Weyand, who was a huge basketball fan and had planned on seeing me play for the U.S. Army Hawaii basketball team. General Weyand reluctantly approved my release. I look back upon this decision as key to my leadership development because I was able to better focus on small-unit tactics, weapons proficiency, and jungle warfare exercises—training that served me well when I deployed to Vietnam.

In the spring of 1965, Ed and I moved out of the BOQ and went to live with Rich Foss, Len Roberge, and Charlie Baroody at their north shore beach house. It was the perfect setting to enjoy the benefits of living in Hawaii and was just a short drive to Schofield Barracks. Early one Sunday morning, Len Roberge and I were returning from Waikiki Beach and noticed that Rich's TR4 sports car was on the lava rocks under the house. I was the first to see the vestibule front door hanging on its hinges and a hole in the roof. We found Rich passed out on his bed. He had been drinking when he placed a call to his company orderly room at Schofield Barracks. While waiting for the duty NCO to come to the phone, he spotted an artillery simulator that we used during training exercises to replicate battlefield explosions. Rich kicked the door open, planning to throw it on the front lawn. But by the time he had pulled off the safety cover and extracted the safety pin, the vestibule door had closed. The simulator bounced off the door and landed on the floor. Hearing a loud whistle, he was conscious enough to run for the nearest bedroom—landing on one of the beds just as the simulator exploded, knocking the door off its hinges and putting a hole in the roof.

We cleaned up the house the next day but deferred the front door and roof repairs to the following week. Unfortunately, our landlady decided to visit before we could arrange for repairs. She was not happy, resulting in our eviction and a bill for damages. Lieutenant Dave Bramlett, West Point Class of '64, a good friend and now a retired four-star general, was one of our successors. His rental agreement included the stipulation that Lieutenant Ardeen R. (Rich) Foss and Lieutenant Robert F. Foley were not allowed on the premises at any time. We rented another place about 200 yards down the beach.

Due to the buildup of American military assistance in South Vietnam, the 25th Infantry Division staff was continuously reviewing plans consistent with the division's role as the strategic force for the Pacific Theater. In late 1965, with increased emphasis on preparing for possible deployment to Vietnam, our new battalion commander, Lieutenant Colonel Harley F. Mooney, implemented extensive training in counterinsurgency, search and destroy operations, and airmobile assaults. His proactive leadership style clearly made the difference in getting us ready for combat operations in Vietnam. Leading up to our deployment, we would see him in the field observing, evaluating, and providing guidance on tactical situations, such as attacking fortified machine gun positions. We appreciated his sense of urgency and respected his credibility as a soldier. He had served as a rifle platoon leader and infantry company commander during the Korean War, receiving the Silver Star, two Bronze Stars, and three Purple Hearts for his valorous actions in combat. Although he walked around with a noticeable limp due to a chronic leg ailment from his wartime wounds, he set the example as a tough, dedicated leader every day.

In November, while I was the battalion staff duty officer, Sergeant Major Hugh O'Reilly, the honorary regimental sergeant major, walked into the headquarters. He had been stationed in Japan with the Wolfhounds as part of the occupation force after World War II. On Christmas Day 1949, then Platoon Sergeant O'Reilly, along with a dozen Wolfhound soldiers, accompanied a Red Cross representative during a visit to the Holy Family Home—an orphanage in Osaka established by the Sisters of Charity of Saint Vincent de Paul. Sergeant O'Reilly was so struck by the children's extremely poor living conditions that he took up a collection and returned on New Year's morning to donate $143 to the orphanage.[2] This began an informal association between the 27th Infantry Regiment and the Holy Family Home that has lasted more than 70 years. In his capacity as the honorary regimental sergeant major, this extraordinary non-commissioned officer spent every day in the barracks area. It was a delight to see his face light up when I asked him about the orphans in Osaka. Before he departed that night, I told him that I would like to visit the orphanage someday. He said, "If you're serious, I can make all the arrangements."

Two weeks later, I was on an all-expenses paid flight to Tokyo with a connecting flight to Osaka—compliments of Japan Airlines. Upon landing in Tokyo, a stewardess told me the captain and his crew wanted to meet me in the crew lounge. The captain thanked me for visiting the Holy Family Home and complimented the Wolfhound regiment for this unique program, which honored the orphans and the Japanese people. I indicated my trip would not have been possible without the support of Japan Airlines. The captain asked me where I was stationed. When I told him Schofield Barracks, he said, "Yes, I remember it well. I flew over Schofield Barracks on my way to Pearl Harbor when I was a Navy pilot." With visions of Japanese bombers attacking the battleships docked at Pearl Harbor on December 7, 1941, I took my time trying to absorb the magnitude of what he had just said. Before I could respond, he acknowledged how times had changed as evidenced by the 27th Infantry support to the Holy Family Home—an enduring example of the peace and friendship between Japan and America today. The co-pilot added that this chance meeting was truly historic since it was December 7, 1965, and we were celebrating American soldier support to Japanese orphans exactly 14 years after the attack on Pearl Harbor. When one of the stewardesses mentioned that she and other crew members flew to Hawaii at times, I gave her my telephone number and asked that she call the next time they were in Honolulu.

Upon my arrival in Osaka, I was pleasantly surprised with the warm reception I received from the orphans. And they were elated to see such a tall Wolfhound. As I went to several cribs and picked up babies, I was smothered with hugs. I remember having one orphan in each arm and two with their arms wrapped around my legs. I departed with a lasting image of the amazing goodness realized by the 27th Infantry Regiment's association with the Holy Family Home. I spent my last day sightseeing in Tokyo and went to the officers' club at Camp Zama for dinner where I met a civilian intelligence specialist. When I told him that I was stationed with the 25th Infantry Division, he said, "I suppose you've heard that your division has been alerted for deployment to Vietnam." This was news to me, and I was glad to be on a flight to Honolulu in the morning.

At Schofield Barracks, I reported to my company commander, Captain Mack Howard, who told me I was no longer the Bravo company executive officer. Lieutenant Colonel Mooney had reassigned me to be the 4.2-inch mortar platoon leader. Since the mortars, vehicles, and equipment were packed up and the soldiers, including Platoon Sergeant Nishimura, were on leave until after New Year's Day, I made plans to fly home to Boston. On the day of my flight, the Japan Airlines stewardess with whom I had spoken in Tokyo called to see if we could meet that night at "The Top of The Ilikai" for Mai Tais. This is what bachelor lieutenants call bad timing.

After a few days in Boston and dinner in New York City with Ed Meyers, I flew back to Honolulu. We spent our final days attending local parties and swimming at Waikiki Beach. Because we were scheduled to depart from Pearl Harbor on a troop ship at noon on January 4, I made plans to spend my last night at Waikiki Beach. After embarkation and the ship orientation, I asked my company commander, Captain Fred Turner, if I could leave the ship and be back before it sailed. He said that no personnel were authorized to leave the ship for any reason, adding, "Once on board, everyone stays." I thought this was overly restrictive and was tempted to sneak off for a few hours but thought better of it and went to sleep in an extremely narrow berth hanging from the bulkhead. When I woke up the next morning, I sensed that we were underway. I got dressed, went to the main deck, and saw that Hawaii was nowhere in sight. The captain had decided to take advantage of tidal data and cast off at midnight. In a flash, I knew how fortunate I was not to have left the ship. Missing a troop movement is a serious offense. As a minimum, my military career would have been over.

## CHAPTER 6

# The Vietnam War

In 1966, the buildup of American forces in Vietnam was just beginning. I never felt anxious about deploying to Southeast Asia, nor did my junior officer friends. We were always preparing to accomplish the purpose of the U.S. Army—to fight and win our nation's wars. In Hawaii, we had been training extensively in the mountainous, jungle terrain and were looking forward to using our skills in a meaningful way. When the time came, like all soldiers, we did not want to be left behind. Our vocation in life was the profession of arms. We were not thinking about American geopolitical objectives or the national military strategy. Instead, we were focused on accomplishing the unit mission and taking care of our soldiers. As so clearly expressed in the West Point motto "Duty, Honor, Country," we were participating in the Vietnam War because it was our duty to do so, it was the honorable thing to do, and we were doing it for our country. Our thoughts were the same when we arrived and when we departed.

Before describing my tour of duty in Vietnam I thought it might be useful to examine how and why America became involved in a conflict that lasted for 25 years—from the U.S. Military Assistance Advisory Group (MAAG) activation in 1950 until the capture of Saigon by the People's Army of Vietnam in 1975. The U.S. Armed Forces' commitment to the Vietnam War began with 38 soldiers, rose to over 500,000 in 1968, and ended with a total cost of almost 60,000 American lives.

In the 1850 to 1880 timeframe, Vietnam was called French Indochina, which included Cochin China, Annam, and Tonkin as well as the border areas of Laos and Cambodia—a land ruled by the French government and occupied by wealthy French colonialists and landowners. By 1940, the Vietnamese had been under French colonial rule for 60 years. Prior to World War II, America had no history of and no interest in establishing any relations with Indochina.[1] In December 1944, President Roosevelt informed Secretary of State Edward R. Stettinius that he did not want to pursue any military effort involving the liberation of Indochina. And in March 1945, Roosevelt stated he would take action against the Japanese in Indochina but there would be no military assistance to the French.[2]

During World War II, the mission of the U.S. Office of Strategic Services (OSS) was to conduct intelligence and counterintelligence operations against Japanese forces in French Indochina.[3] Collaboration between the OSS, Ho Chi Minh, and the Viet Minh guerrillas began with the rescue of Lieutenant Rudolph Shaw, a downed pilot from the U.S. 51st Fighter Group, who was safeguarded from capture by French and Japanese forces until he was returned to his base in Kunming, China.[4] As stated by one military historian:

> Although Ho Chi Minh and many in the higher echelons of the Viet Minh coalition were communist, they merged Marxist philosophy with their own patriotic ideals and certainly could not be considered puppets of either the Soviets or the struggling Chinese Communists.[5]

The Viet Minh desired to be recognized by the United States as the true representative of the people of Vietnam who were fighting against the French and Japanese in their desire to secure a free, independent, and democratic nation.[6]

In August 1945, OSS officers found Ho Chi Minh lying in the corner of a dark room with a high fever, yellow, dry skin, and glassy eyes. He was diagnosed by an OSS medic with malaria, dengue fever, and dysentery—a frail, elderly man close to death. With intensive care by the OSS team, he recovered enough in 10 days to begin walking. The ensuing friendships were evident in a 1945 photograph of OSS officers standing side by side with Ho Chi Minh, a revered leader who became the president of North Vietnam, and Vo Nguyen Giap, who was the North Vietnamese minister of defense during the Vietnam War.[7]

Regrettably, the close working relationships knit together in the jungles of Vietnam between American OSS officers and the two most important leaders of North Vietnam were not leveraged to create an American-Viet Minh coalition. After the OSS dissolution on October 1, 1945, its solidarity with the Viet Minh vanished in the wake of the American and Allies' pursuit of a new world order.

This misfortune was exacerbated by communications to American diplomats from Charles de Gaulle, the leader of the Provisional Government of the French Republic:

> If the public here comes to realize that you are against us in Indochina, there will be terrific disappointment, and nobody really knows to what that will lead. We do not want to become Communist; we do not want to fall into the Russian orbit, but I hope you do not push us into it.[8]

Ho Chi Minh sent telegrams to President Truman, hoping America would intervene in support of Vietnamese independence, but never received any response—a grave disappointment to Ho Chi Minh, who had been schooled in American idealism.[9]

In February 1946, the French and Chinese governments agreed to the complete withdrawal of Chinese troops from northern Indochina. Ho Chi Minh signed an agreement with the French government recognizing northern Indochina as the Democratic Republic of Vietnam—a free, independent, and sovereign state.[10]

In December 1949, the American joint chiefs of staff warned that communist success in China portended the spread of communism throughout Southeast Asia. U.S. Army historian Ronald Spector wrote:

> Should Southeast Asia fall to communism, the Joint Chiefs noted, the security of Japan, India and Australia would be threatened. Indochina was the key because its fall would undoubtedly bring about the fall of Burma and Thailand and probably of the Philippines, Malaya, and Indonesia.[11]

On March 10, 1950, with the French threat of disengaging from Indochina, President Harry S. Truman approved $15 million in military aid to Vietnam.[12] To ensure the requisitioning, control, and distribution of American military supplies, a MAAG of 38 officers and enlisted personnel was established in September 1950.[13] American military weapons and equipment were initially successful in assisting the French to achieve victories against the Viet Minh forces.[14] However, the Viet Minh were too powerful and in May 1954, the French suffered a major collapse at Dien Bien Phu, which led to a negotiated settlement of the First Indochina War in accordance with the Geneva Conventions.[15]

In October 1954, the American joint chiefs of staff approved a program to train the Army of South Vietnam (ARVN) as an extension of the MAAG mission, thereby setting in motion an irreversible chain of events.[16] From February to April 1956, the French government, which had adamantly insisted that American support was essential for France to remain engaged in Vietnam, abolished the French command and withdrew all French troops.[17]

In my view, American Cold War foreign policy was excessively influenced by the "domino theory"—a term coined by President Eisenhower when he compared the situation in Vietnam to a falling domino. If Vietnam comes under communist domination, neighboring countries such as Indochina, Burma, Thailand, and Indonesia would soon follow.[18] While I appreciate the logic behind the domino effect, I think it's unreasonable to presume that the loss of Indochina to communism would bring about the fall of Burma, Thailand, India, Japan, Australia, Malaysia, the Philippines, and Indonesia. Nevertheless, preventing the spread of communism to South Vietnam became a de facto American national security interest due to the domino theory paranoia combined with the American commitment to train the Army of South Vietnam, provide military equipment, and embed American advisors in ARVN units.

In Graham Allison's book, *Destined for War*, he stated: "National interests are plain enough. The survival of the state and its sovereignty in making decisions in its domain—free from coercion from others—are standard fare in discussions of national security."[19] Did America's involvement in Vietnam meet the criteria for state survival free from coercion in its own domain? How significant to the survival of the United States was prevention of a communist South Vietnam? How threatening was communism in Vietnam to the American domain? What coercive measures could threaten the United States by a communist South Vietnam?

In his critical study, *On Strategy*, Colonel Harry G. Summers stressed the importance of the principles of war beginning with the objective: "Every military operation should be directed towards a clearly defined, decisive and attainable objective."[20] The legitimacy of preventing the spread of communism to South Vietnam as a national security interest was crucial in establishing a military strategy that supports the political objective. Was the United States' objective to defend South Vietnam? Was it to deter North Vietnamese aggression? Was it to destroy North Vietnam's ability to wage war? Was it to conduct nation-building while strengthening the South Vietnam Armed Forces?

Covert operations were conducted by South Vietnam against North Vietnam beginning in May 1961 and on January 24, 1964, a U.S. Special Operations Group was established to augment ARVN forces.[21] The American joint chiefs of staff also developed contingency plans to conduct airstrikes along the Ho Chi Minh trail and military industrial targets in North Vietnam.[22]

The initiation of hostilities began with U.S. Navy destroyers operating in the Gulf of Tonkin ostensibly to gather intelligence on North Vietnamese military operations. On August 2, 1964, the destroyer USS *Maddox* had radar sightings and radio intercepts indicating that North Vietnamese patrol boats intended to attack. The *Maddox* fired 283 shells in a mix of fragmentation, high explosive, and star clusters without hitting one enemy patrol boat. The ship's crew admitted that they were short-handed and lacked proper gunnery experience.[23] Four F-8E Crusader jet aircraft with missiles and 20mm cannon from the aircraft carrier *Ticonderoga* engaged three North Vietnamese patrol boats and damaged one. However, all three escaped to a beach at the mouth of the Song Ma River in North Vietnam.[24]

On August 4, during a moonless, starless, zero-visibility night, the USS *Maddox* was joined by the destroyer USS *Turner Joy* off the North Vietnamese coast. Between 7:45 and 9:45 p.m., numerous radar contacts of unidentified aircraft and vessels were reported by both destroyers. With great excitement and general confusion, the destroyers' crews fired over 300 rounds at radar contacts of possible enemy torpedo boats.[25] In an interview with *Stars and Stripes*, Admiral James B. Stockdale, one of the pilots responding to the reports of enemy activity, stated that the attack by North Vietnamese torpedo boats on August 4, 1964, never took place:

> There was an attack by enemy boats against the destroyers Maddox and Turner Joy two days earlier, on Aug 2, Stockdale says, but the report of a second attack Aug 4 was a false alarm. After spending 90 minutes in the air trying to find the attacking boats and later studying radio communications from the ships and alleged intercepts of Vietnamese radio communications, Stockdale concluded that there were "no boats" active against US ships that night.[26]

In the opinion of Commander Herrick, the captain of the USS *Maddox*, it was unlikely for enemy vessels to have been within 10,000 yards of his destroyer on the night of August 4, 1964.[27]

On August 5, 1964, 64 sorties of carrier-based aircraft conducted retaliatory strikes on specific targets in North Vietnam.[28] On August 7, Congress passed the Gulf of Tonkin Resolution granting President Johnson broad powers to conduct combat operations in Southeast Asia.[29] There is one paramount question for which the Johnson administration ought to have been held accountable. Was the Gulf of Tonkin incident a deliberate U.S. government provocation designed to serve as the catalyst America needed to initiate a war with North Vietnam?

To his credit, Secretary of Defense Robert S. McNamara organized a series of symposiums in the 1997–98 timeframe with key American and Democratic Republic of Vietnam military and civilian leaders to examine the hypothesis that Hanoi and Washington had missed opportunities to achieve their geopolitical objective without going to war.[30] In his book *Argument Without End: In Search of Answers to the Vietnam Tragedy*, McNamara said:

> There were, I hypothesized, opportunities either to have avoided the war before it started or to have terminated it long before it had run its course. Were there such opportunities? If so, why were they missed? What lessons can we draw to avoid such tragedies in the 21st century?[31]

Without question, the red flags of opportunity to prevent war with North Vietnam waved on a regular basis, beginning with the OSS leaders' friendship and collaboration with Ho Chi Minh and the Viet Minh at the end of World War II; and again with President Truman's approval of $15 million in military assistance to Vietnam on March 10, 1950; followed by the creation of a MAAG in September 1950; then again with the French defeat by the Viet Minh forces on May 8, 1954; once more in 1954 with the decision by the American Joint Chiefs of Staff to train the South Vietnamese Army; and, finally, in 1956 with the withdrawal of all French troops from Vietnam. At each of these junctures, a detailed assessment of American national security interests should have created significant foreboding on the consequences of continued involvement in Vietnam. Unfortunately, the American piecemeal, mission creep, and rush-to-judgment decision-making established a war footing that surged forward on its own momentum.

One of the North Vietnamese military leaders interviewed during the American and Democratic Republic of Vietnam seminars was General Vo Nguyen Giap, retired four-star general of the Army and former Defense Minister of North Vietnam. Giap's father and first wife were executed by the French and a sister of his died of privation in a French prison. He was the commander of Viet Minh forces during their victory over the French at Dien Bien Phu and was responsible for planning and executing the North Vietnamese Army and Viet Cong forces Tet Offensive against the forces of the South Vietnamese Army, the U.S. Armed forces, and their allies in January 1968.[32] Secretary McNamara asked General Giap about his hypothesis of missed opportunities and lessons learned to avoid such tragedies. In response, General Giap said:

> Lessons are important. I agree. However, you are wrong to call the war a tragedy—to say that it came from missed opportunities. Maybe it was a tragedy for you because yours was a war of aggression in the neocolonialist "style" or fashion of the day for Americans. You wanted to replace the French: you failed; men died; so, yes, it was tragic because they died for a bad cause. But for us, the war against you was a noble sacrifice. We did not want to fight the US. We did not. But you gave us no choice. Our people sacrificed greatly for our cause of freedom and independence. There were no missed opportunities for us.[33]

> According to Giap, the August 2 attack was ordered by a local commander, not by Hanoi, as was assumed in Washington at the time. It was carried out, he said, in retaliation for US-backed South Vietnamese commando raids on two North Vietnamese Islands nearby on 30 and 31 July and in retaliation for the [destroyer] patrols designed to spy electronically on North Vietnamese communications facilities. In addition, the second, "attack" on August 4, which US officials believed was highly probable but were never able to confirm positively, never occurred.[34]

In his study of American leadership during the Vietnam War, H. R. McMaster described President Johnson in this way:

> Preoccupied with the campaign, Lyndon Johnson was determined to make only those decisions that would rebound to his short-term political benefit. They [McNamara and Johnson] used a questionable report of a North Vietnamese attack on American naval vessels to justify the president's policy to the electorate and to defuse Republican senator and presidential candidate Barry Goldwater charges that Lyndon Johnson was irresolute and "soft" in the foreign policy arena.[35]

Unfortunately, President Johnson was motivated by domestic political objectives to the detriment of national security interests and Secretary McNamara attempted to replace the principles of war and military strategy with a doctrine adopted through quantitative analysis. This focus on unrelated objectives and limited support was not destined to achieve victory.

> In McNamara's concept of "graduated pressure," the aim of force was not to impose one's will on the enemy but to communicate with him. Gradually intensifying military action would convey American resolve and thereby convince an adversary to alter his behavior. Johnson found McNamara's strategic concept particularly attractive because it would not jeopardize his domestic political agenda. Although the presidential election was still ten months away, he thought that mishandling Vietnam policy might easily cost him victory. He tried to use American involvement in Vietnam to his advantage. He wanted to be seen as a "moderate" candidate, so he resolved to take only those actions in Vietnam that bolstered that image.[36]

In her book, *Leadership in Turbulent Times*, Doris Kearns Goodwin indicated that President Johnson chose to ignore those advisors who argued that South Vietnam was not a vital national security interest.[37] His military strategic planning lacked coherence and conviction as he was focused on a domestic agenda that featured civil rights as his vision for the Great Society. His piecemeal approach to the situation in Vietnam gave him ownership of the war over time. Facing such a costly struggle, he told Congress no more than was necessary, which led to concealing from the public the true story of America's involvement in Vietnam.[38]

> In the end, no statesman can successfully pursue a war policy unless he has instilled a sense of shared direction and purpose, unless people know what to expect and what is expected of them. By all these standards of candor and collaboration between a leader and the people in the critical time of war, Lyndon Johnson had failed.[39]

In chapter one of his book, *On War*, Carl von Clausewitz asserts that the object of war is to impose one's will to the point of rendering the enemy powerless.[40] War is using other means to continue a nation's policy; is not to be carried out by military commanders unless it is in pursuit of political objectives; and should not be conducted in isolation from national security interests.[41] Clausewitz also maintains that "only great strength of will can lead to the objective."[42]

On December 19, 1777, during the American Revolutionary War, 11,000 Continental Army soldiers arrived at Valley Forge in severe winter weather—many with no shoes, no socks, no hats, no coats.[43] These patriots who left their shops, their farms, their homes, and their families to go to a place where there was no food, no shelter, and no pay reinforces the tenet that the will of the people to defend freedom and independence ought never be discounted.

The catalyst for America's participation in World War II was an attack by Japan on Pearl Harbor. Going to war was a vital national security interest characterized by a clearly defined objective, the complete support of the American people, and full mobilization of the U.S. Armed Forces backed by American industry. In less than four years, America and its allies compelled the unconditional surrender of Germany and Japan.

The catalyst for the Vietnam War was faulty information of an attack by North Vietnamese torpedo boats on U.S. Navy destroyers off the coast of North Vietnam. The conditions for declaring war against North Vietnam did not meet the criteria for a national security interest. The war had no clearly defined objective and was characterized by limited U.S. Armed Forces' participation, a growing anti-war movement, and a loss of national will at home. Over a period of 25 years, the United States of America lost the war and South Vietnam was unified with North Vietnam to create one communist state—the Socialist Republic of Vietnam.

## CHAPTER 7

# Rifle Company Commander

On our second day aboard the USS *General Nelsen M. Walker*, I decided to conduct physical training (PT) for the mortar platoon between two smokestacks on the top deck. After five minutes of attempting to keep our balance while the ship succumbed to roll, pitch, and yaw, I realized that PT for 35 soldiers on a ship at sea was not a good idea. Instead, I stopped and briefed them on everything I knew about our deployment to Vietnam.

On January 18, 1966, General Westmoreland, Commanding General of Military Assistance Command Vietnam, Colonel Lynwood M. Johnson, 2nd Brigade Commander, 25th Infantry Division, and Major Karl Lange, Executive Officer of 2nd Battalion, 27th Infantry, welcomed us as we disembarked in landing craft at Vung Tau, South Vietnam.[1] After movement by truck to Bien Hoa airfield, we linked up with our vehicles, weapon systems, and equipment and traveled by convoy to Cu Chi—the new home of the 25th Infantry Division. During the first few days, we filled sandbags, built bunkers, and constructed firing platforms for the mortars. Although the heavy mortar platoon was well back from the front lines, we had two soldiers wounded in the first two days due to Viet Cong (VC) mortar fire. The wounds were superficial. Nevertheless, we learned that the battlefield was a perilous place regardless of proximity to the enemy.

Walking toward the division helipad one day, Colonel Johnson pulled up in his jeep and told me there was a fire in my platoon area and I had better get over there right away. I ran straight to the mortar position, leaped over the concertina wire, and saw Platoon Sergeant Nishimura pointing toward smoke coming from one of the ammunition bunkers. Reaching the bunker, I saw a pile of rags burning on a stack of mortar ammunition. I jumped into the bunker, scooped up the rags, and threw them outside. Concerned the mortar rounds could overheat and explode, I carefully picked up a round, carried it outside and laid it on the ground. When Platoon Sergeant Nishimura arrived with the rest of the platoon, we moved all ammunition out of the bunker and promptly established new policies on storage of ammunition and cleaning equipment.

The four months that I spent as the battalion 4.2-inch mortar platoon leader were relatively quiet since we were relegated to a static firing position inside Cu Chi base camp. Because of our vehicular, ammunition, and logistical requirements, moving by road made us a good target for a VC ambush. Therefore, our standard mission was to provide supporting fires, primarily at night, for the front-line units located along the base camp perimeter.

In June, I flew to Hong Kong for five days of R&R (rest and recuperation) in a luxury hotel with a hot shower, good food, and drinks. When I returned to Saigon, I called battalion headquarters about transportation to Cu Chi and was told I had been promoted to captain and assigned to the battalion operations section. My promotion ceremony was brief. Major John Wesley "Wes" Loffert, the battalion operations officer, said, "Here's a copy of your orders and a set of captain's bars. You're the S3 Air (assistant operations officer). Now get to work."

I spent most of my time coordinating company airmobile operations and responding to situation reports from the companies conducting patrolling and search and destroy operations. Since battalion mortar platoon leader called for a first lieutenant, moving to a job as a battalion staff officer was a natural progression for a new captain. An assignment as the S3 Air not only allowed me to gain experience at the battalion level but also afforded the operations officer and battalion commander time to evaluate my qualifications to be a company commander.

While listening to situation reports coming in over the radio in the battalion Tactical Operations Center (TOC), I occasionally made remarks about our company commanders' lack of aggressiveness. One day, unknown to me, Major Loffert and the battalion commander, Lieutenant Colonel Boyd T. Bashore, were listening on the other side of the TOC. The next morning, Lieutenant Colonel Bashore told me to report to Alpha Company. Because I had been conducting morning inspections along the bunker line, I asked if there was a specific area that he wanted me to check. He gave me a surprised look and said, "I want you to command that outfit." Sensing it would be wise not to ask any more questions, I said, "Yes sir," saluted, and left his office. On August 5, 1966, I became the commanding officer of Alpha Company, 2nd Battalion, 27th Infantry (Wolfhounds). I was fortunate to have excellent leaders, beginning with my executive officer, First Lieutenant Jim Day, and First Sergeant Edward L. Fulghum.

In walking through the company area on my first day, I came across six soldiers in their squad tents with venereal disease (VD) picked up from contacts in the village of Cu Chi. The doctors had prescribed antibiotics and bed rest for seven days. Understandably, Alpha Company soldiers saw this as "getting over"—being rewarded for bad behavior. I assigned the problem to Lieutenant Day, who devised a plan which I approved for the next heliborne assault. On the morning of the operation, he shepherded the VD patients in combat gear on trucks with the rest of the company seemingly to stand by while the company lifted off from the division helipad. Instead, they were loaded aboard the helicopters in their assigned squads and went on the airmobile assault with their fellow soldiers. The VD patients were uncomfortable walking through the rice paddies but from that day forward, Alpha Company had a new policy—soldiers with VD would participate in all duty, including combat assaults. Even though the company VD rate went to zero, I was visited by two upset doctors, who went away without convincing me to change my policy.

My first airmobile assault was conducted in the Mekong Delta. While walking along a narrow finger of land with water on both sides, we received fire from the far bank of a river. With no cover anywhere on land, we jumped in the water and returned fire. Since we could not maneuver across the river, I called for artillery fire on the enemy positions, which caused the Viet Cong to withdraw. It took us another hour to find a good piece of dry land on which to spend the night. As we began changing socks, we found some new friends on our legs—leeches—which had plenty of time to get fat on our blood. Because they have tiny teeth, pulling them off was not a good idea as their teeth could remain in the skin and cause an infection. However, they would immediately drop off if you squirted mosquito repellant on their heads or placed a lighted cigarette next to them.

Early in my command, several NCOs recommended we not wear rank on our uniforms and helmets because enemy snipers focused on leaders. We lived with our soldiers 24 hours a day—we knew them and they knew us. I approved the recommendation that all soldiers in Alpha Company would not wear any rank, nametag, U.S. Army, or other insignia on our uniforms while conducting missions outside the Cu Chi base camp.

During combat operations, the battalion standard operating procedure (SOP) required us to change location after three days to prevent the VC from obtaining a read on our defensive configuration. I gave latitude to the platoon leaders in organizing their defenses but insisted that the night positions be different from what the VC could observe during daylight hours. Fifty-caliber and M-60 machine guns were repositioned to new locations at night but continued coverage of the most dangerous enemy avenues of approach. On one operation, First Platoon placed a single strand of concertina wire 20 yards in front of their fighting positions during the day. As darkness fell, Lieutenant Graves added two more strands of wire, creating a triple concertina obstacle that included trip flares and Claymore mines (remotely activated anti-personnel mines that shot tiny steel balls out 100 yards in a 60-degree arc). Then he placed a single strand of wire another 20 yards in front of the triple concertina obstacle. That night, a substantial VC force attempted an assault into First Platoon sector by cutting the single strand of concertina wire. Thinking they had cut the only wire barrier, the VC stood up and charged straight into the triple concertina obstacle. When the trip flares went off, First Platoon soldiers had a clear view of the VC silhouetted in the wire obstacle, struggling to get free. They pressed the Claymore mine triggers and opened fire with rifles and machine guns. The enemy abruptly ended their assault.

Simultaneously, a VC element approached Second Platoon sector in a tight crouched formation on the left side of a raised dirt road to avoid the 50-caliber machine gun that they thought was on the right-hand side of the road. However, it had been moved to the left-hand side after dark. When the VC got to about 30 yards from the machine gun position, the gunner commenced firing using his AN/PVS-1 "Starlight Scope" night sight. The VC immediately withdrew as 50-caliber machine gun rounds ripped through their formation. An enemy mortar position had also been set up to support the assault. As soon as one round fired, we identified the location and silenced the mortar with machine gun fire and grenade launchers. The enemy scattered. At the first hint of daylight, we conducted a battlefield assessment, retrieving VC rifles, mortar ammunition, and uniform items. Alpha Company's defense worked to perfection with 20 dead Viet Cong and no friendly casualties. The positive results of this engagement reinforced the effectiveness of aggressive tactics, deception, and innovation even in a defensive configuration. It also demonstrated the benefits of empowerment—providing subordinate leaders the opportunity to gain confidence in accomplishing their duties without being over-supervised.

Continually searching for battlefield innovations, Major Loffert, our battalion operations officer, suggested we employ ducks to provide security at night. In theory, the ducks would alert us by quacking if any VC tried to sneak into our defensive perimeter. After we distributed the ducks, Lieutenant Graves asked one question, "Are you serious about this?" I didn't impart any specific instructions except the ducks should be tethered in front of their fighting positions so they wouldn't waddle off. That night, I heard quacking along the company perimeter followed by sharp explosions. The next morning, I walked the front-line trace to see how the concept worked. The soldiers had tied the ducks to Claymore mines. Upon hearing a quack, the soldiers triggered the Claymore mines, hoping to kill any VC attempting to infiltrate. By morning, all ducks but one had been killed in action. This last duck chose to remain silent right up to its eventual demise as duck stew for the Vietnamese interpreter that night.

On one occasion, in preparing for a heliborne assault from a battalion field site, I selected a broad rice paddy as the landing zone (LZ). The standard operating procedure required our soldiers to remain concealed in a wood line until the aircraft were inbound to the LZ—reducing exposure time to five minutes while loading the helicopters. When it was time for the aircraft to begin their descent, the company moved in eight-man loads to the LZ and lined up in a crouched position ready to board. On this day, however, the sky was clear. No "wop wop" helicopter sound could be heard. I moved to the center of the LZ and called the airlift commander, who apologized for being late and indicated the aircraft would be there shortly. But the five minutes had elapsed, and I was not happy. While backing up to let the aircraft land, I proceeded to tell the airlift commander over the radio how I felt about them being late

Not watching where I was walking and weighted down with my M-16 rifle, magazines, and hand grenades, I dropped straight into a well located at the corner of the rice paddy. Because I sank in over my head, my two radio telephone operators (RTOs) pulled me out, but my M-16 was still in the well. I removed my equipment and helmet and dove back in. First Sergeant Fulghum and the battalion commander, Lieutenant Colonel Bashore, had walked over to the LZ in time to see Captain Foley diving into a well while the troops were loading the helicopters. Turning to First Sergeant Fulghum, Lieutenant Colonel Bashore said, "What the hell is your company commander doing?" My first sergeant said, "I'll find out, sir," He ran across the LZ, grabbed my mud-covered M-16, and handed me another one. I picked up my map case and began squishing my way to the helicopters now loaded with smiling soldiers who had just witnessed their commanding officer get a good dunking. I also felt a sharp pain in my left knee from my size 16 boot getting caught on the lip of the well as I fell in.

When we returned to the field site that afternoon, the company medic taped ice on my swollen left knee. I laid on the ground with my back against a sandbag bunker keeping my leg elevated on two other sandbags. It was early evening and I noticed that several NCOs were gathered in front of me. I looked over at First Sergeant Fulghum and said, "Are you having a meeting, Top?" Before he could respond, the NCOs began singing a song based on the nursery rhyme, "Ding Dong Dell." I can only remember the first line, "Ding Dong Dell, there's a captain in the well." When they finished, I said with a hint of sarcasm, "Very funny." At that moment, I looked to my left and spotted a bamboo viper about 10 feet away, coming straight at me. I only remember saying "Holy shit," as I pushed straight up with my good leg and did a back flip over the sandbags. As the snake slithered right over the spot where I had been sitting, I heard a deafening "Blam! Blam!" next to my right ear. First Sergeant Fulghum was standing there with his shotgun and calmly said, "Dead snake." The NCOs responded with uncontrolled laughter. Thankfully, this was the last exhilarating interlude to occur on that fun-filled day.

In addition to helicopter airlift and gunship support, we appreciated the medical evacuation helicopters referred to as "DUSTOFF birds" (Dedicated, Unhesitating Service To Our Fighting Forces). They arrived with medics onboard ready to begin treatment on the way to a military hospital. One day, we called for the medical evacuation of two wounded soldiers in the middle of a heavy firefight with Viet Cong elements. In minutes, a DUSTOFF chopper arrived. We had thrown a smoke grenade to mark the LZ, but I told the aircraft commander to remain airborne until we could suppress the enemy fire. His response was, "Roger, sir, but we have a job to do so if it's all the same to you, we're coming on in." The DUSTOFF was on the ground in seconds, picked up the wounded soldiers, and flew away under intense enemy fire. I'll never forget the gallantry of the DUSTOFF crews and how well these great soldiers lived up to their motto every day.

While concerned with every casualty, we couldn't afford to worry about those killed during the heat of battle. To someone who has never experienced combat, this may appear to be a callous sentiment, but leaders couldn't take time out for mourning the loss of a soldier in the middle of a firefight. Decisions are split second and we owed it to our soldiers to stay ahead of the game. It didn't take much to lose momentum in the close fight and soldiers needed to see leaders taking decisive action when the going got tough. It wasn't only the competent employment of maneuver forces and indirect fire support that made the difference. It was also the example set by leaders. Only when things settled down could we allow ourselves the opportunity to grieve.

One of the most important lessons I learned as a young company commander was having the courage to say "No." One night, I was tasked by the battalion staff to send out a squad-size (eight-man) patrol to establish a listening post (LP) along a suspected enemy avenue of approach. Due to recent casualties, I did not have any NCOs available who could lead the patrol. Although I was pressured to accept the tasking, I held fast, and the mission went to another company. Unfortunately, the patrol from the other unit departed friendly lines with an inexperienced young sergeant who did not establish the LP at the designated location. Instead, he placed the patrol closer to the battalion perimeter so they could run back quickly if attacked. In addition, the sergeant told his soldiers to go to sleep and he would stand the first watch. Regrettably, the sergeant also went to sleep. During the night, a VC element attacked their position, killing four, wounding two, and taking the sergeant and another soldier captive. We have a moral obligation as leaders to ensure the safety and security of the soldiers entrusted to our care at all times. Many decisions in combat are split second, but when time is available, it's prudent to consider the risks involved in tasking soldiers to independent missions. In addition, we must be tough enough to withstand inordinate pressure from superiors, peers, and subordinates who may not like the decisions we make or the positions we take.

Although it was standard procedure to fly in and out of operational areas, we never lost sight of our ability to displace without helicopters. One time, when my company couldn't obtain airlift support, we were forced to return to Cu Chi on foot. I knew we would eventually be moving in darkness, but I was comfortable navigating with map and compass (the Global Positioning System didn't exist in 1966). Anticipating VC activity on the way back, I directed my artillery forward observer (FO) to plan for fires on suspected enemy locations between our company location and the Cu Chi base camp. Precision firing was essential since we were moving directly toward the firing battery and any round fired long could drop right on the company. I told the FO to obtain assurance from the battery commander that the fire missions could be executed properly. A few minutes later, my FO told me the battery commander was on the radio and wanted to speak to me. He said, "Hey 'Files'—this is Jack." I immediately recognized the voice. It was Jack O'Donnell, my plebe year roommate. He was the only classmate who called me "Files"—a nickname indicating that I was boning files, i.e., studying hard to get ahead of my classmates. He was the commander of Alpha Battery, 1-8 Artillery, assigned that night to fire in direct support of us. He told me not to worry. He would confirm the accuracy of every round fired until we were safely inside base camp. It's always nice to have a West Point classmate and former roommate looking out for you when you are making a night movement through enemy territory.

## CHAPTER 8

# Operation *Attleboro*

On Wednesday, November 2, 1966, after a six-day search and destroy operation, I landed with Alpha Company at the 25th Division airfield. We wanted nothing more than a shower, hot meal, rest, and recuperation. As the first order of business, the non-commissioned officers supervised the storage of ammunition, hand grenades, and sensitive items, followed by the cleaning and maintenance of weapons and equipment. That evening, after post-operation procedures were complete, First Sergeant Fulghum released the company for dinner and access to the beer tent.

The next day, the battalion operations officer sent me a warning order.

"Get your company ready for an airmobile assault to War Zone C to reinforce 1st Battalion, 27th Infantry. Details are sketchy, but you will be deploying later today."

"Why us? We just returned from a six-day operation."

"Because you are available, and the need is urgent."

Details were indeed sketchy but from previous operations in War Zone C we knew that the area of operation consisted of dense, heavily wooded jungle terrain with triple canopy trees, where visibility was limited to 10–15 yards and artillery had to be adjusted by sound instead of direct observation.

What we did not know was enemy intent. In 1966, the Central Office for South Vietnam (COSVN) governed the communist strategy for the North Vietnamese Army (NVA) and Viet Cong forces operating in South Vietnam. COSVN was not located in a building or a fixed site. On the contrary, it was comprised of NVA and VC leaders who lived in jungle huts and were continually on the move to avoid detection.[1]

The COSVN commander, General Nguyen Chi Thanh, believed that success in South Vietnam could only be achieved by the loss of so many American lives that the growing anti-war movement in the United States would force America to abandon the war. In Hanoi during the summer of 1966, General Thanh met with General Vo Nguyen Giap. General Thanh recommended that a major offensive be conducted against American forces in South Vietnam. Comfortable with the hit-and-run tactics employed by the VC and wary of American military firepower, General Giap initially expressed reluctance to give his support but ultimately approved the concept.[2]

For this unprecedented military campaign, General Thanh selected Tay Ninh Province, a geographical salient sharing its northern border with Cambodia, approximately 50 miles northwest of Saigon. Located at the southern end of the Ho Chi Minh Trail, this elaborate network of mountain and jungle paths through Laos and Cambodia was used by the NVA to infiltrate troops and military supplies to South Vietnam. General Thanh appointed Senior Colonel Hoang Cam, Commander of the elite 9th Viet Cong Division, to oversee the operation. Colonel Cam designated the 271st and 272nd Regiments, augmented by the 101st North Vietnamese Army Regiment, as the principal combatants in the order of battle.[3]

American intelligence indicated that the VC had constructed base camps, storage sites, and staging areas in the jungles of Tay Ninh Province. In the summer of 1966, General Westmoreland placed the newly arrived 196th Light Infantry Brigade (LIB) near the provincial capital of Tay Ninh City to ensure the approaches to Saigon were well protected.

In mid-October 1966, the 196th LIB commenced Operation *Attleboro*, a series of small-unit operations designed to provide a break-in period in an area presumed to be occupied by relatively few VC. While one battalion remained at the base camp for security, the brigade headquarters and two infantry battalions deployed to the middle of an old Michelin rubber plantation near an abandoned airfield.[4] There was no indication that the operation would quickly involve five infantry battalions and that November 5, 1966, would be the most difficult and devastating day faced by the soldiers of Alpha Company, 2nd Battalion, 27th Infantry. Before it was over, elements of the 1st Infantry Division, the 25th Infantry Division, the 11th Armored Cavalry Regiment, the 173rd Airborne Brigade, and three South Vietnamese Army battalions were engaged in a massive hunt for NVA and VC forces belonging to the 9th Viet Cong Division. When Operation *Attleboro* concluded on November 25, there were 155 American soldiers killed in action (KIA) and a reported 1,016 VC/NVA killed, with most of the 9th VC Division desperately evading the American forces they had been sent out to destroy.[5]

Brigadier General Edward H. deSaussure, the 196th LIB commander, had served in the Pacific Theater during World War II, and thereafter was assigned primarily to guided missile units. He was a field artillery officer involved in his first infantry command. His top priority was to build the brigade base camp, conduct operations to obtain intelligence on enemy activities, and gain familiarization with the surrounding terrain. During the first few months of search and destroy operations, the 196th uncovered large caches of VC weapons, ammunition, and medical supplies. One storage area contained 843 tons of rice, which the 196th began returning to the peasant farmers from whom it had been taken.[6]

At the end of October, the 196th received reports that the 9th Viet Cong Division was headed toward Saigon and might pass through Dau Tieng, a small village just east of Tay Ninh City. General deSaussure requested reinforcements through its higher headquarters, II Field Force, which tasked the 25th Infantry Division to provide the requisite support. On November 1, 1966, 1st Battalion, 27th Infantry (1/27), was placed under the operational control of the 196th Light Infantry Brigade.[7]

On November 2, at 7:00 p.m., Major Guy S. Meloy, the 1/27 battalion commander, attended a briefing in the 196th LIB tactical operations center located at the airfield near Dau Tieng. The brigade operations officer gave a short presentation using a map mounted on an easel to illustrate the scheme of maneuver. The plan called for two of Meloy's units, Charlie Company and Bravo Company, to conduct airmobile assaults on opposite sides of the brigade area of operations—5,000 yards apart. And he had no unit available for reinforcements because Alpha Company, 1st Battalion, 27th Infantry (A/1-27), was in brigade reserve. In addition, there were four companies from two other battalions—2nd Battalion, 1st Infantry (2-1), and 4th Battalion, 31st Infantry (4-31)—conducting independent operations in between his two companies.[8]

Information included in the Army standard five-paragraph field order, such as the estimate of the situation and concept of the operation, were missing from the 196th LIB presentation. Major Meloy argued vehemently that the plan violated basic tactical doctrine, lacked unity of effort, and was devoid of standard control measures. He requested reconsideration of the plan with emphasis on developing a concise mission statement and a clear understanding of the commander's intent. General deSaussure stated that the plan would stand as is and walked out of the briefing tent.[9]

On the following morning, Charlie Company, 1st Battalion, 27th Infantry (C/1-27), conducted an airmobile assault into the northwest corner of the brigade area of operations. While moving from the landing zone to the nearest wood line through 4-foot-high elephant grass, the company was engaged by VC forces with automatic weapons, rocket-propelled grenades, and snipers in trees. The company commander and first sergeant of C/1-27 were killed. Two platoon leaders and two platoon sergeants were severely wounded. A medical evacuation helicopter was hit and exploded on the ground, killing one crew member. Only one officer in C/1-27 was not wounded—a newly arrived second lieutenant.[10]

Major Meloy quickly took command of the battle, requesting release of A/1-27 and Charlie Company, 3rd Battalion, 21st Infantry (C/3-21), from brigade reserve to reinforce C/1-27. After a heavy concentration of artillery fire, A/1-27 and C/3-21 conducted an envelopment of the VC positions. In Meloy's words:

> The attacks began at 3:35 p.m. and ended 90 minutes later. The VC had been overpowered and, typical of their tactics, had left to fight another day. When A/1-27 and C/3-21 linked up in the northeast sector of the Viet Cong defense, we discovered the largest and most elaborate enemy base camp I had ever seen. No question that is why the VC had defended it so tenaciously and with so much firepower.[11]

On the morning of November 4, Task Force 1/27 advanced to the northeast with A/1-27 leading. After 1000 yards of trudging through dense undergrowth, A/1-27 ran into intense enemy automatic weapons fire reinforced by snipers in trees. Major

Meloy moved C/3-21 and C/1-27 to positions on either side of A/1-27 to form a defensive perimeter and called for close air support and artillery fire.

> Adjusting fires was a challenge because in the dense jungle we could not see more than 30 feet, so we had to adjust artillery and designate airstrikes on instinct and sound and coordination of action on the radio was almost impossible due to the volume of fire and ear-shattering battle noises.[12]

At 1:36 p.m., the enemy fired mortar rounds into the 1-27 defensive perimeter, wounding Major Meloy in the right elbow, shoulder, and left knee. At 2:00 p.m., the enemy launched an attack on the right flank, followed by a frontal attack on A/1-27. The Wolfhounds successfully fought off these attacks with the help of artillery and close air support.[13]

At 2:54 p.m., my battalion commander, Lieutenant Colonel William C. (Bill) Barott, called Major Meloy from his helicopter. Barott told Meloy that 2nd Battalion, 27th Infantry (2-27), was ordered by General deSaussure to reinforce 1-27. In addition, Barrot was directed to relieve Meloy so he could be medically evacuated. Major Meloy was stunned. He had not requested reinforcements and considered his wounds to be minor. After providing Barott with grid coordinates for a landing zone, Meloy said, "From the LZ go due east to an open field, then north to approach my position."[14]

At 5:41 p.m., Barott called Meloy on the radio, stating: "There are VC between you and me. I am with Charlie Company. Am going to try to retrace route and go around VC."[15] Unfortunately, instead of heading due east and then north from the LZ, Lieutenant Colonel Barott and C/2-27 went north first and then due east, which put them right behind the enemy bunker system.

Although this was a tragic mistake, confusion is not uncommon in fast-moving combat situations. Major Meloy was sending his message on the radio over the sounds of weapons firing and explosions and Lieutenant Colonel Barott was listening to the radio communication in a helicopter while competing with the high-pitched sound of turbine engines and the slap of rotor blades. In hindsight, Major Meloy should have designated a team of soldiers to guide Lieutenant Colonel Barott and C/2-27 from their landing zone to the 1-27 location.

At 6:47 p.m., Private First Class William Wallace, Lieutenant Colonel Barott's RTO, notified Major Meloy that Lieutenant Colonel Barott and Captain Gerald L. Currier, C/2-27 company commander, were KIA. In attempting to retrace their steps, the battalion command element and C/2-27 ran straight into several enemy firing lanes. The surviving soldiers were hunkered down in an old B-52 bomb crater. Since it was getting dark, Major Meloy instructed Private First Class Wallace to tell everyone to lay low—no noise and no firing of weapons unless the VC made an attack on their position.[16]

"The situation in C/2-27 when Barott was killed, and the company became trapped behind VC defenses was the pivotal point of the entire battle."[17] Major Meloy had planned to break contact and destroy the enemy with artillery and close air support. That was no longer an option. He had to maintain contact and break through the enemy positions if they were to have any chance of rescuing C/2-27 and evacuating their casualties. Believing there was a gap in the enemy lines, he ordered Captain Thompson, the company commander of C/2-1, to infiltrate through the gap and evacuate C/2-27 to the west. He emphasized that they should withdraw if enemy contact was made. At 9:00 p.m., C/2-1 commenced movement and was quickly caught in a very confusing, bloody night fight. Captain Thompson broke contact, suffering five KIA and 13 wounded in action (WIA).[18]

Back in Cu Chi on November 3, after receiving the battalion warning order, I discussed the situation with Lieutenant Day and First Sergeant Fulghum. We decided to immediately gather Alpha Company in the mess hall. Although I normally briefed the leaders separately, I wanted these great Wolfhound soldiers to hear the bad news directly from me. As I explained our new mission, I could see the looks of disappointment on their faces. But as soon as I mentioned that our fellow Wolfhounds were in trouble, their demeanor changed. They understood the situation and quietly moved back to their squad areas to get ready. I met with the platoon leaders and platoon sergeants to provide instructions for liftoff at 6:00 p.m.

While boarding helicopters at the division airfield, my good friend, Mack Howard, ran up and yelled over the noise of the helicopter engines, "Keep your head down, it's getting rough up there." As we took off, I thought Mack did not run from division headquarters to the airfield for no reason. When he was the company commander for B/2-27 in Hawaii, I was his executive officer. We had watched each other's back on many occasions.

Upon landing at Dau Tieng, I placed the company in a wooded area with instructions to rise early and continue constructing sandbag bunkers. The next morning, I briefed my platoon leaders in a tent belonging to the C/1-27 commander and first sergeant who had been killed the previous day. After the meeting, I looked down at the footlocker across from me and saw stenciled on the front, "Captain Fred Henderson"—my West Point classmate. I heard a rumor when I arrived in Vietnam that infantry platoon leaders lasted about six months before being killed or wounded. I never thought to ask how long infantry company commanders would last.

Around noon on November 4, the 196th LIB executive officer notified me to meet with General deSaussure on the Dau Tieng airstrip. They needed a rifle platoon right away for an airmobile assault to secure a downed helicopter. I told the commanding general that a routine VC tactic in the Ho Bo and Boi Loi woods was to ambush reinforcements sent to the aid of a smaller unit. Not wanting to take a chance with one platoon, I recommended that my entire company be assigned the mission. General deSaussure said there were not enough helicopters and walked away. I told the brigade executive officer (XO) that I was not going to send one platoon. If he wanted it done, he would have to get someone else. He told me to wait on the airstrip and ran to catch up with General deSaussure.

The brigade XO quickly returned with approval to send the entire company in two airlifts. As soon as the second flight landed, an enemy force from a nearby wood line engaged us with automatic weapons and rifle grenades. While calling in artillery, I maneuvered two platoons against the VC positions, leaving one platoon to secure the helicopter. The VC quickly vanished, the helicopter was recovered, and we returned to Dau Tieng with no casualties. Later that evening, we were airlifted into the 1-27 defensive perimeter.

At 1:00 a.m. on November 5, I reported to Major Meloy to receive an operations order. He told me to pass through the 1-27 perimeter defense, break through the enemy bunker system, link up with C/2-27, form a corridor back through the enemy sector, and evacuate the company to friendly front lines. In addition to being tasked with an extraordinarily complex mission, Major Meloy informed me that we would be fighting against North Vietnamese regulars. And he was convinced if we didn't take immediate action, C/2-27 would be annihilated in the morning. One final piece of unwelcome news: due to the proximity of C/2-27 to the enemy bunker system, I couldn't employ artillery, close air support, or gunships. We had to do something we had never done before—fight with what we carried in with us.

I sat thinking this was a suicide mission, but if we didn't go, who would? With only a few hours to daylight, I went back to brief my platoon leaders. I told them only that part of the mission that involved breaking through the enemy bunker system. If we were fortunate enough to link up with C/2-27, I wasn't about to come back through enemy lines carrying dead and wounded. Instead, we would head northwest out of the combat zone and arrange for a heliborne pickup at a remote site. There are times when leaders must adapt to changing situations and adjust the mission if following orders is not the right thing to do. There are those who would take exceptions to this belief, but leaders must be tough enough to accept the consequences of disregarding orders when, in their judgment, the success of the mission and soldier welfare are at risk.

At 7:30 a.m., we departed friendly front lines in a column of platoons with First Platoon leading—followed by the command group, Third Platoon, and Second Platoon. I chose this formation because I wanted Lieutenant Harold K. Graves, First Platoon leader, up front. He was a tough combat veteran who would aggressively confront the enemy. I also needed maximum flexibility to maneuver with the other two platoons when we made enemy contact. After moving just 30 yards, the enemy hit us with a fusillade of automatic weapons fire, rifle grenades, and direct fire from snipers in trees. The initial burst came from the right flank of First Platoon, resulting in eight casualties. I ordered Lieutenant Graves to lay down a base of fire while I moved Third Platoon to the left flank. I held Second Platoon in reserve until I could develop a more accurate picture of the situation.

The deafening noise of our rifle and machine gun fire on top of the enemy weapons fire and grenade explosions made it difficult to hear leaders shouting orders. My primary objective was to continue the momentum of our attack. At the first burst of enemy fire, soldiers look to their leaders. If leaders hit the ground, soldiers hit the ground. I did not want to get pinned down. During the assault, Specialist Fourth Class John W. Lynch, one of my RTOs, was hit in the knee. I helped remove his web gear, turned him over to the medics to receive first aid, and gave the radio to another soldier. When I moved forward again, Specialist Fourth Class Rick Stevens, my second RTO was wounded. After engaging several snipers in trees, Stevens was running to catch up with me when he was hit by machine gun fire.

Lieutenant Graves sent Private First Class Charles D. "Chuck" Dean, an outstanding soldier from First Platoon, to describe to me the tunnels of fire the enemy had cut through the vegetation in front of their bunkers. Because these lanes were waist high, they were difficult to identify. Soldiers had to crouch or crawl on the ground to discover them. Any soldiers who walked into a firing lane or tried to provide aid to a wounded soldier lying in a firing lane became a target for enemy machine guns. Although I sent this information out by runner to the other two platoons, I knew we were in a bad situation. Amid the shouting of orders were cries for medics. Casualties were mounting and due to the dense vegetation, I couldn't tell what progress was being made. From my basketball days I knew that after receiving a pass, you can dribble, shoot, pass, or take it to the hoop. If you hold the ball and do nothing, the defensive read changes. Combat's no different. The enemy adapts to your movement until you dictate the course of events on your terms.

While Dean was sketching out a map of the NVA bunker locations on the ground, an M-60 machine gunner to our right front was hit in the legs and fell, unable to move. Now I was angry as hell. I picked up the machine gun and told Dean to help me link as much ammunition as we could in a continuous belt, which I placed around my neck. I told him, "You're my assistant gunner. Get the rest of the ammo and let's go."

Dean ran through heavy enemy fire, grabbed two more belts of M-60 ammunition, and returned leading several other Wolfhounds. In addition to carrying his M-79 grenade launcher, Dean carried the M-60 ammunition and stayed right with me. He not only displayed outstanding courage, but he provided the leadership to clearly make a difference by telling Alpha Company soldiers to follow us as we moved forward. He would receive the Silver Star for his courageous actions that day.

I took off straight for the sound of the enemy guns. I moved as fast as my long legs would carry me but the thick foliage and fallen trees made any kind of rushing assault difficult. Although I advanced steadily forward in a matter of minutes, it seemed like it was taking forever. I stopped thinking about command and control of Alpha Company. Instead, I was focused solely on taking out the enemy machine guns.

When I finally came upon the NVA positions, I fired the machine gun at three bunkers to my right front and continued a steady rate of fire at every bit of movement along the trench line. Dean was firing his grenade launcher directly at the bunkers. As I turned, I could see my soldiers coming in behind me taking up firing positions. In minutes, there was a surge of soldiers moving forward, throwing hand grenades into the trenches and firing their weapons at the enemy bunkers.

Making my way along the trench system, I was wounded by an enemy grenade. I forgot momentarily that a 6-foot 7-inch company commander makes a good target. There was profuse bleeding from my left side, but the adrenaline was surging too fast for me to feel much pain. When I looked down at the barrel of my machine gun, there were only about 10 rounds left. One of my NCOs grabbed the M-60 and said, "Sir, we got this now." He was right. I was not supposed to be fighting this battle by myself. I had a 100-man rifle company to command and control. As more soldiers arrived, including Lieutenant Price with Second Platoon, a deadly barrage of friendly fire was unleashed at the NVA positions, and the enemy promptly withdrew.

Although all three platoons made it to the enemy bunker and trench system, we didn't have the firepower or manpower to continue. We had taken heavy casualties and we were running low on ammunition. It was about 11:00 a.m. and we had been in the fight for three and a half hours. While I was contemplating what to do next, Major Loffert, the battalion operations officer and acting battalion commander called on the radio and directed that we conduct an orderly withdrawal. He told me that due to our assault, the NVA uncovered C/2-27 to face us. As a result, an ad hoc task force of three companies under the command of Captain Bob Garrett, commander of B/1-27, was able to sweep in from the north, link up with C/2-27, and evacuate the dead and wounded.

The task force approached C/2-27 with ease. Private First Class Bill Wallace, the RTO for Lieutenant Colonel Barott, indicated that the linkup was surreal. For two days, they had been hugging the ground with automatic weapons fire and explosions all around them, waiting for the VC to attack. Suddenly, with everything quiet, they were looking up at the faces of American soldiers who were motioning for them to get up.[19] C/2-27 was in worse shape than we thought. They had 15 KIA and 70 wounded, requiring the best efforts of three rifle companies to carry them to friendly lines and board medical evacuation helicopters.

After giving instructions to withdraw, I became aware of an eerie silence on the battlefield. We had gone from a cacophony of continuous firing and explosions to an absence of any sounds. I kept thinking, "What the hell happened? Where did the NVA go?" I was spotted by some medics who pulled off my blood-soaked fatigue shirt to extract shrapnel from my back, stop the bleeding, and apply dressings to my wounds.

As I sat on the floorboards of the helicopter during the airlift back to Cu Chi, my thoughts were with these tough Wolfhound soldiers whose indomitable spirit had made all the difference. We had 13 KIA and 31 wounded. With tears rolling down my cheeks, I reflected on how they never wavered, never hesitated. They simply carried out this difficult mission with courage and determination. The Alpha Company Wolfhounds had demonstrated the 27th Infantry Regimental motto—"No fear on earth." They were, to the very last soldier, standing tall that day.

One example of the strength of character of these magnificent Wolfhounds was displayed by the actions of my RTO, Specialist Fourth Class Rick Stevens. Years later, in an email to me, he said:

> After hitting some snipers in the trees, I ran to catch up with you but was hit by a machine gun burst. I knew you needed the radio, but I was laying against a tree and couldn't move. I remember yelling, "Hey Captain Foley." It immediately dawned on me that I was telling any of the enemy within earshot (of which there were a lot) that you were the captain. I just want to say that I'm sorry and that I'm glad I didn't get you killed.[20]

Specialist Stevens was wounded and in pain but was only concerned that he may have put my life in danger. When he found out I was alive 43 years later, he felt a need to apologize. There was no need. I was happy to hear from him and tremendously grateful he was by my side on that difficult day.

I also received an email from Specialist Fourth Class Bob Park, who said:

> I have wanted to contact you for a long time. I doubt that you remember me, but I remember you. I was with you on November 5th during Operation Attleboro. I was knocked down and wounded the same time you were. I don't know if it was the same grenade or not. Things were going way too fast. I know what you did that day saved a lot of lives, including mine, and I never really had a chance to thank you for that. I thank you and my family thanks you. I understand that you stayed in the Army and finally retired as an LTG. You must have had many commands since Alpha Company and you undoubtedly deserved them, but you will always be Captain Foley, CO of Alpha Company to me.[21]

When I reflect on November 5, 1966, I habitually begin with the sudden disappearance of the enemy from the battlefield. The NVA had prepared elaborate defensive positions with concrete bunkers and overhead cover in the middle of the jungle. The waist-high tunnel system with interlocking fields of fire was one of the most innovative tactical concepts we had ever encountered. The NVA soldiers with pith helmets, khaki uniforms, web gear, and combat boots, armed with AK-47s and rocket-propelled grenades, were vastly superior to the VC, who wore black pajamas and sandals, were armed with a variety of weapons, and consistently adopted hit-and-run tactics. If the NVA were so adamant about defending in place, where did they go on November 5, 1966, and why?

Colonel Rod Paschall, U.S. Army Retired, a former Special Forces officer and a respected military historian, was in command of Bravo Company, 2nd Battalion,

27th Infantry, during Operation *Attleboro*. In an article that he wrote about the actions of both Wolfhound battalions, he said:

> Captured documents unraveled the mystery of the sudden lack of enemy resistance on 5 November soon after the violent attack by Alpha Company, 2nd Battalion, 27th Infantry. The documents revealed that the 3rd Battalion of the 101st North Vietnamese Army Regiment that was facing the 1st and 2nd Battalions of the 27th Infantry was so ravaged by the American attacks and firepower that its troops simply fled the battlefield. The report went on to describe that the North Vietnamese were so shaken that it took six days to locate the survivors.[22]

Major Meloy had a distinguished military career rising to the rank of major general and command of the 82nd Airborne Division. After he retired, he wrote an account about 1st Battalion, 27th Infantry, during Operation *Attleboro*. In describing the actions of Alpha Company, 2-27 Infantry, General Meloy said:

> One thing is clear, and there is one thing that always needs to be recognized and never forgotten about the fight that A/2-27 had that morning. And that is the courage, pride, training, esprit, discipline, and sheer individual as well as collective guts of the A/2-27 soldiers and leaders on the morning of 5 November match any ever displayed on any battlefield of any war in the Army's history.[23]

In looking at lessons learned from the Wolfhounds' participation in Operation *Attleboro*, I began with an analysis of 1st Battalion, 27th Infantry, when it was placed under the operational control of the 196th LIB. After the briefing on the evening of November 2, Major Meloy made it clear to Brigadier General deSaussure that he resolutely opposed the operational concept and laid out cogent reasons why the plan was defective. But the destiny of 1-27 was sealed when General deSaussure walked out of the briefing tent, stated the discussion was over, his decision was final, and the plan would stand as is.[24]

What options did Major Meloy have at this point? Should he have taken time right after the briefing to develop an alternative concept with the other battalion commanders for consideration by General deSaussure? Should he have refused to participate in the operation? Should he have asked his parent brigade commander, Colonel Thomas L. Tarpley, for intervention with General deSaussure? Any parent brigade commander would have been very upset if he knew that one of his battalion commanders under the operational control of another command was not comfortable with his orders. Unfortunately, Major Meloy's conformity with a plan that he later described as "ludicrous" was compounded over the next 72 hours by the inexperience of the 196th LIB staff and by the incompetence of a guided missile-trained brigade commander conducting a large-scale infantry operation.

Colonel Charles K. Nulsen, U.S. Army Retired, who commanded 3rd Battalion, 21st Infantry, one of the 196th LIB units participating in Operation *Attleboro*, wrote an article entitled "A flawed battle plan turned a combat training exercise in War Zone C into a bloody battle during the fall of 1966." Colonel Nulsen stated that:

Major Meloy violently objected to the battle plan. He felt that, although it may have looked impressive on the map and seemed logical in briefings, the plan did not consider the realities of infantry movement in dense, overgrown jungle and the extreme difficulty of maintaining control of many small, separated maneuver elements in that environment. As it transpired, the next three days exposed the flaws of the battle plan. Battalions were split by four to five kilometers; companies were lost; communications between battalion headquarters and brigade staff were non-existent during critical times; and in the final phase of the battle, one battalion commander was commanding 11 companies while another battalion commander was left to command only his headquarters elements.[25]

When Major Meloy lodged protests about the operational concept at the initial operations briefing, General deSaussure should have asked for opinions from the other commanders and staff to resolve any issues. Because he was a career artilleryman commanding an infantry brigade, he ought to have welcomed the experience and judgment of his infantry battalion commanders. In addition, the 196th LIB had the latitude to establish their own timelines. General deSaussure could have delayed the operation a day or two to develop a better plan.

On November 6, the 1-27 and 2-27 Infantry Battalions were pulled out of the operation and flown back to Cu Chi. Simultaneously, the 1st Infantry Division, commanded by Major General William E. DePuy, took command of Operation *Attleboro* and Brigadier General deSaussure was relieved of command.

In my view, the leaders who "get it" carve out time to listen, ask questions, and establish the proper climate for the free flow of information. But determining the right course of action is not enough. Leaders must also have the courage to say no when the mission has unacceptable risk, when essential resources are not provided, or when following orders is simply not an option. A solid background in moral-ethical reasoning is essential for leaders to feel confident in asserting their beliefs when faced with difficult situations. They can't walk by the red flags of ethical turmoil and then maintain, during damage recovery, there were no indicators. Without question, a comprehensive values-based education for our leaders is a key component in fulfilling the purpose of the U.S. Army to fight and win our nation's wars.

When General John A. Wickham, Jr. was the Army chief of staff in 1985, he published a pamphlet entitled *Guideposts for a Proud and Ready Army*. In it he stated: "At a time when we are all blessed with so much opportunity and challenge, I believe we should rededicate ourselves to the fundamentals responsible for the Army's success—the core values that have served our institution and our nation so well."[26]

On Sunday morning, November 6, 1966, Brigadier General G. G. O'Connor, acting commander of the 25th Infantry Division, flew to Dau Tieng and presented me, Private First Class Charles D. Dean, and Private First Class William H. Wallace with the Silver Star. He also awarded the Bronze Star for Valor to Staff Sergeant James Powe and Platoon Sergeant Floro Revera. On Tuesday, November 8, the *Boston Globe* and *Boston Herald* published stories about Operation *Attleboro* indicating that I had been awarded the Silver Star and would be recommended for the Medal

Captain Robert F. Foley wearing a Silver Star for his actions during Operation *Attleboro*.

of Honor by my company. Since I had convinced my parents that I had a desk job in battalion headquarters, they were astonished to see my picture in the newspaper wearing a helmet with a rifle over my shoulder. The photo clearly shows me following the Alpha Company uniform policy—no rank on my helmet and no rank, nametag, U.S. Army, or other insignia on my jungle fatigues.

Concerned with reports that I had been wounded; my mother reached out to the Army for clarification. When the Department of the Army Casualty Branch sent a message to the 25th Infantry Division requesting information on my welfare, I was advised to write my mother. Because regular telephone service was not available and a letter in the mail would take several days, I decided to call home through the Military Auxiliary Radio System (MARS) station at Cu Chi. MARS used a phone patch connection over short-wave radio through an amateur HAM radio operator who requested assistance from a telephone company operator in placing a collect call to my parents. This was cumbersome at best—exacerbated by the requirement to say "Over" so the radio operator would know when to switch back and forth from the transmit to the receive mode. It was fortunate that I spoke first and was able to tell my mother that I was fine. When it was her turn to speak, she kept talking and never said, "Over."

Since all soldiers who deployed to Vietnam from Hawaii in January had completed their mandatory one-year tour of duty, we began receiving reassignment orders to stateside units. I was assigned as commanding officer of a basic training company at Fort Dix, New Jersey. In the final weeks at Cu Chi, I prepared Alpha Company for the change of command, obtained my permanent change of station orders, and was placed on the manifest for a flight from Saigon to Travis Air Force Base, California. I was not informed of any pending awards beyond the Silver Star I received in the jungle near Dau Tieng but years later I came across a DA Form 638 (Recommendation for Award) signed on November 15, 1966, by Lieutenant Colonel Henry R. Shelton, battalion commander of 2nd Battalion, 27th Infantry, recommending me for the Medal of Honor.

## CHAPTER 9

# Two Decisions

On December 21, 1966, I climbed aboard a helicopter headed for Tan Son Nhut Air Base in Saigon to connect with a Pan American charter flight back to the United States. I was amused when the crew chief instructed me to sit in the center of the helicopter and buckle my seatbelt. As a rifle company commander, I sat on the floorboards until we were ready to land and then stood on the skids outside the aircraft with my arm around the center pole so I could check for enemy activity and the suitability of the landing zone.

As our Boeing 707 lifted off, everyone onboard broke out with cheers and applause. After landing at Travis Air Force Base in California I went straight to my BOQ room—a welcome luxury from the austere living conditions in Vietnam. Without unpacking, I indulged in a long, hot shower, enjoyed a deep sleep in a double bed, and left the next day for home. Since I was not thrilled at the prospect of being assigned to Fort Dix, New Jersey, I asked my good friend, Mack Howard, for advice. This led to my reassignment as an infantry instructor at the U.S. Army Engineer School, Fort Belvoir, Virginia.

At the end of February 1967, I moved into a townhouse in Alexandria with Rich Foss. Although I was immersed in instructor certification and teaching assignments for the first few weeks, one Saturday evening, Rich and I headed for an upscale bar in Georgetown. While crossing the 14th Street bridge it dawned on us that we didn't have much money—not even enough to pay the cover charge. We turned around and drove to a party hosted by my classmate, Rodger Bivens, at his apartment in Mount Vernon. Upon arrival, I went straight to the bar while Rich struck up a conversation with Jeanie Brown, an art teacher, who came to the party with her friend, Julie Languasco.

This was Memorial Day weekend and Rodger had asked Julie to bring some friends since there would be many officers at the party who had recently returned from Vietnam. She rounded up two carloads of her girlfriends to attend. Seeing nothing but wall-to-wall women with a few guys sitting at the bar, her friends departed. However, Jeanie persuaded Julie to stay so she could continue talking to

Rich. Julie's weekend Rehoboth Beach cottage reservations had been cancelled and this party was, in her estimation, a disaster. She went looking for Rodger to give him a piece of her mind, but he was nowhere to be found. About midnight, when I walked over to Rich indicating I was ready to go, I was introduced to Julie. Not in a good mood and attempting to be playful, she mimicked my Boston accent and teased me about my height, none of which I found amusing. As a result, our chance meeting did not engender any mutual attraction.

I woke up the next day ready to play tennis with Rich at Fort Myer. When he announced that he had arranged for us to play doubles with Jeanie and Julie at Hains Point, a U.S. National Park Service recreation area on the Potomac River in southwest Washington, D.C., I said, "No way, I'm not going." But after recognizing how important it was to him, I gave in. We drove to Julie's residence—a remarkable three-story penthouse apartment that she shared with three other teachers. While I was seated on a long blue sofa in the living room, Julie noticed my size 16 basketball sneakers from cadet days with "FOLEY" printed in black letters on the sides. She started to laugh and said, "Why do you have your name on your shoes, are you afraid you might lose them?" When I gave Rich a déjà vu look, he urged us to head for the tennis courts. When it was my turn to serve, I aimed straight at Julie with extra force and, to my surprise, she returned every shot the same way. I began looking at her differently, gaining respect for her athletic skills and her competitive nature. During a soda break, she flicked tiny bits of crushed ice at me to "cool me off," she said. I quickly realized Julie was not bad-looking and had a spunky demeanor. We spent the rest of the day enjoying one another's company with no idea it would be the first of many days in a fun-filled yet serious relationship.

During a party at Julie's apartment in June, she described her summer plans to fly to Italy by way of Pan American Flight Number One—a daily flight circling the globe with the option to stay wherever the plane landed for any length of time. Since she would be in Honolulu when I was visiting my friend Bob Corboy, I offered to meet her at the airport. I was at the gate well before her scheduled arrival, but, at the last minute, I returned to the terminal to pick up an orchid lei. When I met her walking toward the baggage claim area, she said, "You're late." And the lei I had placed around her neck was dripping wet from the water spray at the vendor's stand. It was not a good start, but I recovered with Mai Tais and dinner at the Top of the Ilikai Hotel. For the next three days, we had a fabulous time playing tennis, swimming, having dinner at Fort DeRussy, and taking evening walks along Waikiki Beach.

Since I had given considerable thought to whether I wanted to make the Army a career or transition to a civilian occupation, Bob Corboy set up an interview for me with his boss, Frank Crum, the Honolulu branch manager for New York Life Insurance. At the end of our 90-minute session, Frank said, "Bob, I would be happy to bring you into our training program right now, but I think you love the Army. You should see how animated you get when you talk about your sergeants and your soldiers." He was right and his observation played a major role in my subsequent decision to remain on active duty.

Julie sent me a postcard from every country she visited. As soon as she returned, we went to Gettysburg to walk the battlefields. When we came back to the car, she was shocked to see my keys in the ignition and the doors locked but was very impressed when I pulled a spare key out of my wallet. Since I was the principal speaker for a large-scale outdoor demonstration, she asked me if she could attend and was disappointed when I told her the demonstration was only for Department of Defense personnel and their guests. Not to be dissuaded, she convinced her friend, John Gallagher, a Navy commander, to escort her to the site. Standing beside the podium watching the crowd arrive, I thought it strange to see a Navy officer in uniform coming up the hill until I recognized a person whom I knew walking in high heels beside him.

It did not take me long to realize I was deeply in love with Julie. She was smart, fun, and beautiful. I kept thinking that if I didn't act soon, she would marry someone else. But when I proposed, her response was, "Oh, Bob, don't be silly. I hardly know you." She said she treasured her independence and was not ready to take such a big step.

In April 1968, my West Point classmate, Jay Westermeier, dropped by my apartment. He was assigned to the U.S. Army Awards and Decorations Branch in the Pentagon and told me that I would receive the Medal of Honor from President Lyndon B. Johnson in the White House on the first of May. I was stunned because I had not heard anything through official channels in the 18 months since I had left Vietnam. When I arrived home in December 1966, my mother showed me Boston newspaper articles that indicated I would be recommended for the Medal of Honor, but I had dismissed them as news media hyperbole.

My award recommendation had been approved by the chain of command beginning with Colonel Marvin D. Fuller, commanding officer, 2nd Brigade, 25th Infantry Division; Major General Fred C. Weyand, commanding general, 25th Infantry Division; and General William C. Westmoreland, commanding general, U.S. Army Military Assistance Command, Vietnam. It also received approval from the Senior Army Decorations Board, the joint chiefs of staff, the secretary of the Army, and secretary of defense before going to the president for final confirmation.

Since I did not like making speeches, attending formal affairs, or conversing with senior leaders, I was more than apprehensive about what the immediate future might bring. Jay told me I needed to quickly prepare a list of family members, friends, and fellow soldiers I wished to invite to the ceremony. The ensuing days were a blur. My parents and I moved into a suite of rooms at the Madison Hotel located a few blocks from the White House. Two non-commissioned officers took my dress uniform to be cleaned and pressed. They pinned on all insignia and decorations, measuring the exact locations with a ruler. Soldiers from the Old Guard Regiment were assigned as escorts and drivers. A limousine was scheduled to take us to the White House and a separate limousine designated to pick up Julie at her apartment in southwest Washington.

My father was overcome with tears while we rode to the White House in a big limousine, escorted by police cars and motorcycles with blue lights flashing and sirens wailing. We were ushered into the red room, where we met the president, General Harold K. Johnson, the Army chief of staff, and General Earle G. Wheeler, the chairman of the joint chiefs of staff. Right on cue, I faced the uncomfortable task of making introductions and speaking with senior government officials. But I smiled as the president and my mother engaged in a lengthy discussion about the floral arrangements in the red room.

It was a memorable but intimidating experience walking into the East Room with the president of the United States while the band played ruffles and flourishes followed by "Hail to the Chief." As the press pool cameras flashed, I stepped on the platform beside the podium bearing the presidential seal and faced an audience comprised of members of Congress, general officers, family, friends, and fellow soldiers. Seated in the front row were my mother and father. My brother, his family, and Julie were seated right behind them.

On the rostrum beside me was Sergeant John F. Baker, an outstanding soldier in my company who was also receiving the Medal of Honor. Two weeks before we deployed on Operation *Attleboro*, then Private First Class Baker, an artillery cannoneer from the battery across the road in Cu Chi, asked First Sergeant Fulghum if he could join Alpha Company because he wanted to see some action. As evidenced by his citation, which described how he had led repeated assaults against enemy positions and killed several enemy snipers, he saw plenty of action that day.

President Johnson made remarks, our citations were read, and the president placed the Medal of Honor around our necks. We made quite a pair with Sergeant Baker standing at 5 feet 2 inches in height and me at 6 feet 7 inches. In a video of the ceremony, the narrator said:

> Multiple awards for the Medal of Honor for the same action once common in the Civil War are almost unheard of now. These two awards say much about the intensity of that battle and of the special courage it took to face so fanatical an enemy. And these medals too, should dispel any lingering myths about heroic stature.[1]

At the conclusion of the ceremony, the president went over to meet my brother Bill, his wife Barbara, their daughters Karen and Kristen, and Julie. We were all surprised when Kristen, age three, refused to shake the president's hand and crawled under a chair. When the president departed, my parents and I were escorted to the foyer outside the East Room, where a receiving line was set up. We were able to greet all our guests, which included relatives, high school friends, and West Point classmates. It was a blur of soundbites, but I remember breaking into a huge smile when I spotted Mel Wenner, my high school basketball coach, speaking with George Hunter, my West Point basketball coach—two gentlemen who taught me about the will to win, good sportsmanship, and strength of character. After about 20 minutes, the White House staff directed us to the exits.

At the luncheon in the Madison Hotel immediately following the ceremony, I visited with soldiers from the 25th Infantry Division I had not seen since our time in Vietnam, including Major General G. G. O'Connor, Colonel Thomas L. Tarpley, Lieutenant Colonel Henry R. Shelton, Major Wes Loffert, Captain Malcolm J. Howard, Captain David B. Price, Lieutenant Harold K. Graves, First Sergeant Edward L. Fulghum, and Specialist John Lynch. The day ended with a reception in our suite of rooms at the Madison, where I finally got to relax with my West Point and Belmont High School classmates, immediate family, and relatives.

In the weeks following the ceremony, I went to New York City with my parents and Julie to meet Ed Sullivan on his show. I served as the keynote speaker for an outdoor United States savings bond rally held at the Pentagon courtyard and was guest speaker on Armed Forces Day at Aberdeen Proving Ground. I also threw out the first pitch at one of the Washington Senators baseball games. Because my parents had recently moved to Kissimmee, Florida, the town officials put together a "Welcome Home" series of events. We flew on a private jet, and were met by the mayor and his wife, citizens of Kissimmee, and school children waving small American flags. Over the next few days, I made several appearances, including a parade featuring cowboys on horseback and a water-skiing performance at Cypress Gardens. With the support of the town officials, my mother and father moved into a bigger house with a sunroom and a backyard containing grapefruit trees.

At the end of May, I received orders to attend the Armor Officer Advanced Course at Fort Knox, Kentucky. This was a major turning point. My five-year commitment on active duty was complete, leaving me free to remain in the Army or resign from active duty and pursue a career as a civilian. I thought back on the previous five years and decided I had enjoyed it all—the terrific officers, NCOs, and soldiers, the camaraderie, leadership responsibilities, medical benefits, post exchange, and commissary privileges, the social life on Army posts as well as opportunities to travel and live in different countries. In comparison to a career working at a desk in the corporate world, my choice was easy. I headed to Fort Knox.

With a clear understanding of making the Army a career, I again asked Julie for her hand in marriage, fully divulging my love for her and my vision of us going through life together. Still hesitant about getting married, she was unable to say "yes" and cried as I left for Fort Knox. I was disheartened but hopeful that someday she would change her mind. We kept in touch with letters and phone calls, and we met at weddings of mutual friends, but with each passing month we seemed to grow further apart. The year went by quickly and just before graduation in May 1969, I received orders to be a company tactical officer at West Point, which came with attending graduate school to obtain a master's degree in business administration at Fairleigh-Dickinson University (FDU) in New Jersey.

Company tactical officers at the U.S. Military Academy are the key component in accomplishing the mission for developing leaders of character. They supervise a company of 120 cadets (freshmen to seniors) and are responsible for discipline, leadership development, military training, physical fitness, and moral-ethical growth. In addition, they are held accountable for the evaluation and performance counseling of individual cadets in confirming their qualifications to become commissioned officers.

I went to school full time that summer and stayed with my good friend Ed Meyers, who lived a short drive from the school campus. One evening in June when I returned from class, Ed told me that Julie had called and wanted to talk to me. I was surprised. After her rejection of my two previous marriage proposals, I thought things were pretty much over for us. Two days later, on the way to school, I stopped at a pay phone and dialed her number.

When she answered, I said, "Ed Meyers told me you called. What do you want?"

"Well, I haven't heard from you for some time and wanted to know how you are doing.

"Julie, what do you want?"

"I just called to talk and catch up on what you are doing."

"Julie, I'm calling from a pay phone on a busy highway and I'm on my way to class. What do you want?"

"I want to get married."

"To whom?"

"To you, silly."

"Right, I bet you'll change your mind in the morning."

"No, I won't."

I detected a firm and convincing tone in her response that led me to drive to Washington, D.C. that weekend so we could talk in person. On the way to the FDU campus, I thought about this totally unexpected turn of events. Did she just propose to me? I was surprised yet delighted, skeptical yet excited, and very much looking forward to seeing her. Our conversation Friday evening was all positive and we subsequently made plans to get married at West Point in September. I asked Julie why she called me after we had gone our separate ways for the better part of a year. She said that she loved me, missed me, was ready to get married, and knew I was serious about my future when she learned I was studying for a master's degree. Her worst fear was that she was too late, and I might be engaged to someone else.

## CHAPTER 10

# About Face

Julie and I crammed her belongings, including several plants, into my Chevrolet two-door sedan and her tiny Fiat 600. We drove from southwest Washington, D.C. to a rooming house in Highland Falls just outside Thayer Gate at West Point. On the very first day, Julie found a friend in Mary Maher, sister of Marty Maher, the legendary Army master sergeant and swimming coach who was portrayed by Tyrone Power in the 1955 movie *The Long Gray Line*. I moved into the BOQ in Lincoln Hall and began my duties as a company tactical officer. Julie began teaching in Newburgh, planning our wedding at the West Point Catholic chapel, and arranging our reception at the Officers' Club.

September 27, 1969, was a beautiful day. We exchanged vows surrounded by family members, friends, and West Point classmates. My parents flew in from Florida. Julie's mother, sister, and brother drove from New York City, and her Aunt Evelina Bergoglio arrived from Torino, Italy. Brother Bill was best man, Jeanie Brown was maid of honor, Julie's brother, Adrian, walked her down the aisle, and eight first class cadets from Company E, 3rd Regiment, served as saber bearers. Father Edwin F. O'Brien, a young adjunct priest, celebrated the wedding ceremony and Mass. We happily followed his ecclesiastical career from the time he became an Army chaplain with the 82nd Airborne Division and later became the archbishop of the Military Services followed by archbishop of Baltimore. In 2012, we were delighted to attend his consistory in Rome hosted by Pope Benedict, at which he was appointed His Eminence Edwin Cardinal O'Brien.

Our honeymoon in Bermuda was warm, sunny, and relaxing until the day we decided to rent motor scooters and tour around the island. We were riding single file down a busy road when it began to rain. As soon as Julie saw a dump truck approaching, she moved closer to the left side of the road, skidded into a side rail, and tumbled onto the sidewalk. I ran to her side; afraid she might be seriously injured. Seemingly out of nowhere, an ambulance arrived and took us to the emergency room, where she received 16 stitches in her leg. I was miserable thinking how I had failed to properly care for my new bride. We tried to make the best of the situation, but Julie was in so much pain she could hardly walk. We cut short our honeymoon and flew home.

The basement BOQ room was not designed for newlyweds. It had one twin bed, a circular shower with no curtain, a half window in a corner kitchen, a stove out of commission, and a living room with wedding gifts piled high on the floor. It even came equipped with a mouse, who outsmarted our every attempt to trap him, so we gave up and let him stay. I could not help thinking Julie left behind a beautiful penthouse apartment on the top three floors of a building that included a private rooftop garden with a panoramic view of the nation's capital to live in this spartan sub-basement—an inauspicious start to Army married life. Although she never complained, Julie had to walk up a long flight of stairs on her injured leg every day and drive to Newburgh, where she taught 1st grade.

This predicament could have been easily avoided in the summer when West Point conducted its annual housing drawing for married personnel. Because I was single, I was excluded from participating in the drawing by bureaucratic organizers, who would not budge when I pointed out that I would soon be married. Moreover, the regulation stipulated that company tactical officers were required to live on post. When Brigadier General Sam S. Walker, the commandant of cadets, was told about our situation he directed that the Family Housing Office assign us the next available set of quarters. In the interim, we moved out of the basement to a larger BOQ room and were pleased to move into the next set of available quarters, which happened to be a spacious three-bedroom townhouse on Tillman Place.

The week I returned from Bermuda, Lieutenant Colonel James F. Miley, the regimental executive officer, invited me to join him for a walk through the Company E3 area. I was professionally embarrassed at the signs of indiscipline and low standards prominently displayed in cadet rooms, gym lockers, and common areas. I scheduled an inspection the following Saturday. In one room, I found a second classman who had earlier stood inspection in his own room. He wanted to see if I would remember him when he showed up in another room. He didn't think it was funny when I accused him of attempting to deceive the inspecting officer. After finding a cadet in the same room wearing someone else's nametag and another cadet displaying a classmate's pair of shoes under his bed, I stopped the inspection and asked the company commander for an explanation. He told me these second classmen had successfully played the same tricks on the previous tactical officer and were surprised when they got caught by me. I told him these antics had clear implications to the cadet honor code. The remainder of the inspection did not go well for the company. With my 6-foot 7-inch height, I could not only see to the rear of the shelves in the wardrobe closets but had the reach to extract unauthorized items such as beer, coffee pots, and civilian clothes. By the end of the day, several cadets were over their demerit allowance, and many would be walking punishment tours on the area.

On Monday morning, I inspected the company trunk room with the cadet in charge of quarters and found bottles of liquor, wine, and six-packs of beer hidden in suitcases. I lined up the prohibited items on the floor and ordered the first classmen to report to me as soon as they returned from class. I watched as they emptied the alcoholic beverages down the drain. At lunch, I observed a table of cadets in Company E3 with no rank on their collars. By the evening meal, cadets with indiscipline issues were seated with their respective chains of command. I told the company commander to prepare a written plan of action that would hold the first classmen accountable for the proper standards of conduct for all cadets in the company. I now had their undivided attention.

There was also a culture of indifference evident in more than a few second classmen in the company. One of them was caught consuming beer in the barracks. While considering the appropriate punishment, I discovered he had exceeded his demerit allowance—a situation that had occurred on two previous occasions. However, no expulsion action had been taken because his father, grandfather, and great-grandfather were West Point graduates. I put together a recommendation for dismissal that was approved by the superintendent. After he was discharged, I sent a letter to other second classmen in the company who possessed a record of misconduct directing they submit a letter to me citing their commitment to the highest standards of excellence in conduct, honor, academics, and athletics. In short order, one of them was involved in a misconduct incident. When he came to my office, I showed him a copy of my recommendation for his dismissal. He burst into tears and pleaded with me for another chance. I told him I would defer action on this incident, but any future misconduct would result in an automatic recommendation for dismissal. This not only turned him around, but it also captured the attention of every other second classman. Good order and discipline had returned to Company E3.

I subsequently discovered that the previous commandant of cadets, Brigadier General Bernard W. Rogers, who became the Army chief of staff and later the supreme allied commander in Europe, had rated Company E3 number 36 out of 36 in conduct and assigned me as the tactical officer to straighten things out. It would have been enormously helpful if Colonel Marion C. Ross, the regimental commander, and Lieutenant Colonel Miley, the executive officer, had made me aware of this cornerstone of intelligence as I was making plans to assume my duties. I never did find out why this information was kept from me.

In October 1970, Julie announced that she was pregnant. I was so happy that I bought her a shaded silver Persian kitten. She was thrilled but the post veterinarian indicated the cat had some serious ailments and recommended we return it to the pet shop. Julie would have none of that. Shahnaz was nursed back to health, had six beautiful kittens of her own, and lived to be 20 years old.

General Walker promoted me to major in January 1970 and the West Point Elementary School hired Julie to teach 1st grade in a building across the street from our quarters. Armed with lessons learned from the previous year, I challenged the Company E3 cadet leaders to establish a goal that they could take pride in accomplishing. They responded with enthusiasm, winning the Corps of Cadets Intramural Flag Football Championship, which set the tone for a positive climate during the remainder of the academic year.

On June 24, 1971, Julie and I were delighted to welcome our first child, Mark Bradford Foley, into the world. He was a handsome baby with a sunny disposition who loved to play and laugh but who also had a serious side.

For academic year (AY) 1971–72, I was assigned as the regimental personnel and logistics officer and continued my classes at Fairleigh-Dickinson two nights a week. In January 1972, I graduated with an MBA (*cum laude*) from Fairleigh Dickinson University. In April, I learned that my next assignment would be senior aide-de-camp to Lieutenant General Richard T. Knowles, commanding general (CG) of I Corps Republic of Korea/United States (ROK/US) Group with headquarters in Uijeongbu, Korea. Since this one-year assignment was unaccompanied (without family members), we moved to Cornwall, New York. There, we welcomed another wonderful son, David Clifford Foley, on August 5, 1972. I reported for duty in Korea five days after he was born, leaving Julie in Cornwall with Adriana, our au pair girl from Italy, though Julie had her mother and sister close by in New York City. Shortly after I departed for Korea, our new baby boy had a medical emergency resulting from a botched procedure at the post hospital. At Julie's insistence, David was flown from Cornwall airfield to Walter Reed Medical Center in Washington, D.C. Upon arrival, he was examined by a team of doctors, and, after an emergency baptism, the procedure was done correctly. Julie said Dave charmed all the doctors and nurses in the ward by smiling and cooing at them. However, the incident gave Julie such a scare that she refused to bring him home until he was completely healed.

Uijeongbu is 30 miles south of the Demilitarized Zone (DMZ) and 50 miles north of Seoul. My tour of duty as aide-de-camp was educational and gratifying. I was responsible for accurate and timely communication within the headquarters staff, outside agencies, and subordinate commands to ensure the CG had reliable, rapid telecommunications and secure networks. I developed the CG's weekly and long-range calendars, scheduled meetings, and arranged for vehicular and helicopter transportation to visit units in the field. I also provided advice on a range of issues, including protocol, soldier concerns, and American/ROK relations. In addition, I was the golfing partner for the CG, who normally played nine holes of golf at the end of every weekday in Uijeongbu and all day on Sunday in Seoul—rain or shine.

General Knowles was a respected commander and military strategist who instilled a sense of urgency in American and Republic of Korea Army (ROKA) leaders regarding their wartime responsibilities for the defense of South Korea. The junior aide-de-camp was Captain Pat Toffler—a smart West Point graduate, Class of 1968, who later served as director of plans, policy, and analysis at West Point. Captain

Il Soon Shin, the Korean aide-de-camp, a graduate of both the Korea Military Academy and the U.S. Military Academy, became a four-star general and deputy commander of Combined Forces Command Korea. One of my principal duties was to coordinate General Knowles's calendar with Major Kim Dong Jin, who was the executive officer to the deputy commanding general of I Corps (ROK/ US) Group. I had a close working relationship with Major Kim as well as getting to know him socially at evening receptions and dinner. This friendship continued when we were classmates in the Command and General Staff College (CGSC) at Fort Leavenworth, Kansas. I had no idea how influential this relationship would be until 20 years later when I was assigned as assistant division commander for the 2nd Infantry Division in Korea.

In April, I learned that my next assignment would be a student at CGSC. Since Julie's mother and sister spent the summer with Aunt Evelina every year in San Remo, a beautiful resort city on the Italian Riviera, we decided to join them for part of the summer. Julie and the boys traveled from New York City to Italy, and I flew to Nice by way of Detroit, New York City, and Frankfurt, then took the train to San Remo. At the end of a splendid month relaxing on the beach we flew to New York City, picked up the car and the cat in Forest Hills, and drove to Fort Leavenworth. Our first stop was the emergency room, where both boys were prescribed antibiotics for their ear infections. We then went to the housing office and signed for a townhouse in Kickapoo Village.

CGSC was a one-year course designed to educate us in subjects such as joint and combined land warfare, strategic planning, operations, intelligence, logistics, and communications. My tablemate in our 50-person seminar was Major Hubert G. Smith (now Lieutenant General Smith, U.S. Army Retired). Julie and I became great friends with Hugh and his wife, Nancy. We also reconnected with several West Point classmates, including Mike and Kay Keaveney, Bill and Sue Boice, and Tom and Judy Karr. In addition, we became good friends with Major Cesare Pucci, who became the chief of staff of the Italian Army, and Major Kim Dong Jin, whose last assignment on active duty was chairman of the joint chiefs of staff for the Korean Armed Forces.

In April 1974, I received orders to be the operations officer of the 1st Battalion, 7th Infantry, in Aschaffenburg, Germany. We sold our 1967 Chevrolet, placed our household goods in storage, and looked forward to our first tour of duty in Europe.

## CHAPTER 11

# Battalion Operations Officer

Before reporting for duty in Germany we again stayed with Julie's mother and sister in San Remo. Julie and the boys remained at the beach all summer, but after three weeks I took an overnight train to Frankfurt, bringing the cat with me in her pink travel case. I was met at the end of a 17-hour overnight journey by Captain Harold Stitt, the Battalion Assistant S-3. Not feeling well, I asked him to drive me directly to the medical clinic in Aschaffenburg where I was diagnosed with strep throat. I was given penicillin and placed on 48 hours of bed rest.

When I reported to the 1st Battalion, 7th Infantry, headquarters at Graves Kaserne, the commanding officer, Lieutenant Colonel William Cummins, outlined the challenges he envisioned for the battalion over the next few months, including deploying the battalion to major training areas, conducting company-level tactical exercises, enhancing the maintenance readiness of vehicles and major weapons systems, managing the shortage of officers and NCOs from the drain of personnel to support the war in Vietnam, and reducing the amount of soldier drug and alcohol abuse.

Thenceforth, I was decisively engaged with deployments to Schweinfurt for company-size operations followed by movement to Wildflecken for live fire exercises. Deployment of a mechanized infantry battalion with M113 armored personnel carriers (APCs) included wheel vehicle convoys over German highways and travel by rail for the APCs. With my busy schedule and infrequent access to telephones at major training areas, I didn't get around to calling Julie. But I found a telephone right away when I received a telegram that read, "Call Aug 14, seven p.m. You in doghouse. Julie." First and foremost, she wanted to hear my voice, but she also wanted information on the availability of housing to determine how soon she could travel with the boys to Germany.

There was a long waiting list for family quarters, but temporary accommodations, originally designed for the maids of Wehrmacht officer families during World War II, were ready for occupancy on the fourth floor of a residential building. I moved into this unique set of quarters consisting of a kitchen, bathroom, dining area, and a long, narrow hallway with six small bedrooms.

The night before I planned to pick up Julie and the boys in Frankfurt, I couldn't find the cat. Her box in the bathroom was next to a tiny door in the wall, which she had opened. Hearing her meow from somewhere in the attic, I knew I had a problem. I wasn't going to show up at the train station and try to explain to Julie why the cat was missing. Time was of the essence. With no better options, I made a hole in the ceiling large enough for me to squeeze through and spotted Shahnaz with my flashlight. However, she wouldn't let me near her. It was late when I called Captain Stitt, who found the situation hilarious but promptly came to my assistance. We crawled across horizontal beams, being careful not to put any weight on the apartment ceilings below us. After catching Shahnaz, I accidentally stepped on a fold-down ladder, partially lowering it into the bedroom of a senior non-commissioned officer. Since he and his wife were in bed, he angrily yanked the ladder down yelling "What the hell's going on?" I apologized profusely and related the whole story. He told us that he was just about to call the military police to report voices in the attic. The next day, I picked up the family. We traveled by train to Aschaffenburg and took a taxi to our temporary quarters.

With the rainy weather in Germany, the boys stayed indoors most of the time, but they enjoyed racing up and down the long hallway on their new tricycles. The building had no elevators and no washers and dryers for families in temporary quarters. On the first laundry day Julie walked down three flights of stairs and put the boys in the stroller with the laundry bag. She then held up an umbrella and walked to Jaeger Kaserne, located on the other side of a busy thoroughfare. I promptly purchased a Volkswagen hatchback sedan. Six months later, we moved into a second-floor apartment with three bedrooms and a combination dining and living room, located in the dependent housing area. We felt comfortable in our new home—the boys were enrolled in pre-school and Julie was hired to teach at the Aschaffenburg American Elementary School.

Our battalion commander, a very capable but serious, no-nonsense officer, was quick to get upset if things didn't go well. I sensed that some of the officers and NCOs were intimidated by his leadership style, but I understood his intent. He was anxious to get results and I was certain I could help to accomplish his agenda.

At the next Hail and Farewell dinner for officers and spouses, Lieutenant Colonel Cummins asked the principal staff to stand and give a synopsis of activities in their functional area. They all gave brief and earnest reports. When it was my turn, I stood up and said, "Since I'm new here, I really don't know what's happened in the past, I'm totally confused about what's going on now and I have absolutely no idea what we're planning to do in the future." I then sat down. Everyone except Lieutenant Colonel Cummins roared with laughter. Before he could say anything, I jumped up and said, "Just kidding, sir." He smiled as I proceeded to give a detailed report regarding battalion operations and training. From then on, I leveraged this event in generating a more relaxed atmosphere.

After the first six months as a battalion operations officer, I concluded that the instruction we received at Fort Leavenworth was lacking in battalion-level operations and institutional values. Convinced that the CGSC leadership would appreciate getting feedback on their core curriculum, I wrote a letter to the commandant, Major General John H. Cushman. I suggested that much of the CGSC experience was not relevant to the operational needs and leadership challenges we faced at battalion level. General Cushman responded to my areas of concern with positive and precise language:

> The center of gravity of our common curriculum tactics instruction has been shifted to the lower echelons, emphasizing battalion and brigade operations. This trend will carry into Academic Year 1976 where the execution at these echelons will be stressed to an even greater degree. In the realm of leadership, we have developed a new course of study entitled the Profession of Arms.[1]

This reinforced my belief that senior officers placed great value on feedback from leaders at the company and battalion level. Not only did I continue providing insights and recommendations to senior leaders throughout my Army career, but I also adopted a standard policy of asking for the opinions of subordinates at every opportunity. When an issue was raised at command and staff meetings, my first response was, "What do you recommend? I then went around the table to obtain everyone's ideas. At times, I pushed back from the table to see if the leaders could reach a consensus. In the meantime, I was simultaneously evaluating my leaders' ability to articulate their points of view.

The commanding general of the 3rd Infantry Division, Major General Edward C. "Shy" Meyer, was a dynamic and well-respected leader who encouraged creative thinking. During a training meeting held at the Division Headquarters in the fall of 1974, he discussed a training wheel concept designed to inspire commanders and staff in planning one year out. Intrigued with this unique approach, I spent the next week completing a 1st Battalion, 7th Infantry, training wheel. Lieutenant Colonel Cummins liked it so much he invited General Meyer to our headquarters to receive a briefing. General Meyer sat in his chair, put his feet up, and listened intently. I told him that the training wheel was an effective management tool that promoted long-range planning and enabled an immediate assessment on the feasibility of scheduled activities. He asked several pertinent questions and said the division would publish our training wheel and adopt it as the model for the division.

During a trip to Berlin, we had dinner with Lieutenant Tim Wray and his family. Tim had been one of my cadet company commanders when I was a tactical officer at West Point. We also had dinner with Major Stu Sherard and his wife, Betty Ann. Stu was my teammate and captain of the 1961–62 Army basketball team. Julie and I were impressed with the single-family homes in the Berlin American Community, which came with Persian rugs, curtains, silver, china, and crystal. Before departing, I had an extensive conversation with Brigadier General R. Dean Tice, the Berlin brigade commander, about the infantry training we were doing in Aschaffenburg.

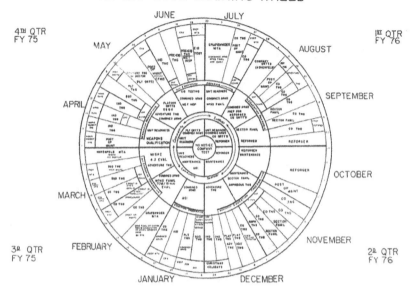

1st Battalion, 7th Infantry Training Wheel.

Soon after our trip, I was told that I was under consideration to become the next assistant division operations officer in the 3rd Infantry Division. Since I had been a battalion operations officer for less than a year, I was not happy at the thought of being on the division staff. Coincidentally, General Tice called to offer me a job as an infantry battalion executive officer in Berlin. I told him I was interested but I might have difficulty getting released. He said he would speak to General Meyer. A few days later, General Meyer visited 3rd Brigade and scheduled an appointment to talk to me. That same morning, Julie called me at the office. She was upset because a lady from the Community Housing Office had knocked on our apartment door with a couple who wanted to see the quarters because they understood we would be moving to Würzburg. To put it mildly, I was not happy with this disturbing sequence of events.

My meeting with General Meyer that afternoon would turn out to be one of the most difficult leadership challenges I had to confront in my 11 years on active duty. I had the utmost respect for General Meyer—he was a charismatic and inspirational leader. Subordinate leaders wanted to do anything he asked simply because of his extraordinary command presence and natural leadership ability. He spoke with authority, conviction, and integrity. Yet I was struck with the need to remain at battalion level, where I felt I could make my best contribution, and stay in Aschaffenburg, where I could best care for my young family, who had just settled comfortably in the military community housing complex.

When I saw General Meyer that afternoon, he emphasized the importance of my assignment at division headquarters as the assistant division operations officer for training. Although I appreciated his consideration in meeting with me, I was caught up in the emotions of the past few days and did not want to be on the division staff. I told him that I had been in the job for only nine months, I loved being with soldiers at battalion level, and my family had just settled into new quarters. After a brief discussion, he said, "What do you want me to do?" I'm not sure to this day why I said, "Send me to Berlin." But as soon as I blurted it out, he stood up, jammed his cap on his head and walked out. His final words as he left the room were, "I'll let you know." In a subsequent phone call, General Tice told me that General Meyer chewed him out for proselytizing in his division.

That afternoon, I told Major Larry Dacunto, our battalion executive officer, that I might have ended my career because I had just upset two general officers. He countered with, "Don't worry, Bob, it's a big Army." But it turned out to be a small Army. I was not assigned to the 3rd Infantry Division staff and didn't go to Berlin. I remained the operations officer of 1st Battalion, 7th Infantry for a second year and was selected to command 1st Battalion, 4th Infantry for two additional years in Aschaffenburg where I worked for General Tice when he took command of the 3rd Infantry Division. Three years later, I was assigned to the Pentagon as chief, Europe/Africa/Middle East Branch working for Lieutenant General Meyer who, at the time, was the Army Deputy Chief of Staff for Operations and a few months later became the Army chief of staff.

I was distressed for some time over rejecting General Meyer's plans for me to join the 3rd Infantry Division staff in Würzburg. I felt I had offended someone for whom I had the utmost respect. However, I was not unhappy with holding fast to what I felt was right for me and my family. What's more, remaining in Aschaffenburg and becoming a battalion commander was an outcome that could not have been better. After I wrote General Meyer a letter informing him of my selection for battalion command and thanking him for keeping me in the 3rd Infantry Division, he sent me a letter of congratulations stating how delighted he was that his career counseling had worked out for at least one soldier. When I reported to the Pentagon in the summer of 1979, I ran into General Meyer at a meeting. He picked me out of the crowd and publicly welcomed me to the office of the Army Deputy Chief for Operations. I felt that I had earned his trust and confidence because I was not afraid to stand up for what I thought was right. Subsequently, he selected me to preside at a swearing-in ceremony at the 200-year anniversary celebration of the American victory over the British at Yorktown and later appointed me director of Army Emergency Relief (AER) when he served as AER president. The lesson I learned was to have the courage of your convictions.

In January 1976, I was assigned as chief of staff for the REFORGER 1976 Umpire Control Group. REFORGER is an acronym for Return of Forces to Germany—a military exercise based on the strategic concept of U.S. Armed Forces deploying from the continental United States to Germany in response to a Warsaw Pact threat against Western Europe. My job was to prepare the rules of engagement for controlling opposing forces in the war games. The exercise was conducted in September of each year and gave brigade-size units the opportunity for limited maneuver across the German countryside. While continuing to live in Aschaffenburg for the next nine months, I made the daily commute to REFORGER headquarters in Kitzingen.

On July 2, 1976, I was promoted to lieutenant colonel by Brigadier General Rufus Lazelle. Julie, who was pregnant with Sara, came from Italy with four-year-old David, while Mark stayed at the beach with his cousins. After the exercise was complete, I attended an after-action review for the VII Corps commanding general, Lieutenant General Frederick J. Kroesen, and his staff on REFORGER 1976. Following the briefing, General Kroesen asked to see me in his office. On my way down the corridor, Major General Pat Crizer, the commanding general of 3rd Infantry Division and the assistant division commander, Brigadier General Robert M. Elton, pulled me aside and told me General Kroesen was planning to assign me as a staff officer in VII Corps headquarters. They said to tell him that I could not accept the VII Corps position as I would be taking command of 1st Battalion, 4th Infantry, in Aschaffenburg in November. Since this was news to me, I said, "I am?" When I reported to General Kroesen in his office, he came right to the point by saying he wanted me to be the VII Corps assistant operations officer. He was surprised when I told him that I would be commanding a battalion in 3rd Infantry Division. But he graciously congratulated me and wished me the very best in my new assignment.

## CHAPTER 12

# Moscow and Leningrad

Beginning with my time as a cadet at West Point, I developed a special interest in Russia. In the second semester of senior year, I took a course on the history of Russia. Books I have read include *Catherine the Great* and *Nicholas and Alexandra* by Robert K. Massie, *The 900 Days: The Siege of Leningrad* by Harrison E. Salisbury, *What is to be Done?* by Vladimir I. Lenin, and *Red Famine: Stalin's War on Ukraine* by Anne Applebaum. In July 1974, when I was the operations officer of the 1st Battalion, 7th Infantry, in Germany, we had a wartime responsibility outlined in the U.S. Army Europe contingency plans to defend against an invasion by Warsaw Pact forces. U.S. Army units stationed in Germany were required to periodically review their plans, as a part of the General Defense Plan (GDP) set against the potential threat of military formations from Albania, Bulgaria, Czechoslovakia, East Germany, Hungary, Poland, Romania, and the Soviet Union. In my examination of plans for the 1st Battalion, 7th Infantry, I found that our commanders gave the enemy situation a cursory look, placing their major emphasis on positioning of friendly forces. I was reminded of the teachings in Sun Tzu's *The Art of War*—a study of military operations in ancient China that includes a predominance of one important tenet: "knowing the enemy." Before approving plans or engaging in military exercises, I have always asked, "What's the threat?" For me, it never made sense to develop a scheme of maneuver and a fire support plan unless you are focused on a specific enemy disposition of forces and it's critical to continually gather intelligence on the changing enemy situation. Because I was stationed in Europe, I thought it would be beneficial to visit Russia and enhance my understanding of Soviet intentions and capabilities—and I was right.

In June 1975, Julie and I booked an American Express eight-day tour to Russia. In preparation for our trip, we read about the Czarist regime, the Bolshevik Revolution, and Marxist-Leninist ideology. Theoretically, the Russian Five-Year Plan, a central planning process for industrial and agricultural production that was established by Joseph Stalin in 1928, evolved from the Marxist-Leninist ideology: "From each according to their ability to each according to their needs." Colossal

Russian bureaucracies used scientific data to determine the output for categories of food such as wheat, meat, and corn. This included estimates on the number of tractors and trucks needed on collective farms in each region of the Soviet Union. The inefficiencies inherent in this socialist way of life were obvious everywhere we went and broadly defied the logic of supply and demand economic principles characteristic of capitalist countries.

We flew from Frankfurt to Helsinki on Lufthansa airline and from Helsinki to Leningrad on Aeroflot airline. In Russia, we landed on a bumpy airfield with grass and weeds growing through cracks in the concrete. Much to our surprise, Victoria, our INTOURIST guide, took us to state-sanctioned sites that had been in place prior to the Bolshevik Revolution in 1917. We saw prerevolutionary palaces and the Hermitage Museum displaying gilded carriages and unique treasures of the Czarist era. We also visited the battleship *Aurora*, docked next to the Hotel Leningrad, where we stayed.

During one of our tours, Victoria asked me if she could read my *Time* magazine while we were on the bus. When I told her she could keep it, she refused my offer, saying she didn't want to get caught with it. Since she had not read *The Gulag Archipelago* by Aleksandr Solzhenitsyn, I told her I would send her a copy. Again, she declined, saying she would never receive it. Julie and I had read about the vast censorship system that controlled the flow of information to the 133 million citizens living in Russia in 1975 but having this confirmed by our tour guide was mind-boggling. When I asked Victoria about the possibility of visiting the Red Army Museum in Moscow, she told me it was closed during the summer months.

After we arrived in Moscow, I asked Irina, our new INTOURIST guide, about the Red Army Museum. She told me it was closed for renovations. Suspicious, I decided to find out for myself. On the second day in Moscow, our group was scheduled for a cruise on the Neva River, followed by a tour through the Moscow subway. I asked Julie to tell Irina that I was sick and would remain in my hotel room for the day. After the group departed, I purchased a Moscow city map and hopped on a bus headed for the Red Army Museum. I found it open for visitors and free of charge. Entering the main building, I paused to stare at the captured World War II German flags with swastikas displayed from one end of the huge foyer to the other—a stark reminder of Russian deep-seated animosity toward Germany.

Groups of Young Pioneers with their red scarves and white shirts marched through the museum under the watchful eyes of their chaperones. I wandered into a theater to watch a film about the final days of World War II, featuring Soviet soldiers turning Berlin into rubble as they fought the remnants of the Wehrmacht. I stopped at a large glass case filled with thousands of Iron Crosses, presumably taken from dead German soldiers or prisoners of war. With a general familiarization of the U.S. Army Europe defense plans, I was mesmerized by the static displays and photos of Russian soldiers trudging behind tanks under cover of darkness on snowy ground wearing chemical protective clothing. This reinforced my belief that, in case of war, NATO forces would face Warsaw Pact formations attacking at night in the dead of winter using chemical weapons.

During a city tour of Moscow, we saw a man who appeared to be unconscious lying on the sidewalk while scores of Muscovites stepped briskly by him. Irina explained that Russian citizens routinely did not stop to help strangers on the street for fear of being charged as accomplices to some type of wrongdoing. I had another opportunity to witness this "don't get involved" mindset early one morning while strolling around Moscow. I came to a large building resembling a military barracks with sally ports leading to a courtyard. It was eerily quiet as I meandered through the entrance, hesitating momentarily at the center of the enclosed area. I was determined to take a few photos before anyone showed up but, all at once, whistles blew and hundreds of Russian soldiers in uniform came streaming out of the barracks. It suddenly occurred to me that I was a towering U.S. Army officer with a camera around my neck standing in the middle of a Russian Army reveille formation. As I made my way to the sally port, I expected at any moment to be stopped by someone in authority, but my presence was completely ignored. I breathed a sigh of relief as I turned the corner and strode expeditiously back to our hotel. I can only imagine the consequences had I been detained.

The immense failure of central planning was reinforced when we observed food markets with only chickens to purchase; hundreds of women waiting to buy Western-style men's shirts in a line that went from the second floor of the GUM department store to the street; and people queueing up at kiosks to obtain information on where to buy food and merchandise the next day.

I think Julie accurately captured the life of a Russian citizen in her diary when she indicated that the Russian people appeared to exist rather than live. In Julie's eyes, every day brought forth an outpouring of people wearing plain work clothes, moving quickly and earnestly but never smiling. They gave the impression of being good people with the same needs and concerns as anyone else but seemed to be carrying the burden of their past with them. We wondered if they were content with simply having a job, enough food, clothing, and a place to live. Although it was difficult to read their thoughts, they must have noticed the tourists' stylish and colorful clothes, good shoes, expensive cameras, and leather handbags. We wondered what they were thinking, and whether they believed what they were being told about us.[1]

I had the opportunity to walk around Moscow and Leningrad early in the morning and peek in doorways to see life beyond the tours of museums, monuments, palaces, and forts built during the Czarist regimes. Not much opulence since 1917, except

Lenin's Tomb. The hundreds of drab apartment buildings looked like the New York City housing projects. We came away from our trip happy to be American citizens and fortified with a deep appreciation for freedom and democracy.

In November 2017, I read *Gorbachev: His Life and Times* by William Taubman, which revealed how central planning struggled from 1980 until dissolution of the Soviet Union on December 25, 1991. Gorbachev decided the focus during his first two years as General Secretary would be "Acceleration of scientific-technological progress."[2] Unfortunately, acceleration did not work within the framework of the Five-Year Plan:

> "By the end of November 1985, only fifty-one percent of construction projects had come online. Agricultural output, too, was less than expected, partly because 30 percent of the fodder was allowed to rot." In a visit to the town of Kuibyshev in early April, Gorbachev "found the textile industry backward, housing scarce, food rationed, one movie theater for 600,000 people, 17,000 children without places in Kindergarten, and, despite all this, any manifestation of initiative is punished."[3]

As Gorbachev was pondering this bad news, tragedy struck. On April 26, 1986, nuclear reactor number four at the atomic power station near the town of Pripyat in Ukraine exploded.[4] This was a major turning point for him. His belief in *perestroika* (a restructuring of the Soviet political and economic systems) and *glasnost* (openness and transparency, including freedom of speech, expression, and criticism) had the potential for eliminating authoritarian rule, providing unprecedented reformation, and setting the stage for the creation of a democratic form of government. But Mikhail Gorbachev was forced to resign from office as president of Russia and Communist Party general secretary in December 1991 before he could institute the measures necessary to empower the goodness of representation in government, a free-market system, and "unalienable rights" to achieve his vision of greatness for the Russian people.

In her book, *Red Famine*, Anne Applebaum describes the horrors brought upon Ukraine in the early 1930s by Joseph Stalin, a ruthless dictator, who was then Secretary General of the Communist Party of the Soviet Union. His policy of transforming the peasantry from landowners to collective farming ended in abject failure and caused widespread famine in the USSR. Stalin subsequently ordered the collection of all available food in Ukraine and had it shipped to Russia, resulting in more than 3 million Ukrainian citizens dying of starvation. In her book, published in 2017, Applebaum warned that Russia is destined to end Ukrainian independence through forced annexation, as done in the Crimea. Understanding Russia's intent to destroy the Ukrainian peasantry almost 100 years ago, it is disturbing, disillusioning, and disheartening to watch history replicate itself as so clearly demonstrated by Vladimir Putin's invasion of Ukraine in 2022.[5] Wars are won through bold and aggressive action, not cautious pessimism, but failing to heed historical lessons is not a new phenomenon. George Santayana, a philosopher, and writer born in Spain in 1863, wrote, "Those who cannot learn from history are doomed to repeat it." After signing a pact of peace with Adolf Hitler in 1938, British Prime Minister Neville Chamberlain declared, "peace for our time," and later found out that, "appeasement doesn't work."

## CHAPTER 13

# Battalion Commander

At the Frankfurt Army Hospital on November 2, 1976, Julie gave birth to Sara Caroline Foley—a gorgeous baby with long black hair, bright blue eyes, and a sweet little cry. Two weeks later, in a ceremony at Fiori Kaserne, I assumed command of 1st Battalion, 4th Infantry. Because Sara was waking up several times at night, Julie's mother was a huge help caring for the new baby and looking after the boys. But when Nonna went home to New York, Julie was not sleeping well, and things took a turn for the worse when Sara was diagnosed with bronchiolitis. Subsequently, Julie developed a severe case of post-natal depression and Aunt Evelina told her to fly to Torino with Sara right away. Joan McCrory, a neighbor and registered nurse, wisely suggested that taking Sara to Italy would exacerbate the cause of Julie's depression and kindly offered to take Sara into her home. Although reluctant to leave her new baby and family behind, Julie concluded that the only solution was to get away and recuperate as soon as possible.

Because we were preparing for deployment on a major winter exercise, the battalion ladies went into action. They came to our quarters, brought food, packed Julie's suitcase, and booked her on a flight from Frankfurt to Torino. Joan McCrory came to get Sara; David stayed with Harold and Virginia Stitt; Mark moved in with Larry and Emilie Dacunto; and my West Point classmate, Tom Karr, and his wife, Judy, took our cat.

I had planned on driving Julie to the airport. However, on the day she was scheduled to depart, I came down with a fever and stomach virus. The battalion was conducting a rail and road movement from Aschaffenburg to the field site for the winter exercise and I was lying in bed too weak to move. With tears rolling down her cheeks, Julie was rubbing my forehead telling me that everything was going to be okay. The ladies drove her to the airport, and I went to sleep.

Major General Pat W. Crizer, who replaced General Meyer as the commanding general of 3rd Infantry Division, had the reputation of being a tough taskmaster, as evidenced by the three battalion commanders he had relieved before I took command. While reading a copy of *Stars and Stripes* in the division Tactical Operations Center,

General Crizer was disturbed by an article indicating that Lieutenant Colonel Robert F. Foley was in Washington, D.C. with other Medal of Honor recipients at the inauguration of President Carter. He found it incredible that one of his battalion commanders was not with his soldiers on the winter exercise and directed his staff to find me. They immediately began making calls to Washington, D.C.

Meanwhile, I felt better and made my way to the battalion field location, which was about a two-hour drive from Aschaffenburg. About mid-morning, the division commander's aide-de-camp called from the command helicopter requesting confirmation on our location. He said they were flying over the area confirmed as the battalion location but could not see one tank or armored personnel carrier in the snow-covered fields. We popped red smoke. After General Crizer landed, he said he was glad to see me as *Stars and Stripes* had indicated I was at the presidential inauguration. Surprised, I told him that it never occurred to me to be away from my battalion during the exercise. After seeing our tanks and APCs covered with winter camouflage patterns and our soldiers wearing white camouflage uniforms, he understood why it was difficult to spot us from the air and appreciated our efforts at conducting realistic training. I learned that he later received a report from his staff confirming my location to be at the Howard Johnson's Motor Lodge in Arlington, Virginia. I'm sure he had fun with that.

In response to the environmental concerns of the local *Forstmeister*, General Crizer provided guidance to brigade and battalion commanders prohibiting soldiers from starting fires during the exercise. While flying in his helicopter on the second day of maneuvers, he spotted a group of my soldiers standing around a fire next to their M114 scout APC. The vehicle had lost power and the soldiers were stranded with no heat and no communications. Upon landing and finding the soldiers were assigned to my battalion, he came looking for me. He found me supervising a tank recovery operation and said he thought he'd made it clear there would be no fires. I told him I had modified his guidance, directing that no fires be started unless the soldiers felt they were in danger of hyperthermia or frostbite. General Crizer said, "Yeah, that's what they told me. That was good guidance, Commander. I just passed it on to all units in the division."

Ten days later, when the battalion redeployed to Aschaffenburg, I drove to the Frankfurt airport—happy to pick up a smiling Julie. We went straight to Joan McGrory's quarters to reunite Sara with her mom. She looked wonderful, as did Mark, David, and the cat. We would not have been able to overcome this adversity without the help of our friends and neighbors. This is a classic example of the Army family covenant. Wherever Army families go, especially overseas, they live in a tight community where assistance is but a phone call away.

While inspecting vehicle maintenance one day, I noticed many of the APCs in the battalion motor pool were missing the rubber shrouds which were designed to cover the top half of the roadwheels and track. When I was told the shrouds were removed because they were damaged when the APCs hit trees, I said, "Stop hitting trees." Because the shrouds provided an amphibious capability, I directed they be reinstalled on all the APCs in the battalion. Drain plugs were replaced, bilge pumps certified, and in 90 days, the APCs swam across a local training area pond.

One of the most important attributes a commander can acquire is the ability to select good leaders. I had an organization chart sitting on an A-frame in my office that identified the commander, executive officer, primary staff, company commanders, first sergeants, platoon leaders, and platoon sergeants. I continually referred to the chart—reviewing in my mind what changes I should make as vacancies occurred. I believed in giving officers and NCOs time to prove themselves in leading our soldiers, but I wasted no time in directing their removal if they weren't qualified or performing to standard.

Early in my tenure, I was faced with finding an assignment for a sergeant first class who was retiring and planned on living in Germany. He spoke German and his wife was born in Germany. Tired of seeing soldiers spend their free time in the barracks, I asked him to establish a travel office. This modest beginning grew into a weekly arrival of buses at Fiori Kaserne, picking up soldiers and their families for trips to places of interest in Europe. During Oktoberfest, buses gathered up soldiers in the morning, drove to Munich, and brought them back at 3:00 a.m. the next day—a good way to prevent driving under the influence of alcohol (DUIs). Every soldier in the battalion had an official Warrior Travel Club business card. Regrettably, toward the end of my command tour, the division staff judge advocate informed me that the success of our club created a disproportionate level of competition with local tour companies and would have to be terminated consistent with the Status of Forces Agreements (SOFA). Although the travel club was discontinued, everyone was pleased at how much it benefited soldiers and their families for almost two years.

An important aspect of a successful battalion is the contribution made by the battalion spouses. Julie coordinated numerous activities to generate spirit, camaraderie, and fun in the battalion. The community news that she received from the brigade commander's wife was passed on through a series of monthly coffees hosted by wives of the company commanders. In case of an emergency, especially when the battalion was in the field, Julie activated the telephone tree. Occasionally, she assisted with domestic problems and requested help from the battalion chaplain as needed. The ladies rallied volunteers to support events such as the community carnival, children's Christmas party, Easter egg hunt, and fund-raising bake sales. Newly arrived spouses received a battalion pin from Julie and a home-delivered welcoming plant from the battalion executive officer's wife. I can still visualize the huge "Welcome Home Warriors" banner the spouses made to hang across the front gate of Fiori Kaserne when we returned from lengthy field exercises. One time, at a luncheon for first sergeants' wives at our quarters, Julie asked for recommendations on places to visit—specifically for the women who did not have a car. This generated a trip involving 42 ladies in a caravan of roomy cars to carry back the items purchased from German wicker, porcelain, and crystal factories.

When the Officer's Club needed a revitalization, the battalion was assigned the foyer and bathrooms. The ladies painted the foyer, redecorated the windows with curtains, had new lights and flower boxes installed, and Linda Long, a talented artist, painted a full-length World War I "Doughboy" on the men's room door and a lady in an evening gown on the ladies' room door. At the Officer's Club Spring Formal for 300 officers, spouses, and German guests, the ladies sent out invitations, made place cards, booked a dance band, ordered table centerpieces, hired a photographer, and placed potted shrubs and hanging plants as background scenery—all for only $7 per couple. One night, they held a potluck dinner and auction to raise money for the children's Christmas party and brought a "white elephant gift" to donate for the cause. After extending the drinking hour, they raised $321.

When it was the battalion's turn to sponsor the Wives' Club luncheon for the community, the spouses decided to put on a fur coat fashion show and found a furrier to lend them the coats. Sergeant Talbott, the club manager, built a 2-foot-high runway. Military police and battalion soldiers accompanied the wives to pick up $45,000 worth of fur coats. They remained on guard at the show and escorted them back to the furrier. Mary Lynn Landgraf and Glenice Gile wrote a fabulous Dior-type script. Glenice, Sandy Leysath, Sylvia Tovar, Vicki Kay, Suzi Ohgren, Lydia Harding, and Mary Lynn modeled the furs while Julie coordinated the script with the models. Julie modeled a blue fox fur coat during the grand finale, when all the ladies walked around wearing their favorite fur coat. The show was a huge success, receiving front-page headlines in the local newspaper.

For our Dining-in at the Officer's Club, we invited Major General Tice, the new division commander, as the guest speaker. When I went to the club to check on last-minute preparations, he came to our quarters to change into his formal attire. While he was getting ready, 16 battalion wives arrived—heading for their own "dining out." He went around shaking hands with everyone and told them how he had tried to request my assignment to Berlin but was told by General Meyer he could have any officer in the division except Bob Foley. When Julie asked General Tice if he would rather go out with the ladies, he gave her a big hug.

The most enjoyable Warrior Battalion event was the quarterly Hail and Farewell normally held at a local *Gasthaus*. I presented a garter to all new wives bearing the battalion red and green colors and a scroll describing the "Order of the Garter." Certificates of Non-Achievement were presented to the officers (mostly lieutenants) who had committed a minor faux pas in the past 90 days. The "rubber duck award" was a rotating award presented to the officer who had committed the biggest blunder since the last Hail and Farewell. The awardee had to carry the duck with him at every battalion function or buy drinks for all officers in attendance. I received the rubber duck award for riding in a military vehicle that took a wrong turn on the *Autobahn*. This was the official reason given but it was primarily because I had never received the rubber duck in the past.

At a subsequent brigade parade with the officers in dress green uniforms, I asked Julie to carry the rubber duck in her purse in case the parade evolved into an official battalion function. Right on cue, the officers devised a scheme to drop by the Officer's Club with the spouses before going home. On the way to the club, I took the duck from Julie and placed it under my armpit inside my dress coat. Several officers challenged me to produce the duck. I asked them if they really wanted to do this, knowing if they were wrong, they had to buy the drinks. The officers suspected I was stalling for time as there was no way I could have the rubber duck in any of my dress green uniform pockets. When they gathered around the bar eager to order their free drinks, I opened my dress coat and pulled out the rubber duck from under my arm.

At the Wildflecken Training Area, we created a squad live fire exercise employing machine guns, 81mm mortars and light anti-tank weapons. The soldiers in each squad prepared fighting positions, engaged an array of targets, and were evaluated on target identification, accuracy, and fire control. When General Bernard M. Rogers, the Army chief of staff, came to visit our training site, I met him in my APC at the bottom of a long, winding dirt road that went up a steep hill. His escort officer, a colonel from U.S. Army Europe Headquarters, asked about a heated staff car. I told him a sedan would never make it up the hill to the training site and General Rogers didn't seem to mind riding in the back of an APC. Since the firing range was closed due to inclement weather, I briefed General Rogers on the training objectives and invited him to jump into the foxholes to talk with our soldiers.

He climbed down into each fighting position and obtained a firsthand account from soldiers, fire team leaders, and squad leaders on establishing a static defense. He even had the opportunity to talk to one of the truck drivers who had driven our soldiers to the range. General Rogers said, "What's your job, soldier?"

"Sir, I'm a truck driver."

"Do you enjoy your job?"

"I love it—it's a real get over." (It's easy compared to other jobs.)

General Rogers smiled but reminded this great soldier how important it was to drive other soldiers safely to their destination. He then left to visit the next unit on his schedule. Since we never received clearance to fire, the escort officer departed saying, "I hope you do better for lunch." When General Rogers and his party returned, the colonel just about lost it when he saw we were having C-Rations (combat rations). As General Rogers entered our small tent, the mess sergeant placed a case of C-Rations on the table and opened it from the bottom, so the contents of each box were not visible.

General Rogers said, "How do we know what's in each box?"

"Sir, the mess sergeant is following standard procedure for soldiers to pick up a box so the chow line can move quickly, but we can flip the box over."

"No, don't do that. I'll follow the soldier protocol. I just hope I don't pick ham and lima beans."

To the dismay of the escort officer, General Rogers picked ham and lima beans. I offered him a second choice, but he refused and ate crackers for lunch. We had a lively and productive discussion based on my guidance for the company commanders to speak candidly about their problems. The next day, I received a telephone call from the division chief of staff, who wanted me to know that General Rogers told General Blanchard, the commanding general of U.S. Army Europe, that 1st Battalion, 4th Infantry, had the best training he had witnessed during his visit. He appreciated the candid assessment of company-level issues and indicated that our battalion had an outstanding command climate.

I was blessed with terrific company commanders and their wives—Charlie and Chris Williams (Alpha Company), Greg and Glenice Gile (Bravo Company), Bruce Arlinghaus (Charlie Company), Jim and Cherie Gribschaw (Combat Support Company), Tom and Gail Mitchell (Combat Support Company), and Gary and Charlene Enos (Headquarters Company). I also had a superb battalion motor officer named Mike Quirk and two phenomenal executive officers and their wives—Brian and Linda Long and Bruce and Vicki Kay. In addition, I can't say enough about my outstanding operations officer, Bill Landgraf, and his wife, Mary Lynn.

We have fond memories of our four years in Europe. Julie and the children spent five straight summers on the Italian Riviera at Zia Evelina's beach, where our children played with their Italian cousins. Although I was in major training areas for most of the summer, I periodically took the overnight train to San Remo for short vacations. Since her mother, sister, aunts, and cousins were available to babysit, Julie and I took train trips to Rapallo, Santa Margherita, and Portofino in Italy as well as Cannes, Nice, Monte Carlo, and Saint-Tropez in France.

From Aschaffenburg, we made use of every long weekend by taking short trips to scenic and historic areas throughout Europe. We took the boys to the U.S. Armed Forces Recreation Center in Garmisch-Partenkirchen and Berchtesgaden in the Bavarian Alps—a pristine area dominated by the Zugspitze, which peaks at 9,718 feet. We loved the tidy German homes with flower window boxes and charming restaurants serving delicious *Wiener Schnitzel* and *Bratwurst*. Julie was thrilled to attend the *Passion Play* in Oberammergau, which was performed by local townspeople once every 10 years.

Outside a *Gasthaus* one night, we were approached by a German gentleman who showed us a wallet filled with dollars, Deutsche Marks, and a soldier ID card. He had found it on the street and asked if we could locate the owner. We thanked him for his kindness and took the wallet to the Military Police station. The soldier was there when we arrived and was greatly relieved to see his wallet again. This episode had a big impact on Mark and David, who followed the event, wide-eyed, every step of the way. They appreciated the importance of honesty, especially coming from a stranger in a foreign country.

Before Sara was born, we took the boys to the *Kris Kringle Mart* in Nuremberg, Oktoberfest in Munich, ate at the Hotel Zum Ritter in Heidelberg, and took the funicular railway to the ruins of Heidelberg Castle. We visited the Mercedes-Benz factory in Stuttgart and ate inside the Fernsehturm restaurant at the top of a 700-foot spire overlooking the city. We visited Madurodam, the miniature city in the Hague, and the Keukenhof tulip gardens in Amsterdam with its fabulous petting zoo. We saw the dykes and windmills of Holland and drove through Safariland in Arnhem, where lions and giraffes roamed free. We visited Luxembourg, one of the smallest countries in Europe, where Julie purchased a large, white Moroccan bird cage she saw in a shop window.

One weekend, we took the overnight train from Frankfurt to West Berlin. The boys were excited to see Russian and East German soldiers with weapons over their shoulders inspecting the compartment of our train when we crossed the border into East Germany. With the boys safely deposited in the Berlin Community Command nursery, Julie and I had an unforgettable experience visiting East Berlin. We were given lengthy stares as we entered separately through Checkpoint Charlie near the Brandenburg Gate. We were astonished to see old, drab buildings with shell holes from World War II in sharp contrast to the modern steel structures and bright lights of West Berlin. Most noticeable were the East German agents, who followed us everywhere we went.

Although I didn't have the time to become fluent in German or Italian, speaking both languages would have made living in Europe much more enjoyable. Fortunately, Julie spoke Italian and French, and I learned a few useful expressions, such as "*Ein Bier und ein Speisekarte, bitte.*" ("A beer and a menu, please.")

But I did speak some Italian, which I put to good use one night in San Remo when I went to the promenade to order ice cream from one of the cart vendors.

I said, "*Buona sera, signor. Un gelato, per piacere.*" ("Good evening, Sir. An ice cream, please.")

The vendor said, "Okay, what kind?"

"*Cioccolato.*" ("Chocolate.")

"How many scoops?"

"*Due per piacere e quanto costa?*" ("Two please, and how much will that cost?")

"One thousand lire."

In departing I said, "*Grazie, signor, buona sera.*" ("Thank you, Sir, good evening.")

He responded with, "You are welcome. Good night."

Absolutely hilarious, and neither one of us cracked a smile.

In April 1978, I was selected to attend the Naval War College and turned the battalion over to Lieutenant Colonel Bill Landgraf. After the change of command

and three weeks of vacation in San Remo, we flew to Boston, where I purchased a new Chevrolet four-door sedan and drove to Newport, Rhode Island—a small, picturesque town founded in 1639. It was the largest of four original settlements located on Narragansett Bay—the scene of bustling commercial sailing ships and a key port city during the American Revolution. The British used Newport for three years as a naval base. After departing for New York City, they were replaced by a 6,000-man French expeditionary force under the Comte de Rochambeau. In 1781, Rochambeau moved south to support George Washington and the American Continental Army. Admiral de Grasse, with a powerful French fleet, established a blockade and conquered the British fleet at the battle of Chesapeake Bay. This proved to be the turning point in the Revolutionary War as George Washington and the Continental Army defeated Lord Cornwallis and the British at Yorktown.[1]

Upon arrival at the college, we signed for the upstairs unit of a two-story townhouse with a spectacular view of Narragansett Bay. Mark and David were enrolled in the Sisters of St. Joseph of Cluny, a private, Catholic elementary school, and Sara registered for preschool. I surprised my Italian wife by purchasing another Fiat for her and was astonished to discover that she never liked the first Fiat and didn't want another one. Too late—the purchase was nonrefundable.

## CHAPTER 14

# Naval War College

Prior to the first day of academics, we were required to read *The History of the Peloponnesian War* by Thucydides—an Athenian general and historian who wrote a comprehensive account of the 27 year conflict between Athens and Sparta (430–404 BC). Our 10-person seminars were facilitated by two PhD professors, who guided the classroom discussions, evaluated our verbal contentions, and graded the 10-page, double-spaced, typewritten essays we submitted every two weeks. Our first essay question was "To what extent did Athens and Sparta pursue military strategies consistent with their political objectives during the various phases of the Peloponnesian War?"[1] I was comfortable writing a response but did not anticipate such a comprehensive grading system.

A copy of my essay was provided to my seminar classmates, who were graded on their critique of my essay, while my grade was based upon how well I could rebut their critique. In addition, I received a separate grade for the essay, bountifully marked up by the professors. Grades were on a 4.0 system, and I received a 3.5 for my first paper. My professor wrote, "The essay certainly is definite in answering the question and makes quite good use of supportive material. Your style is very readable, and you should have few problems with the written requirements of the course."[2] With the extensive list of required reading and writing assignments, I established a routine for studying in my alcove for most of the day—Monday through Friday.

In addition to the core curriculum, I signed up for Foundations of Moral Obligation, a 10-week elective course, taught by Vice Admiral James B. Stockdale and Dr. Joseph G. Brennan. Dr. Brennan was a professor emeritus of philosophy at Columbia University's Barnard College and a Navy veteran who served in North Africa, Italy, and Southern France during World War II. Admiral Stockdale was president of the Naval War College, a U.S. Navy fighter pilot, and a Medal of Honor recipient who spent eight years as a prisoner of war in North Vietnam. He was held in solitary confinement, endured beatings, wore leg irons, and had a broken shoulder and leg, which his captors refused to treat. Nevertheless, he exercised courageous leadership on behalf of his fellow prisoners.

Five years after his release from captivity, Admiral Stockdale wrote an article describing the consequences involved in collaboration with the enemy. He tells the story of a prisoner who thrived on adulation and was willing to compromise his ethical principles and abandon loyalty to his cell mates for favorable treatment from his captors.[3] "He was obsessed with success. When the going got tough, he decided expediency was preferable to principle. The man was a classic opportunist. He befriended and worked for the enemy to the detriment of his fellow Americans."[4] Although this man tried to come back, he was never accepted. After release from prison camp, he was involved in an accident that looked very much like suicide.[5]

Our studies in moral philosophy included Aristotle (384–322 BC), who believed that character was a habit—the daily choice of right over wrong. We were introduced to Immanuel Kant's theory of motivation and John Stuart Mill's theory of consequences. Kant was born in Konigsberg, East Prussia in 1724 and believed that acts of true moral worth must be based upon what "ought" to be done—free of personal benefit, gain, reward, or expedient measures.[6] John Stuart Mill was born in London in 1806 and believed that an act of true moral worth was measured entirely on whether the actions contribute to the greater good. Mill concluded that the motivation behind the act was not a factor in the results achieved if a person's actions create a happy ending for all concerned.[7]

In comparing the two philosophies, Admiral Stockdale passed on a simple yet palpable illustration. A woman is standing at the edge of the ocean yelling for someone to help her daughter, who is drowning. A man runs by her, jumps in the water, and rescues the girl. A second scenario has a man running up to the woman offering to help if he is paid $500. The woman agrees, and the man saves her daughter. John Stuart Mill would argue that both examples are acts of true moral worth, whereas Immanuel Kant would contend that only the illustration of the man who jumped in without any reward or benefit is an act of true moral worth.

Admiral Stockdale cautioned us not to attempt the assimilation of theories such as utilitarianism or dialectical materialism. Instead, he advised us to concentrate on understanding the ethical principles involved in values-based decision-making. The course greatly reinforced my sense of professional ethics, the strength of character essential in overcoming adversity, and the importance of values in the words we speak, the decisions we make, and the actions we take.

While I was proceeding to class one day wearing my green service dress uniform, the dean appeared in the hallway. He said, "Colonel Foley, we want you to be the captain and coach of the Naval War College basketball team this year. Your mission is to beat Army during the annual Jim Thorpe sports competition at the Army War College." I looked down at my uniform and said, "Why would I want to do that?" After recovering from my surprise tasking, I dutifully organized a team of Army, Navy, Air Force, and Marine Corps officers who didn't possess exceptional basketball skills but were tough competitors. We won games more through physical intimidation than skill and made it to the finals in the basketball tournament at Carlisle Barracks but lost to the Army War College in a squeaker.

In February 1979, I learned my next assignment would be at the Pentagon. After spending a weekend looking at real estate in Virginia, Julie and I bought our first home—a two-story colonial in Fairfax with three bedrooms and a two-car garage situated on a cul-de-sac with Metro bus access to the Pentagon. Right after graduation, we left Newport for a brief stay with Julie's best friend, Carolyn Worrall, and her family in East Greenwich, Rhode Island. The overthrow of the Shah of Iran and the establishment of the Islamic Republic in the spring of 1979 interrupted the flow of oil worldwide, increased the price of gasoline, and caused long lines at gas stations. To drive to Virginia, we had to go through New York and New Jersey, which had imposed odd-even gas rationing. If the last digit of your license plate was an odd number, you could only obtain gas on an odd calendar day and vice versa. Even with this constraint, we made it to Virginia with no problems and moved right into our new home.

Julie continued her teaching career at Parklawn Elementary School, Sara was enrolled in pre-school at Lord of Life, and Mark and David were in 3rd and 2nd grades at Laurel Ridge Elementary School. Fairfax County had excellent youth sports programs with parents serving as coaches. However, I was disappointed at the first basketball practice held for the team Mark and David had joined. Although I appreciated the fathers who volunteered their time and energy to coach the youth teams, many didn't know much about basketball. The coach for Mark and David's team brought only one basketball for 10 players. He placed them in a line and told them to dribble to the basket and shoot. Most of the boys couldn't do either. After missing the basket, they would chase the ball and carry it back to the next boy in line. In a one-hour practice, Mark and David spent 90 percent of the time standing in line. I put up a basket with a backboard over the garage, taught the boys fundamental skills, and from then on signed up to coach their teams.

As Chief, Europe-Africa-Middle East Branch in the office of Deputy Chief of Staff for Operations in the basement of the Pentagon, my job was to supervise the preparation of briefings and decision memorandums for senior leader meetings. The best part of my day was reading my five-year-old daughter's handwritten note on a napkin that came with the sandwich she made for me every day. "Don't work too hard, don't let the boss boss you, drive carefully, smile, come home early, I love you." At the end of the day, she would call and say, "Are you coming home now? Jingle your keys. See you soon. I love you." After two years in the Pentagon, I was reassigned to Colonel's Division at the U.S. Army Military Personnel Center in Alexandria,

Virginia. Our mission was to assign colonels to commands worldwide—an enjoyable and rewarding duty as I was able to match senior-level officers with the right assignment based upon their qualifications and experience.

In the fall of 1982, I took the boys to see an Army-Air Force football game at West Point and stayed with my classmate, John Ellerson, who was assigned to the Department of Tactics and had quarters on post. John was captain of the Army football team during our senior year and retired as a major general. Mark and David were impressed with the Corps of Cadets at the Saturday morning review on the Plain and were enthralled with the low-level flyover of several Air Force bomber and fighter aircraft. At the game, I pointed out our mascots, the Army mules, standing inside the stadium but the boys were more interested in the Air Force falcons diving to snatch the lure that their handlers threw up in the air. The Air Force football team consistently passed the ball down the field for touchdowns and won the game 27 to 9.

As we were driving down the New Jersey turnpike on the way back to Virginia, I asked the boys if they might like to go to West Point someday. After a moment of silence, Mark said he was thinking of going to the Air Force Academy. Dave was non-committal, but I apparently planted the seed about the academies very well because Dave graduated from West Point with the Class of 1994 and Mark graduated from the Air Force Academy with the Class of 1995.

On October 1, 1982, I was promoted to colonel. Subsequently, I was selected for brigade command with 3rd Brigade, 3rd Infantry Division. Lieutenant General Maxwell D. Thurman, the deputy chief of staff for personnel, along with Major General Robert Arter, the commanding general, U.S. Army Military Personnel Center (MILPERCEN), supervised the slating process. General Thurman said my assignment was a model for the Army because I would command a brigade in a community where I had previously served for four years. From the summer of 1974 to the summer of 1978, I was the operations officer of the 1st Battalion, 7th Infantry, and commander of the 1st Battalion, 4th Infantry—the two subordinate infantry battalions of the 3rd Brigade located in Aschaffenburg, Germany.

Since the change of command date was scheduled for the summer of 1985, I was assigned, in the interim, to be chief of the Bradley Fighting Vehicle (BFV) Fielding Team in Vilseck, Germany. The BFV was a 40-ton, tracked infantry personnel carrier that carried a squad of nine soldiers and had a top speed of 41mph. It had a turret-mounted 25mm cannon, a coaxial 7.62mm machine gun and a tube-launched, optically tracked, wire-guided (TOW) missile launcher capable of engaging targets at 4,046 yards. It was also designed with an amphibious capability for crossing water obstacles.

Before departing for Germany, I visited the BFV manufacturing facility at the headquarters of Food Machinery Corporation (FMC) in San Jose, California. I was given a standard VIP tour to learn about the vehicle production process. During a break, I went on my own to the employee cafeteria and asked several employees about the BFV. I was given a good report on all aspects except one—the fuel tank. The BFV was designed with a doughnut-shaped, fiberglass fuel cell located at the bottom of the turret. In the production line, workers would occasionally drop a bolt or screwdriver onto the floor of the turret, which punctured the fiberglass fuel cell as the turret swiveled. To replace the fuel cell, the BFV was taken off the production line. The turret had to be removed—a four-hour job requiring a crane and specialty mechanics. Two of the employees led me to a huge warehouse, where I saw about 20 BFVs in various stages of fuel cell replacement. I thanked them and provided assurance that their identity would not be revealed. When I showed the warehouse to my tour guides, they were astonished. I told them soldiers can also drop tools, bolts, and ammunition casings on the turret floor. I recommended they develop a modification to prevent falling objects from puncturing the fuel cell. I shared this information with Major General Donald P. Whalen, the BFV systems program manager. He directed that modification kits be sent to BFV units and integrated into the assembly line at FMC.

One of the best ways to find out what is really going on is to take a walk around the organization, talking to front-line employees or soldiers who build or operate the equipment. Never rely on briefings. There may well be obstacles to you personally checking on the manufacturing process or business operations, but leaders need to adopt unorthodox techniques to find out. If you want to know the status of pride, professionalism, and high standards in an organization, check places like the corporate rest rooms for cleanliness and graffiti, food service facilities and parking space availability for personnel with disabilities and pregnant women. It's called leadership by "walking around."

On the way back from California, I stopped at Fort Hood to receive an orientation by the Continental United States (CONUS) Bradley Fielding Team. While a passenger in one of the Bradleys conducting amphibious operations on a lake, I witnessed how important it was for the crew to understand the vehicle capability in going from water to land. When the vehicle missed the egress point, the driver and Bradley commander tried to drive the vehicle up a steep bank. The BFV slid back into the water and began to sink. Fortunately, the lake at that location was not too deep, but the vehicle was stuck and partially submerged.

This incident emphasized the importance of extensive training for Bradley drivers and commanders in conducting amphibious operations. I also learned that ingress and egress points must be on firm ground and have a gradual slope wide enough to accommodate BFVs, which have difficulty with speed and direction. I decided to conduct extensive river crossing operations when I got to my new assignment so I would fully understand the capability of the BFV for crossing rivers in Germany.

## CHAPTER 15

# Brigade Commander

Upon arrival in Vilseck, we moved into a local *Gasthaus* until government quarters were available. I purchased a silver Mercedes four-door diesel sedan and Julie took a job at the elementary school. The boys enrolled in 6th and 7th grades, happily playing on German soccer teams, and Sara began 2nd grade.

After my "sinking experience" at Fort Hood, I vowed to be an expert on the swim capability of the BFV. I began by performing the duties of a Bradley commander in crossing the Main River at a ferry site near Frankfurt. Following a day of several river crossings and a few excursions up and down the river alongside barge traffic, I concluded that with proper training, under the right conditions, a BFV commander and driver could safely cross rivers in Germany for training exercises. However, the complicated efforts to prepare and operate a BFV for a river crossing under enemy fire would be extremely difficult, time consuming, and dangerous.

Prior to entering the water, a flotation curtain stored inside the outer armor of the BFV had to be opened and deployed around the top half of the vehicle to prevent water from flowing into the engine and crew compartments. Before entering the water, drain plugs had to be secured and bilge pumps turned on. Because the driver couldn't see where the vehicle was going, the Bradley commander gave directions through the vehicle intercom system. The maneuverability and speed of the BFV were achieved through rotation of the tracks in the water. Maximum revolutions per minute (RPM) had to be applied just as the vehicle entered the water and attained full flotation because the current would immediately begin to move the vehicle downstream. The vehicle must be steered upstream to land at the far-side egress point, where both tracks should hit land together. If one track hits the ground first, the side with the dominant impulsion would turn the vehicle back into the water, where the current would propel it downstream or, worst case, the vehicle could capsize.

After three months of *Gasthaus* living, we moved into comfortable government quarters and our household goods were delivered. We had just about emptied all the boxes and were looking forward to two years of relative family stability when I received a telephone call from the commanding general of the 3rd Infantry

Division. He told me that I would replace Colonel Thomas A. Rhame, the 2nd Brigade commander who had been selected for reassignment as chief of staff of the 3rd Armored Division in Frankfurt. Tom was replacing Colonel Gordon R. Sullivan, who had been selected for promotion to brigadier general.

I took command of 2nd Brigade, which comprised two Abrams Main Battle Tank battalions and one BFV battalion at Harvey Barracks in Kitzingen on November 30, 1983. After moving into quarters in January, I traveled to Fort Leavenworth, Kansas and Fort Benning, Georgia for mandatory pre-command training. This time away from brigade responsibilities right after taking command was frustrating to me and clearly disadvantageous to the brigade. In May 1984, after completing an assessment of my first six months in command, the 3rd Infantry Division inspector general told me the soldiers in my brigade didn't know who I was. In unambiguous language, I explained to him why soldiers would not be familiar with me when I was required to spend so much time away from Kitzingen.

Right on cue, I was selected to escort General J. Lawton Collins, senior surviving World War II D-Day commander for the 40-year anniversary of the Allied invasion in France. I flew from Frankfurt to Paris then drove to Normandy to begin a reconnaissance of General Collins's itinerary, which included a visit to the historic chateau that served as VII Corps headquarters and General Collins's residence after the Allied landings. The owners of the estate, Count D'Agnoix and Madame DeFeral, were happy to provide comfortable living accommodation for the 88-year-old general, who needed a walker to get around and a pulley to get out of bed. When I met with Lieutenant General David E. Grange, the director of American D-Day events, he thought it providential that I possessed all the escort officer criteria—a combat veteran and French-speaking brigade commander stationed in Germany. I said, "Sir, you were doing fine until you came to French fluency. I don't speak French." We agreed that I should continue supporting the mission while he found a French-speaking officer to act as an interpreter.

The next day, I picked up General Collins and his daughter at the Paris heliport and flew to Normandy, where we landed on the front lawn of the estate compound. I had at my disposal a UH1H (Huey) helicopter and crew as well as a Mercedes-Benz sedan and driver. In the morning, we flew General Collins to Pointe du Hoc for an interview with Walter Cronkite. This was followed by a meeting with soldiers from the 82nd Airborne Division, who had just completed a parachute jump into Sainte-Mère-Église. Two days later, the French-speaking liaison officer arrived. He was none other than retired Lieutenant General Vernon A. Walters, who had served as United States Ambassador to the United Nations and spoke six languages fluently. He was driven to various activities in his Citroën while I took care of General Collins. Each day was filled with events commemorating the Allied victories over the Wehrmacht forces, including the final ceremony, during which President Reagan met with General Collins.

When I returned to Kitzingen, I was alarmed at the number of 2nd Brigade soldiers cited for vehicle accidents and DUIs. After one of our soldiers was killed in a motorcycle accident, I established a safe driving course. Any soldier reported for DUI or involved in a vehicle traffic accident had to attend an eight-hour course conducted on the first Saturday of every month. I was the primary instructor and if the responsible soldiers didn't make it to class, the company commander or battalion commander attended in their place. After 60 days, the number of moving traffic violations and DUIs went down dramatically and stayed down for the duration of my time in command. We did have one unexpected incident. Julie was stopped by the military police for speeding, but she dutifully went to class and brought a batch of home-baked chocolate chip cookies for the soldiers. The program was so successful that 2nd Brigade received the U.S. Army Europe safe driving award two years in a row.

REFORGER was a large-scale exercise conducted annually in designated areas of Germany where brigade-size units had conditional authority to maneuver over the fields and roads. Soldiers from units in the United States were flown to Germany to link up with their vehicles and major weapons systems located at Prepositioning of Material Configured in Unit Sets (POMCUS) sites.

While preparing for 2nd Brigade to deploy on REFORGER in September 1984, we received a warning order from division headquarters to prepare for the possibility of conducting a river crossing with the BFVs. We continued to ask for implementing instructions, but none were received. Two days prior to the exercise start date I found out, by chance, that the planned swim site was located at a narrow river bypass. Seeing it for the first time, I was astonished. I would never have selected that site. The banks were too steep, the ingress and egress points too confining, and the 10mph river current too fast for a BFV designed to swim at a top speed of 5mph. As former chief of the Europe Bradley Fielding Team and brigade commander responsible for conducting an amphibious operation, I was more than a little disturbed that I was never consulted. While the engineers were attempting to decrease the steep angle of the slopes at the river, I was inspecting the soft, sandy soil. I knew these 40-ton vehicles would sink along the banks of the waterway as the tracks churned up the water-and-sand mixture. It was obvious the engineers were not aware of the BFV's amphibious capability nor the requirements for safe amphibious operations.

That evening, the division commander held a final REFORGER coordination meeting. I was sitting in the front row along with brigade commanders, battalion commanders, and members of the division staff. Roughly 50 officers and NCOs were in attendance. The commanding general began the meeting by stating that he understood some commanders were reluctant to conduct amphibious operations with the BFVs, but he said it was a combat capability for which we needed to train. "Therefore, we will swim Bradleys across the river to start the exercise." I immediately stood up and said, "Sir, I highly recommend that we do not try to swim Bradleys across the river. The crossing site is unacceptable and the current far exceeds the vehicle's capability to safely maneuver in the water. Any attempt would place our soldiers in an extremely dangerous situation."

I could tell by the look on his face he was surprised that I would oppose his guidance in public and was not happy about it. Without saying another word, he turned to his chief of staff and told him to arrange a time for me to brief Lieutenant General John R. Galvin, the VII Corps commander, on why the BFVs couldn't swim across the river. I remember thinking it strange that he would need the corps commander to weigh in on this issue.

The next morning, on the bank of the river at the planned crossing site, I set up a butcher board with charts describing the amphibious capabilities of the Bradley. As I conducted the briefing, the corps commander could see the twin diesel engineer boats struggling to maneuver in the rapid current. I described how the BFV's speed and maneuverability in water were a function of the engine RPM spinning the tracks to provide propulsion to the vehicle. I further explained that in a strong current, the BFV was incapable of controlling the direction and movement essential for successfully accomplishing far-side egress. In addition, I told him that the limited access points on both sides of such a narrow channel severely constrained the ability to conduct a safe crossing. After I completed my briefing, the corps commander spoke to the leaders assembled behind us, including the division commander, the assistant division commanders, brigade commanders, division, and corps staff officers, and the BFV program manager. Lieutenant General Galvin discussed the importance of heeding the lessons of history from experiences in Europe during World War II. He concluded his remarks by saying, "One of the key lessons we learned is to trust the judgment of the commander on the ground. We will not swim Bradleys across the river to commence REFORGER."

In the summer of 1985, Major General George R. Stotser assumed command of the division. He was a terrific soldier and an inspirational commander whose positive leadership and high standards of integrity were deeply appreciated. The outstanding training ethos and upbeat command climate he established across the division made my last five months in command a most enjoyable and rewarding experience.

Throughout my command tour, I worked hard at scheduling activities with our German *Partnerschaft* (partnership) unit, the 24th Panzer Brigade, commanded by Oberst (Colonel) Georg Bernhardt. We conducted mutually reciprocal programs, including weapons familiarization, small-unit training, tactical maneuver leaders' conferences, tank and Bradley/Marder platoon exchanges on REFORGER, and a variety of social events. The value of these programs is realized in the trust, cohesion, friendship, and interpersonal relationships established between soldiers of the American and German armies. For the many soldiers who have been stationed in Germany since the end of World War II, reaching out to German commands and local communities has had enduring benefits in building and maintaining cordial, respectful, and considerate relations.

In the fall, I was notified that 2nd Brigade and the 24th Panzer Brigade would receive the U.S. Army Europe annual brigade level award for the best United States/ Federal Republic of Germany partnership program. General Glenn K. Otis, U.S. Army Europe Commanding General and Lieutenant General Hans-Henning von Sandrat, Chief of Staff of the German Army, presented the awards to me and Oberst Bernhardt at a ceremony held at Wildermuth-Kaserne in Boeblingen with Secretary of the Army John O. Marsh, Jr. in attendance.

My change of command was scheduled for Wednesday, December 18, 1985, with Colonel Mike Davison, an outstanding officer, and a good friend. The airfield runway was the standard location for Kitzingen change of command ceremonies. However, plans were made in the post gymnasium in case of inclement weather. The forecast for the day of the ceremony was for snow and freezing temperatures. By coincidence, I ran into Mike the day before the change of command at the post barber shop, which was packed with soldiers. While waiting, I recommended to Mike that we ask the troops about where to have the ceremony. After he agreed I said, "Let me have your attention. The weather forecast for Friday is for cold temperatures and snow. We have to decide whether to hold the brigade change of command outdoors at the airfield or in the heated gymnasium. What do you think?"

For a moment, there was silence. Suddenly, from the back of the barber shop came the booming voice of a young soldier sitting on the floor. "Sir, we're all-weather warriors, let's go for it." This was followed by immediate applause. I turned to Mike and said, "I think our decision has been made."

On Friday, in thick fog and with 5 inches of snow on the ground, the 2nd Brigade, 3rd Infantry Division, change of command was conducted with precision and ceremonial dignity. My new assignment was Chief of the Operations and Contingency Plans Division in the office of the Army deputy chief of staff for operations and plans at the Pentagon in Washington, D.C.

## CHAPTER 16

# Crisis Management

Since our home in Fairfax was rented until June 1986, we signed a six-month lease on a house in McClean and moved in before Christmas with luggage and sleeping bags. In January, Mark enrolled in Langley High School for the second half of his freshman year. David was in 9th grade at Cooper Junior High and Sara attended Marshall Elementary School to finish 4th grade. With no teaching positions available, Julie went to real estate school. My job at the Pentagon began at 6:00 a.m. and I seldom returned home before 7:00 p.m.

One of my responsibilities as chief of current operations on the Army staff was to coordinate actions in the Army operations center during a crisis. On December 12, 1985, 248 soldiers from the 101st Airborne Division were killed in a fiery crash shortly after Arrow Air flight 1285 took off from Gander, Newfoundland in Canada. The chartered aircraft was returning from the Sinai Desert in Egypt and had refueled in Gander before the final leg to Fort Campbell, Kentucky for the Christmas holidays. The soldiers were completing a six-month deployment with the Multinational Force and Observers, a peacekeeping mission created to ensure Egypt and Israel complied with the 1982 Camp David Accords.[1]

Friends and relatives had gathered at Fort Campbell for the welcome home ceremony. They watched as Colonel John Herrling, the 2nd Brigade commander, walked slowly to the center of the brigade gymnasium and somberly announced that the aircraft carrying the returning soldiers had crashed in Gander and there were no survivors.[2] It's painful to imagine the disbelief, grief, and hysteria that must have engulfed the family members—spouses, children, parents, and siblings who had been waiting patiently to embrace their soldiers.

As the anticipated euphoria of welcoming them home for the Christmas holidays turned into despair, the Fort Campbell family support team, without hesitation, sprang into action. The institutional values of the Army as a family that had long been integrated into the cultural norms of every soldier were fully realized as the 2nd Brigade of the 101st Airborne Division welcome home ceremony was quickly transformed into a headquarters for family support. The division adjutant general took over the division conference room, establishing a full-scale emergency family assistance center. Chaplains, mental health specialists, doctors, and nurses emptied out the post hospital and proceeded to the 2nd Brigade gym, along with commanders and spouses from all over the post. The day care center mobilized voluntary babysitters, who were available to provide around-the-clock relief for parents. A committee was established to meet immediate family needs, such as funds for car repairs, moving expenses, and airline tickets.

Survivor assistance officers across the country were alerted. Congress passed legislation raising the Servicemembers' Group Life Insurance to $50,000. Private and corporate donations poured in from around the nation. Food, clothing, and Christmas toys began arriving. Master Sergeant Terry Du Mers, the non-commissioned officer for coordinating support from agencies such as the Red Cross and Army Community Service, said the support was awesome—all you needed to do was pick up the phone and ask. Church services were held the following Sunday. On Monday in hangar four at the airfield, President Reagan and the first lady visited Fort Campbell, solemnly moving through row upon row of grieving family members.[3]

Looking after families was not the only concern. The 3rd Battalion, 502nd Battalion, commander, command sergeant major, and most of the battalion staff died in the crash. The unit had to be reconstituted quickly as part of the healing process. This took time but the Fort Campbell command, especially Colonel Herrling and his wife, worked tirelessly and with great compassion for the next six months resolving family needs and restoring the battalion to readiness standards.[4]

Two hours after the crash, Major General William G. Moore, director of the operations, mobilization, and readiness directorate, activated a crisis response cell in the Army operations center. We conducted a daily briefing for the senior Army leadership, including the Honorable John O. Marsh Jr, secretary of the Army; General John A. Wickham Jr, Army chief of staff; General Maxwell R. Thurman, vice chief of staff; and Major General Moore.

Based upon previous aviation accidents, Secretary Marsh had given instructions that dental records were never to be carried on the same flight with soldiers. When he asked if the records were on the aircraft there was a long pause until a staff member confirmed that the dental records had indeed been on the plane. Secretary Marsh, a distinguished, mild-mannered gentleman, voiced his extreme frustration at this non-compliance of a direct order and demanded an explanation. There wasn't one, except that somewhere in the excitement of returning home for the holidays, the instructions were overlooked by the chain of command.

> Shortly after he received notice of the tragedy, General Thurman directed that Major General John S. Crosby, assistant deputy chief of staff for personnel, lead a team to the crash site. The mission of the Gander response team was to assist the Royal Canadian Mounted Police in search and recovery operations and arrange for shipment of the remains of the Army's dead to the United States.[5]

Before I arrived, a lieutenant colonel from my staff had been deployed to Gander to work directly with the response team to ensure all operational needs were met. Since the aircraft had just refueled and crashed in flames only minutes after takeoff, it was difficult to identify the remains. In addition, the crash site was in a remote wooded area, the recovery teams were working in below-zero temperatures, and the ground was frozen. After several days of search operations, a colonel from the medical corps briefed General Thurman that the recovery teams had identified all but 30 soldiers and recommended a mass grave be established for the unknown remains. General Thurman stated emphatically there would be no mass grave, and the remains of every soldier would be found. When the colonel told him that it would be impossible as the ground was frozen, he said, "Thaw out the ground."

> The second search and recovery effort at Gander was carried out by 5 four-man teams composed of Army graves registration specialists from Forts Lee and Bragg who arrived at Gander on 8 January 1986. Before the search commenced, a civilian contractor began constructing shelters of wood and plastic over the 350 by 50-meter site. Four to five 150,000 BTU propane jet heaters in the shelters melted the accumulated snow and ice. As each shelter became ready for searching, a graves registration team divided the enclosed area into one-meter-wide lanes with one specialist working each lane. The specialists conducted the search on their hands and knees using brick mason trowels and garden tools to sift through the soil and ash.[6]

All 248 soldiers' remains were recovered, identified, and processed for individual burials. The crash site was closed on May 10, 1986, and has served as a memorial ever since.

Although it was one of the worst air disasters in American history, the U.S. Army, as an institution, can take pride in the rapid, well-organized response provided to the families of the fallen as well as the Army's long-term support for months and even years after the event. The true meaning of the Army family covenant came forth from the hearts and minds of soldiers and family members, who needed no guidance or direction to move briskly to the scene of the stricken families. They just showed up.

In June, we moved back to our house in Fairfax, Virginia. Julie was hired to teach 4th grade at Jermantown Elementary School in Fairfax. Mark and David began their sophomore and freshman years at Robinson High School and Sara was happy to be back at Laurel Ridge Elementary School.

In August, Major General William H. Harrison, the commanding general of the 7th Infantry Division at Fort Ord, California selected me to be his chief of staff with the understanding that I would report for duty in September. While I tried to accommodate his request, I was working on a classified project that prevented my release from the Pentagon for another three months. The family flew out to Fort Ord and moved into quarters in December. I drove across country, arriving just before Christmas. The chief of the General Officer Management Office alerted me that General Harrison was not happy about the three-month delay. My first meeting with him was strained, until I noticed he had a display of ceramic frogs on the shelves behind his desk. As a way of calming the waters, I said, "Sir, I notice that you have an excellent frog collection. Where did they come from?" Without cracking a smile, he quipped, "They were former chiefs of staff." My new boss was going to be okay—he had a sense of humor.

Since the boys were excellent basketball players, I searched for a school with a good basketball program and solid academic credentials. We made a visit to Palma High School, a private, Catholic school located 30 minutes from Fort Ord. Without offering the boys a tryout, the varsity basketball coach told us his team had all the players it needed but Mark and Dave could pick up towels, clean the locker room, and play in a few scrimmages. We promptly scratched Palma off the list. The boys attended Seaside High School, a public school just outside the gate at Fort Ord, where they both played on the varsity basketball team. Their coach, Bob Burleson, was terrific but left Seaside after the 1986–87 season to replace the Palma High School basketball coach, who had been fired.

As fate would have it, Mark would be playing against his old coach in Seaside's first game of the 1987–88 season. I was anxious to see the game, arrived early and, by coincidence, sat in the bleachers with a group of Palma High School parents. When they realized that I was a Seaside High School parent stationed at Fort Ord, they told me that Palma was looking forward to an undefeated season. They even apologized for the drubbing Seaside would take that afternoon but offered, as a consolation, that the boys would learn from it.

Mark used his speed, quickness, and three-point shooting ability to overwhelm the Palma defense. He moved so well without the ball that he was wide open for shots. When Palma fouled him, he calmly sank the free throws. At the end of the first half, Seaside was leading by five points and all the Palma parents were talking about number 14 who had scored so many three-pointers. I was delighted to inform them that number 14 was my son, who hit four more three-pointers in the second half and ended the game with 32 points. Seaside won 65–57. I have always been enormously proud of Mark's basketball skills as well as his calm, winning attitude, but that day was special.

Within six months, General Harrison was promoted to lieutenant general and assigned as I Corps commander at Fort Lewis. This smart, innovative warrior created a division of proud light fighters who proved they could rapidly deploy to any place in the world. He and his wife, Jo, were a great command team—much beloved by the troops. His replacement, Major General Edwin H. Burba, made an immediate contribution to readiness, training, and tactical proficiency. After just one year, he was promoted to lieutenant general and assigned to Korea as the commanding general, Combined Field Army (ROK/US). He was replaced by Major General Carmen J. Cavezza, a charismatic commander who loved leading soldiers and was exceptionally good at it.

The 7th Infantry (Light) was a rapidly deployable division established to airlift light infantry battalions into world crisis spots in a matter of hours. We had no tanks, APCs, or heavy artillery. We either rode in helicopters or walked. On some days, we had only three of our nine infantry battalions at Fort Ord, California—the other six were deployed to faraway places like Korea, South America, and the Sinai desert. Appreciation of the true meaning of a light division is apparent when you walk off the rear ramp of a U.S. Air Force C-147 Starlifter on a remote airfield in Honduras with nothing but a backpack, web gear, canteen, meals ready to eat (MREs), weapon, and helmet—then disappear into the jungle to participate in a combined U.S. Army/Honduran Army exercise. In addition to deployments, we maintained a rigorous physical training program. This was only part of my daily physical exercise as I also played on the division headquarters basketball team.

My job as division chief of staff was to take in all the issues, requests, and reports, sort through them, and send out orders to get things done while the commanding general was in the field with unit commanders ensuring that our wartime mission was being trained to standard. Due to meetings and phone calls during the week, I normally took a box or two of files and decision papers home over the weekend. In my job, I was also called upon to be the master of ceremonies for social events, the commander of troops for Hail and Farewell ceremonies, and the family support group notification officer when battalions were alerted to fly away in just a few hours. Although I had a time-consuming job, I made it a point to leave the office early, meet Julie, and watch our children's basketball games. In my 37 years of service, I never wished that I spent more time with my family because I spent the requisite time attending our children's extracurricular activities.

Julie worked closely with the commanding general's wife and other commander's wives to organize community events such as sports day, the U.S. Army birthday celebration with Martha Raye, the annual division run, the "Walk for the Human Race" fundraiser, and "Special Olympics" with Clint Eastwood, the mayor of Carmel. Since we worked so hard, I was always looking for ways to provide time off for soldiers to be with family and friends. We traditionally authorized a three-day leave on weekends in conjunction with a federal holiday. However, some soldiers drove to San Francisco, Las Vegas, and Los Angeles and had accidents rushing back to sign in before their leave time was up. I convinced the commanding general that we should authorize four-day weekends around federal holidays like Memorial Day, Veterans Day, and the 4th of July to give more time for soldiers to return to Fort Ord. Unfortunately, we had just as many accidents because, with one more day, some soldiers decided to drive to places as far away as Phoenix, Salt Lake City, and Colorado Springs. I learned to never underestimate the ingenuity and perseverance of a young soldier.

After two and a half years as chief of staff, I decided it was time to move on. We had acquired Miss Priss, a shaded silver Persian cat, and two beagles, Daisy and

Maggie. It was 1989 and Mark was graduating from Seaside High School; David was in the 11th grade; and Sara was in the 6th grade at Fort Ord Elementary School. Since Mark was looking at colleges on the east coast and Dave and Sara missed their home in Fairfax, I requested an assignment to the Washington, D.C. area.

We planned to drive both cars across country and accomplish a door-to-door move. Dave flew ahead since he was enrolled in a summer basketball camp in Virginia. We left Fort Ord at the end of June, planning to get a head start on the 4th of July weekend traffic. Julie drove the Mercedes with Sara, Daisy, and Miss Priss. I drove the Citation with Mark and Maggie. We covered 200 miles to Sacramento on the first day and hoped to make it to Salt Lake City, Utah by the next evening.

After one hour of driving up the mountain toward Reno, the Citation began to overheat. I called Julie on our two-way radio system and pulled into the nearest gas station. The mechanic on duty said we had a faulty radiator that he couldn't repair. A tow truck took the Citation to an American Automobile Association (AAA) service station and, after a few hours of poking around, the mechanic admitted he couldn't fix it either. We followed the tow truck back down the mountain to an authorized Chevrolet dealership. The radiator had to be sent to a specialty shop and could not be repaired until the next day. Exhausted, we all piled into the Mercedes and tried to check in at the only motel in the town of Colfax, California (population 1,306). We were turned away because of a no pets policy and drove another 20 miles to Auburn—a former gold mining town—population 13,000. We found a motel, kept the dogs and cat out of sight, and checked in.

The Citation was repaired and ready for pickup at 5:00 p.m. the next day. We stayed one more night in Auburn, leaving early on Friday morning for Salt Lake City. I was watching the temperature gauge very closely—so far, so good—until late in the afternoon when a jerking sensation came from the engine. When I stopped at a service station just outside Salt Lake City, water began pouring out of the engine compartment. The service station attendant looked under the hood and said we needed a new water pump.

The mechanic was a Marine Corps staff sergeant who worked part time at the service station. He said he would replace the water pump in the morning. He even called Tooele Army Depot and made reservations for us to stay overnight. We were delighted with our accommodations in a beautiful suite with two bedrooms, kitchen, and dining room. Concerned that the Citation might not make it to the east coast, Julie and I packed up boxes with non-essential items and mailed them to Virginia. On our way back from dinner, Maggie stepped in hot tar and was in such pain we rushed her to the local veterinarian, who gave her a sedative. When I tried to remove the tar on Maggie's paws she howled in pain and ran under the bed. She recovered but it was a traumatic experience for everyone.

The next morning, when I called about the car, I learned that the sergeant was out of town as his father had died during the night. The service station was shorthanded, but the manager said he would try to get someone to replace the water pump and call us. The car was ready by noon, but the engine was still jerking during acceleration. The manager recommended we get help from a master mechanic at a service station in Tooele. It was now about 2:00 p.m., and I was afraid that we were going to be stuck in Utah until after the 4th of July, which would cause us to miss the moving van scheduled to deliver our household goods on Friday, July 7. I drove to the service station and approached a man leaning over the engine of a car in one of three maintenance bays. When I explained the problem with the engine jerking, he said, "I'm sorry but I have these other cars to repair, and I can't possibly take on another job." After I told him about our dilemma in trying to get across country with my wife, two children, and three pets, he said, "Pull your car into this empty bay and I'll look at it."

After about 30 minutes, he said, "I've checked the spark plugs, distributor, radiator, carburetor, hoses and I can't find the problem." I could sense that this master mechanic was frustrated. Leaning over the engine, he began running his hands along the wiring harness leading from the distributor to the spark plugs. Suddenly, he said, "I'll be damned." He showed me the wire, which had a piece of the protective rubber coating burned away from lying on the hot engine block. The electrical current from the distributor had been grounding against the engine block, resulting in no current to the spark plug. The jerking was caused by the cylinder not firing in conjunction with the other cylinders. He looked at his watch. It was 4:30 p.m. on Saturday afternoon. He quickly removed the old wiring and told me to take it to the auto parts shop on the next block before they closed at 5:00 p.m. "Tell them you want the exact same wiring kit." The parts store had it. When I returned to the station, this good Samaritan was on the phone telling his wife he would not be going out for dinner and would be home late. He installed the new wiring and said, "Let's take it for a test drive." We drove around Tooele for 15 minutes with the engine running smoothly. He had a big smile on his face as he said, "I think we fixed it." After I paid him for the repairs, I offered to give him extra cash for his trouble, but he refused to take it. When I returned to Virginia, I sent him a thank-you note with two 20-dollar bills.

I drove to our suite and prepared for an early morning departure to Colorado Springs, where we planned on staying with our good friends, Mike and Kay Keaveney and their boys Kevin and Keith. In the morning, I began loading the cars. When I placed Miss Priss in the back seat of the Mercedes and reached down to pick up some luggage, she jumped out of the car and ran along the ground toward a vacant building. Because it was dark, she was afraid of every shadow. As she ran around to the other side of the building, I told Mark to catch her if she came his way. Mark's athletic abilities saved the day as he was able to block the cat's path and had the quickness to grab her with both hands just as she was about to jump through an open basement window.

We left Tooele and drove to Colorado Springs, arriving about 8:30 p.m.—almost 16 hours later. We were happy to see the Keaveneys and they made us feel right at home. Soon after we went to bed, the dogs, who had a comfortable place in a fenced-in backyard, began howling in unison. Mark again came to the rescue by volunteering to sleep with the dogs in the back of the Citation. Thinking it might be difficult to make it to Virginia by July 7, we called the crew of our moving van. They had been delayed in San Diego and would not be able to deliver our household goods until Monday, July 10. Thank God.

We could now relax and take our time going home. After reaching Charlestown, West Virginia, we turned north, finally reaching our house in Fairfax, Virginia on Friday afternoon, July 7 and were met there by David. He had no money, but the neighbors were feeding him and had turned on the water and electricity in our house. We had been there about one hour when Daisy bit Dierdre, one of the neighbor's little girls. We were all upset until Julie bought her a stuffed animal. Over the weekend, the boys and I built a fence in the backyard and a doggy door leading from the walkout basement. We let out a huge sigh of relief when the moving van arrived and unloaded our household goods. Sara was delighted to be back in her old house and spent the summer with her friends at our neighborhood pool. She was 13 years old, looking forward to attending Robinson Junior High School and playing basketball on a youth sports team with her dad as the head coach.

Dave played on a summer league basketball team, supervised by Tom Peterson, the Robinson High School coach. David was ecstatic about his prospects for senior year as he liked his coach and was playing with great confidence. Unfortunately, Coach Peterson left before the season began and his replacement was a teacher who didn't know much about basketball and played only the boys he knew. In a televised game against archrival TC Williams, Dave was pulling down rebounds, shooting threes, driving to the basket, and dishing the ball to his teammates—easily the best player on the floor, until the coach pulled him out of the game. The television narrator couldn't understand why he wasn't playing and said, "I can't believe Dave Foley is still sitting on the bench—he must be sick or have a serious injury." Despite not getting well-deserved playing time, Dave averaged 13 points, 7 rebounds, and 5 assists per game as well as shooting 82 percent in free throws and 42 percent in three-point attempts. Dave was frustrated but displayed great strength of character in overcoming this adversity and I was immensely proud and happy for him when he received his appointment to West Point with the Class of 1994.

Mark attended the University of Rochester on a basketball scholarship and played on the varsity team that won the Division III National Championship. When I visited Mark in February 1990, he said he was not happy playing basketball seven days a week, did not like the harsh winters in upstate New York, and wanted to apply to the Air Force Academy. I knew it would be difficult getting him accepted this late,

Cadet Robert F. Foley. (West Point
Association of Graduates Archives)

Captain of the 1962–63 Army basketball team. (#44) (West
Point Association of Graduates Archives)

First Sergeant Chan, Captain Foley, Lieutenant Mike Kowalchik, and Captain Mack Howard at 25th
Infantry Division Base Camp, Cu Chi, South Vietnam, 1966. (Robert F. Foley)

With Sergeant First Class Hunter and Lieutenant
Day at Alpha Company, 2nd Battalion, 27th
Infantry Headquarters, Cu Chi, South Vietnam,
1966. (Robert F. Foley)

Medal of Honor presentation by President Lyndon
B. Johnson at a White House ceremony on May
1, 1968. (Francis L. Wolfe, The White House)

With 25th Infantry Division soldiers after White House Medal of Honor ceremony, May 1, 1968. (U.S. Army)

Welcome by Mrs. Russell B. Thacker, wife of mayor of Kissimmee, Florida with my mother and father on July 3, 1968, for Captain Robert F. Foley Day. (Robert F. Foley)

Wedding Day, September 27, 1969. (West Point Association of Graduates)

Payday talk to soldiers of 1st Battalion, 4th Infantry, in 1977, Fiori Kaserne, Aschaffenburg, Germany. (John A. Varner, Public Information Officer, 1st Battalion, 4th Infantry)

Commemorating the 200-year anniversary of victory at Yorktown with President Ronald Reagan, French President François Mitterrand, Secretary of the Interior James G. Watt, and Congressman Paul Trible, October 19, 1981. (The White House)

Major General Pat W. Crizer, commanding general, 3rd Infantry Division, and Lieutenant Colonel Robert F. Foley, commanding officer of 1st Battalion, 4th Infantry, during winter exercise in Germany, January 1977. (Robert F. Foley)

Meeting with Oberst Bernhardt, commander of 24th Panzer Brigade and Lieutenant Colonel Jack Mountcastle, commander of 3rd Battalion, 63rd Armor, Germany, 1984. (Robert F. Foley)

Congratulating Honduran Army Soldiers at conclusion of 7th Infantry Division combined exercise. (Robert F. Foley)

Second Infantry Division leadership (Korea, 1991). First row: Command Sergeant Major Bob Hall, Brigadier General Herb Lloyd, Major General Terry Scott, Brigadier General Bob Foley, Colonel Mike Sherfield. (U.S. Army Second Infantry Division)

Alumni march to Thayer Monument at West Point in the fall of 1992. (West Point Association of Graduates)

Christmas at West Point in 1993 with Julie, Sara, Dave, and Mark. (Robert F. Foley)

Julie with President George H. W. Bush at West Point before his farewell remarks to the Corps of Cadets, January 5, 1993. (West Point Association of Graduates)

Dave Foley receiving his diploma from his dad at West Point graduation exercises, May 28, 1994. (West Point Association of Graduates)

Cadet Lieutenant Colonel Mark Foley with Second Lieutenant Dave Foley at Mark's graduation from the Air Force Academy, May 31, 1995. (Robert F. Foley)

Sara Foley representing the state of New York at the 1995 Cherry Blossom Festival in Washington, DC. (Robert F. Foley)

With President Clinton at the funeral of Secretary of Commerce Ron Brown, Arlington National Cemetery, April 10, 1996. (Official White House photo, April 10, 1996)

Host to President Clinton at the Tomb of the Unknown Soldier wreath-laying ceremony, Memorial Day, 1996. (U.S. Army Military District of Washington)

1997 Inaugural parade. (U.S. Army Military District of Washington)

Hosting President Oscar Luigi Scalfaro and an Italian delegation for wreath laying at the Tomb of the Unknown Soldier, Arlington National Cemetery, April 2, 1996. (U.S. Army Military District of Washington)

Speaking with Secretary of the Army Togo D. West, Jr. at Arlington National Cemetery. (U.S. Army Military District of Washington)

Promotion to lieutenant general by General Dennis J. Reimer, Army chief of staff, August 5, 1998. (Robert F. Foley)

Retiring as commanding general of Fifth Army with Sara, Julie, and Mark at Fort Sam Houston, San Antonio, Texas, August 12, 2000. (Robert F. Foley)

Speaking at U.S. Army Sergeants Major Academy, Fort Bliss, Texas. (Robert F. Foley)

Talking to West Point cadets prior to meeting with Justice Antonin Scalia at the U.S. Supreme Court. (Robert F. Foley)

2009 West Point Distinguished Graduates: Starry '48, Hughes '46, Foley '63, Shinseki '65, Schwartz '67, and Abizaid '73. (West Point Association of Graduates)

Fiftieth wedding anniversary. (Robert F. Foley)

but I flew to Colorado Springs to meet with the director of admissions. The Class of 1994 was full, but Mark was able to enroll in the Air Force Academy Prep School.

Moving time for military children is always difficult and gets worse as they get older. Changing schools with different academic programs, making new friends, and trying out for teams with an established roster is not easy. Mark, David, and Sara went to a total of nine different schools from 1st grade through high school. But Julie and I could not be prouder of how well they accommodated these moves while maintaining excellent grades and participating in soccer, basketball, and swimming programs.

Our own experience in permanent change of station (PCS) moves increased our awareness of the challenges faced by young soldiers and their families. Typically, in my command positions, Julie made a visit to the family in their new quarters, and I had a policy for soldiers to take the time necessary to move in, set up their house, and get their children in school before reporting to work.

In September 1990, I was assigned to the Pentagon to be the deputy for reserve forces in the Office of the Assistant Secretary of the Army (Manpower and Reserve Affairs). In June 1990, I was selected by the Honorable Kim Wincup, Assistant Secretary of the Army for Manpower and Reserve Affairs, to be his executive officer. Colonel Pete Gleichenhaus, West Point Class of 1960, an Army basketball teammate of mine, asked if I would be interested in becoming the president of the Permanent Technical Committee (PTC) for basketball with CISM (Conseil International du Sport Militaire). CISM was founded in 1948 to provide active-duty military personnel, in countries across the globe, the opportunity to compete internationally with armed forces teams under the motto of "Friendship Through Sports." In 1990, CISM comprised 56 nations participating in 22 sports. The CISM World Basketball Championship was scheduled for September 3–17, 1990, in Dijon, France. After receiving permission from Secretary Wincup to be absent from the office for two weeks, I told Pete I would take the job.

On August 2, 1990, Iraq invaded Kuwait and the UN Security Council passed Resolution 660, condemning the Iraqi invasion, and demanding the unconditional withdrawal of all Iraqi forces occupying Kuwait. In late August, I received a call from the CISM director of basketball operations informing me that the American and Iraqi basketball teams were in the same pool and the American team was scheduled to play Iraq on the first day of the tournament. He wanted to know if I was okay with this development. I said, "Absolutely not—they can't be in the same pool and can't ever play against one another." I told the director to find a solution quickly or I would have to notify authorities in the Department of State and Department of Defense. He called me the next day and said, "We found a solution." Based upon my request, the French Ministry of Foreign Affairs disapproved the visa requests for the Iraqi basketball team.

Because I was at different venues throughout Dijon checking on basketball games and there was a six-hour time difference between Dijon and Washington, it was difficult for my office at the Pentagon to contact me. One evening, I received a message to call Secretary Wincup. When I called, he announced on the speaker phone with the staff present that I was on the brigadier general promotion list. His deputy, Bill Clark, yelled out, "And you are number one on the list." In disbelief, I said, "Sir, can you repeat that?" I had put the notion of ever getting promoted so far out of my mind that it was hard to believe. I immediately called Julie, who had been told by a friend the night before that I was on the list. She was so excited she had stayed up all night. Mark was at the Air Force Academy and Dave was at West Point, so she waited until the next day to contact them. But she did wake up Sara, who said, "That's nice" and promptly went back to sleep.

All my future assignments were managed by the General Officer Management Office (GOMO) in the Pentagon. With the U.S. Army deploying forces to the Persian Gulf in support of Operation *Desert Shield/Desert Storm*, I immediately volunteered to be in the mix—preferably as an assistant division commander. The staff at GOMO explained to me that combatant commanders, understandably, desired to keep together the team they had trained with—especially the senior leaders who were familiar with their subordinate commanders and unit standard operating procedures. Therefore, I was not considered for assignment with a unit deploying to the Persian Gulf but was slated as assistant division commander for support with the 2nd Infantry Division in Korea and received orders to report in February 1991.

## CHAPTER 17

# Assistant Division Commander

Julie was teaching 4th grade in Fairfax; Mark was enrolled at the Air Force Academy Prep School in Colorado Springs, and Dave was in his plebe year at West Point. Sara was happily participating in drama, ballet, and basketball in the 8th grade at Robinson Junior High. She was also on the Springfield cheerleading team, which won the 1990 Class A State Championship for her age group. With so many positive activities, she was understandably upset about moving again and this time "to the other side of the world." But she demonstrated resilience and love for her family in a letter she tucked inside my carry-on bag for the flight to Seoul:

> Hi Daddy. I knew your plane ride was going to be long, so I decided to write you a letter. Thank you for always being there when I was sick and bringing me my soup and tea and yucky Robitussin. I am going to miss you very much when you are in Korea. I will try to take care of Mom the best I can and Miss Priss and the dogs. Mom and I will send you tapes of the basketball games if we can. I will try and write you as much as possible. Korea will be an experience but don't worry about Mom and me, we have each other, and we will be fine…

In July, after placing our household goods in storage and leaving the cars with friends, Julie and Sara flew to Seoul and moved into family housing on Yongsan Army Post. We were fortunate to have Mr. Park, who rode a bicycle in a business suit from his home every morning, changed into work clothes, and performed housekeeping duties in our quarters. Occasionally, he prepared a special Korean meal of *bulgogi*, rice, and *kimchi* for the family. Sara adjusted nicely to her first year of high school, becoming a member of the cheerleading squad and the drama club. She also modeled clothes for a Korean fashion catalog.

Julie loved volunteering in the Chosun Gift Shop, an on-post boutique run by the Wives' Club. Since its charter prohibited competition with Korean commercial enterprises, a rotating group of spouses traveled to Japan, Singapore, Thailand, Taiwan, the Philippines, and Hong Kong, where they purchased items such as jewelry, furniture, rugs, crystal, and pottery for the shop. We still have a camphor chest, silk screens, and cloisonné lamps as well as a small carousel horse, which I am told will hold a plant someday. In addition, vendors at the Itaewon market located within walking distance of the back gate offered jewelry, leather jackets, handbags, scarves, and custom-made clothing. The merchandise was sold at discount prices and included knock-off brands kept in a back room. Julie's skills in the art of negotiation earned her the moniker "Best price Julie."

The 2nd Infantry Division's major weapon systems included Abrams Main Battle Tanks, Bradley Fighting Vehicles, 105mm and 155mm towed and self-propelled howitzers, as well as a full complement of aviation assets to support the defense of the Republic of Korea. Major General Glenn Marsh, the commanding general, and Brigadier General Herb Lloyd, the assistant division commander for maneuver, lived at Camp Casey in the same austere accommodations I had—a small room containing a desk, bed, and bathroom. Because the division was training seven days a week, I scheduled one weekend a month to visit Julie and Sara at our quarters in Yongsan. For security purposes, the vehicle designated for trips to Seoul was a black Chevrolet four-door sedan with built-in anti-terrorist modifications, including bullet-proof windshields, heavy-duty tires, and a high-performance engine. The first time my driver took me to Seoul, we were stuck in traffic. The big, black American vehicle was wedged among a sea of Hyundai cars for an hour—an obvious security risk.

On my next trip home, I took the train from the village of Tong du Chon outside Camp Casey, with plans to switch to the subway for Yongsan and walk to our quarters. While on the train, I continually looked out the window at the platform signs to ensure I would get off at the right station. A young Korean man seated next to me was watching my every move. After several stops, he said, "Where you go?"

I said, "I am going to visit my family in Seoul."

"I go Taegu—see girlfriend. Where you work?"

"Camp Casey."

"Me too, I KATUSA soldier." (Korea Augmentation to the U.S. Army). "What's your rank?" I paused knowing Korean soldiers get nervous around general officers. He again said, "What's your rank?"

I quickly said, "General."

He looked at me with a big smile on his face and said, "Oh yeah, yeah, I hope so, I hope so."

I remember thinking that I must not have looked or sounded like a general. But when I told my story to a Korean officer, he said the KATUSA soldier's response was not about my appearance. In his mind, no American general would be riding the train or subway—he would be in a staff car with a driver. I didn't want to ruin the image of American generals, but I continued to take the train and subway once a month to go home.

In the summer of 1991, General Marsh was replaced by Major General James T. (Terry) Scott, a good friend of mine and an exceptional leader. Due to his experience as a Ranger battalion commander, assistant division commander in Operation *Desert Shield/Desert Storm*, and prior duty in Korea, he made an immediate and positive impact on enhancing the division's warfighting capabilities. Shortly after he took command, we conducted a combined U.S. Army/ROKA command post exercise. On the first day, we experienced language and communications problems that resulted in none of our objectives being accomplished. At the end of the day, General Scott asked me and Herb if we had any ideas on overcoming the difficulties we had encountered.

During my previous assignment in Korea, I had worked closely with Major Kim Dong Jin, who I thought, by this time, might be a high-ranking officer in ROKA. I told my story to three KATUSA soldiers on the division staff, who returned 30 minutes later with big smiles. They had found him. The former Major Kim was a four-star general and chief of staff of the Korean Army. When General Kim came to the phone, he said, "Hello, Bob, this is DJ." He was surprised that I was in Korea and indicated that we should get together for dinner soon. He said, "The staff told me that you are having difficulty with your combined exercise." After I explained our situation, he said, "Continue the training as planned. I'll fix the problem." The next morning, we arrived at the training site to a totally different situation. Every objective was being accomplished. There were no language problems, no communications issues, and no misunderstandings. I thought about the advice provided by General Walter T. (Dutch) Kerwin at the brigadier general orientation class that I had attended before coming to Korea. He said to remember the power of interpersonal relationships. The friendship that I had established with Major Kim Dong Jin when we served together in Korea and when we were fellow students at Fort Leavenworth proved to be immensely beneficial 18 years later.

A major initiative for the 2nd Infantry Division was fielding the BFV to replace the armored personnel carriers that had been first distributed to Army units in 1961. Since I had been the Bradley Fielding Team chief in Germany, I sent a list of issues and a detailed statement of each problem with specific recommendations to the department of the Army BFV office. I asked that a team of experts be sent to Korea to provide responses to each problem. When the 10-person team arrived, our commanders and staff were present in the briefing room as an Army major began a presentation on the general capabilities of the Bradley. I stopped the briefing and displayed our first issue chart on the screen. I looked at the department of the Army civilian heading the team and said, "I need responses to the issues we submitted to you thirty days ago so we can meet our fielding timelines." He said the team wasn't prepared to discuss the issues. I immediately called my West Point classmate, Major General Steve Silvasy, the director of combined and joint operations for United Nations Command, U.S. Forces Korea, and the Eighth Army located in Seoul. When I told him the department of the Army team had come unprepared to assist us, he said, "Send them to me." I knew I could count on Steve, a smart, highly respected general officer who did not appreciate anyone wasting the time of warfighters who trained seven days a week preparing to meet the North Korean threat. Three days later, when the team returned to Camp Casey, they had all the answers.

My good friend Brigadier General Randolph T. Poore had been serving as the assistant chief of staff, G-4 at Eighth Army headquarters in Seoul. He was 47 years old and a standout leader who served two tours in Vietnam with the 173rd Airborne Brigade. He had a master's degree from the University of Alabama and had been the assistant commandant at the U.S. Army Ordnance Center at Aberdeen Proving Ground. Randy, his wife Gloria, and their daughters Julie and Jennifer, lived near us on the base at Yongsan. Friends from a previous assignment, Randy and I gravitated toward one another at social events to talk basketball while Gloria and Julie talked endlessly about everything.

Early in the morning of September 19, Gloria called Julie asking that she join her at the hospital because Randy had fallen during a morning run with his soldiers. They waited in a private room adjacent to the emergency room for about 30 minutes until the doctor came out and told Gloria that the medical team had been unable to save her husband. This shocking news elicited immediate support from Julie, Sandy Schwartz, and several other ladies, who took Gloria home, picked up her daughters from school, ran errands, and made lunch.

Upon receiving the call at Camp Casey that I had been selected as the casualty assistance officer for the Poore family, I flew by helicopter to Yongsan and went to a meeting with the Eighth Army staff. In accordance with Gloria's wishes, arrangements were made within 48 hours to fly Randy, Gloria, and the girls on Northwest Airlines from Seoul to Washington, D.C. While Gloria stayed with Randy's family in Chantilly, Virginia, I met with the Arlington National Cemetery (ANC) staff to discuss the funeral service and burial. Randy was laid to rest with full military honors, I presented the American flag covering Randy's casket to Gloria, and an Arlington Lady presented a letter of condolence from the Army chief of staff. (The Arlington Ladies are a group of volunteers who attend funeral services at ANC to ensure that no soldier, sailor, airman, or Coast Guardsman is buried alone. The Marine Corps has a similar process.) This was an emotional time for all of us, but the Army provided magnificent support to the Poore family.

Several months later, I was again in Washington, D.C. as a member of an officer command selection board for determining a list of officers to fill commands coming available in the following year. This is an important process that ensures battalions and brigades are provided with the most qualified commanders from across the Army. While there, I was informed by Brigadier General Stephen R. Smith, chief of the GOMO, that I was under consideration to be the next commandant of cadets at the U.S. Military Academy. I told General Smith that I wasn't interested since my son, Dave, would be going into his junior year at West Point and I didn't want to interfere with his college life. News travels fast. When I returned to Korea, I was met at the airport by the executive officer to four-star General Robert W. RisCassi, commander in chief of United Nations Command. General RisCassi thought I was the right officer at the right time to be commandant of cadets and wanted me to think about it and get back to him. I very much appreciated his timely intervention because I took time to focus on what turned out to be one of the best decisions in my military career. I went to Camp Casey that night and took a long walk in the snow, contemplating what I ought to do. Julie suggested I call Dave, who didn't hesitate a second in saying he thought it was a terrific idea. I thanked General RisCassi for his advice and told GOMO I would be happy to be considered for the commandant position.

I traveled to West Point in February to interview with the Military Academy superintendent, Lieutenant General Howard D. Graves. I also met with the dean and the chief of staff. After dinner that evening at the superintendent's quarters, I spoke with Gracie Graves in the living room for about 20 minutes while the other guests were in the library with General Graves. Back at the hotel, it occurred to me that I had just been interviewed by the superintendent's wife and I must have done okay because I was promptly notified that I would become the 63rd commandant of cadets.

In June, we sold our Hyundai, cleaned the quarters, and shipped our household goods. I took a Northwest Airlines 13-hour flight to Detroit and on to Virginia to attend a five-day general officer course. I left the cat with Gloria Poore, retrieved one of our cars from Jean Grogan in Fairfax, and made plans to pick up Julie and Sara the following week.

After departing from Seoul and changing planes in Hawaii, Julie and Sara settled in for the flight to Washington, D.C. However, when Julie looked out the window as the cabin door closed, she saw Maggie still sitting in her carrier on the tarmac. She ran up the aisle toward the cockpit yelling, "You can't take off, my dog is not on the plane." After the flight attendant had looked out of the window and verified that Maggie was indeed outside the aircraft, she notified the pilot, who calmly announced:

> Ladies and gentlemen, we are going to have a slight delay while we load one of our passenger's family members aboard the plane. We mistakenly left her dog outside. We will take a few minutes to load it on the plane before we take off. Thank you for your cooperation and understanding.

After I had met Julie, Sara, and Maggie at Dulles Airport, we retrieved Miss Pris from Gloria, picked up our Mercedes from Carolyn Worrall in Rhode Island, and drove to West Point.

The U.S. Military Academy is located on the banks of the Hudson River, 57 miles north of New York City. The river begins in the Adirondack Mountains in upstate New York and runs south for 315 miles, finally emptying into the Atlantic Ocean between New York City and the state of New Jersey.[1] During colonial times, the Hudson River was an important artery of trade from New York City to Albany and became a strategic asset during the Revolutionary War. General George Washington feared the British with their large navy could isolate the northern and southern colonies by cutting off military supplies as well as commercial trade and divide the might of the Continental Army. He was convinced West Point was the lynchpin to command of the Hudson Valley and the most important military tract of land in America.

When members of the Continental Army crossed the frozen river on January 27, 1778, West Point commenced its journey of becoming the oldest continuously occupied post in the United States. A unique component of the West Point fortification was the 500-yard iron chain that stretched across the Hudson River. The chain was placed on log rafts from West Point to Constitution Island, where approaching ships had to negotiate the tight S-curve while fighting changing currents and gusty winds. With multiple cannon guarding both sides of the river, the chain was never tested. Consequently, the West Point fortifications served as a formidable deterrent to British jurisdiction over the Hudson River.[2]

On March 16, 1802, President Thomas Jefferson signed the Military Peace Establishment Act, which directed that the Corps of Engineers be located at West Point with the priority mission of establishing a military academy. On July 28, 1817, Brevet Major Sylvanus Thayer became the fourth superintendent of the U.S. Military Academy. He was a member of the West Point Class of 1808, an academy instructor from 1808 to 1811, and served with distinction during the War of 1812. He proved to be the right person in the right place at the right time. From 1817 to 1833, he founded the Thayer academic system, characterized by small classes of 10–14 cadets, daily recitations, rigorous exams, and an order of merit requiring cadets to transfer from one section to another as their averages rose or fell. He strengthened military discipline, imposed exacting academic standards, and appointed a commandant to supervise the cadets and conduct their military education.[3] During Alumni Weekend in the fall of each year, the superintendent, commandant, dean, cadet first captain, and the oldest graduate lead a procession of graduates to the northwest corner of the Plain. Along with the Glee Club, the alumni sing the West Point Alma Mater as they face a 20-foot-high statue of Sylvanus Thayer. On the base of the statue is a simple inscription, "Colonel Thayer—Father of the Military Academy."

The role of West Point in the growth of our nation began in the Mexican–American War of 1846, during which graduates such as Captain Ulysses S. Grant and Captain Robert E. Lee had their first experience leading soldiers on the battlefield. In the Civil War, 445 West Point graduates were general officers, 294 fought in the Union Army, and 151 fought in the Confederate Army.[4] General John J. Pershing, Class of 1886, was first captain of the Corps of Cadets and served as commander of the American Expeditionary Force on the Western Front in World War I. Many graduates, including Generals Dwight D. Eisenhower, Douglas MacArthur, Omar N. Bradley, and George S. Patton, were instrumental in securing Allied victories during World War II. West Point alumni have also served with distinction in the Korean War, the Vietnam War, and the wars in Iraq and Afghanistan.

In the early years, graduates planned and supervised river, harbor, canal, and railroad construction. During the Civil War, they constructed roads, pontoon bridges, and fortifications for the Union Army. Today, the U.S. Army Corps of Engineers has the nationwide responsibility for civil works such as inland waterway navigation, flood control, environmental protection, hydroelectric power, deep water port maintenance, and geospatial intelligence. In 2021, 12 percent of West Point's graduating class were commissioned in the Corps of Engineers.[5]

Prominent positions in the American government have been held by graduates, such as General Eric K. Shinseki, secretary of Veterans Affairs; General Alexander Haig, secretary of state; Lieutenant General Brent Scowcroft, national security advisor; and Michael R. Pompeo, secretary of state. Eighteen became astronauts, including Frank Borman, Ed White, Michael Collins and Buzz Aldrin.[6] Two became presidents of the United States—Ulysses S. Grant and Dwight D. Eisenhower.

## CHAPTER 18

# Commandant of Cadets

Being appointed commandant of cadets was an honor I never envisioned would happen when I graduated eighth from the bottom of my class. Nevertheless, it was the most enjoyable and rewarding assignment in my 37 years on active duty. Because of my unimpressive academic credentials there was understandable speculation as to how I was selected. Was it my experience playing Division I intercollegiate athletics, my combat record in Vietnam, or my previous assignment as a company tactical officer? These factors were probably considered but, in a humorous vein, I have told the story that it was primarily due to my academic standing. Let me explain. Grades were based upon a 2.0 to 3.0 system. Below 2.0 was failing and 3.0 was the highest grade possible. Our grades were displayed each week in the sally port close to the barracks. Most of the time when I checked my grades, I was proficient, if only by a slight margin.

All was well until the end of senior year, when we rehearsed graduation exercises in Gillis Field House. As we filed into our seats designated by academic standing, I was horrified to see so many of my classmates in the rows in front of me. I could barely see the dais. I immediately looked to the row behind me and there wasn't one. I have, therefore, told my classmates and other audiences that I was selected to be the 63rd commandant of cadets because anyone who sat as far back as I did on graduation day fully understood the meaning of the Long Gray Line.

Lest my inductive reasoning not be convincing, there is precedence. Rene E. DeRussy, the successor to Sylvanus Thayer, was the last man in his Class of 1812. Yet he served as superintendent of the U.S. Military Academy from 1833 to 1838, rose to the rank of colonel during the Civil War, and was appointed brevet brigadier general on March 13, 1865.[1]

On June 22, 1992, I was sworn in as commandant of cadets at a ceremony in Eisenhower (Ike) Hall—a building with five floors, an auditorium for seating 4,432 people, and large rooms designed to accommodate luncheons, football game rallies, and cadet formal dances. We moved into the commandant's quarters, a three-story, six-bedroom, Georgian colonial house with four fireplaces, a dining room, living room, wraparound front porch, and large back yard. Built in 1819, it's the oldest set of quarters on post and is situated at the edge of the Plain overlooking the Hudson River—a stone's throw from the revolutionary cannon and chain links on display at Trophy Point. Dave was beginning his junior year at West Point, Mark was a sophomore at the Air Force Academy, and Sara was in her sophomore year at James L. O'Neill High School in neighboring Highland Falls.

Dave was happy to have his dad as commandant and his family living so close. There wasn't any downside for him that I know of and plenty of enjoyable moments. When I walked through the barracks area as cadets were on their way to class, I was greeted with salutes and multiple voices saying, "Good morning, sir, good morning, sir, good morning, sir...." Occasionally, I would smile as I heard "Good morning, Pop"—knowing Dave was in that sea of gray uniforms somewhere. At times, Dave would receive thanks for changes I made in policy. For example, cadet regulations authorized a specific number of weekend passes for each cadet by year group. These opportunities to get away on Friday afternoon after classes until Sunday evening were prized possessions. Because the Corps of Cadets had done so well raising their grade point average, volunteering for community service, and achieving the goals of each of the 36 cadet companies during AY 1992–93, I awarded one additional weekend leave for all cadets for AY 1993–94. When the brigade adjutant announced from the Poop Deck in the Mess Hall that I had authorized one additional weekend, Dave was mobbed by his classmates, who hugged him and said, "Way to go, Dave."

Lieutenant General Graves, the superintendent, had previously served as commandant of the U.S. Army War College and assistant to the chairman of the joint chiefs of staff. He graduated second out of 534 cadets in the Class of 1961, was a Rhodes Scholar, and earned a Master of Arts and a Master of Letters at Oxford University. The superintendent had extensive governance responsibilities, including strategic planning, campus infrastructure management, and supervision of intercollegiate athletics. General Graves was an outstanding leader and a distinguished gentleman who possessed a compelling vision of how things ought to be. He and Gracie were a beloved team who inspired everyone with their goodness and charismatic leadership style.

Intellectual development was the responsibility of Brigadier General Gerald G. Galloway, dean of the Academic Board, who had three master's degrees and a PhD. General Galloway was not only the driving force behind the college curriculum, but he also developed sound solutions to complex problems, possessed exceptional leadership skills, and was well respected by staff, faculty, and the Corps of Cadets. He and his wife, Diane, were invaluable members of the academy leadership team.

The commandant of cadets was responsible for "the administration, discipline, leadership, character development, military training, physical fitness and moral-ethical growth of the Corps of Cadets."[2] This may appear to be a daunting task but my two years as a company tactical officer and one year as the 3rd Regiment personnel and logistics officer in the U.S. Corps of Cadets, as well as the experience of serving in various command and staff positions for the previous 29 years, fully prepared me for the job.

However, I could not have accomplished my duties without Julie's proactive and positive support. She prepared accommodations for overnight guests such as Admiral James B. Stockdale when he was a candidate for vice president of the United States. She coordinated receptions for faculty, cadets, parents, and guests in Quarters 101 for Plebe-Parent Weekend, Yearling Winter Weekend, 500th Night, Ring Weekend, 100th Night, home football game tailgate parties, and graduation week. She was also a great sounding board regarding policy, programs, and events for the Corps of Cadets.

The superintendent's guidance to me was to run things as I saw fit but to keep him informed. I could not have asked for a better charter as it was an indication of the trust and confidence he placed in my judgment and leadership abilities. My immediate task was to determine how best to implement the commandant of cadet's responsibilities in supporting the purpose and mission of the United States Military Academy:

Purpose
To provide the Nation
with leaders of character
who serve the common defense.


Mission
To educate and train the Corps of Cadets
so that each graduate shall have
the attributes essential to professional growth
as an officer of the Regular Army
and to inspire each to a lifetime of service
to the Nation.[3]

The military development program in existence when I arrived was a progressive and sequential process with each period of instruction building on the previous session, allowing for maturity and growth at successive levels. Each block of instruction represented a leadership experience formally evaluated by the cadet and officer chains of command using 12 leader dimensions:

| | |
|---|---|
| Professional Ethics | Consideration of Others |
| Teamwork | Developing Subordinates |
| Oral/Written Communications | Planning and Organizing |
| Duty Motivation | Military Bearing |
| Delegating | Supervising |
| Decision-making | Influencing Others |

Evaluations were made a matter of record using a form similar to the U.S. Army Officer Efficiency Report, providing raw data for a military grade, and were the key element in providing feedback to cadets during counseling sessions by company tactical officers and tactical non-commissioned officers.[4]

During New Cadet Barracks in the summer of 1992, the new cadets in the Class of 1996 were organized into eight companies of roughly 150 cadets, with members of the first and second class serving as cadre members. I went to work right away evaluating how well the mission was being accomplished by observing activities such as morning physical fitness, which included push-ups, sit-ups, and running in formation; classroom instruction on West Point values; meal formations; barracks room inspections; and rifle drill on the Plain. I concluded that summer training for the Class of 1996 was being conducted to standard and cadet leaders were going about their duties in a professional manner. I was concerned, however, that excessive regulatory requirements were suppressing cadet individual spirit.

Coincidentally, I received a letter from Lieutenant General (Retired) Dave R. Palmer, USMA superintendent from 1986 to 1991, indicating that spirit in the Corps of Cadets was a major factor in reaching the highest standards of excellence in any endeavor and was critical in college athletic competition. In the January 1987 *Assembly* magazine, he wrote:

> The first class is charged each year with designing, organizing, and implementing spirit support by the Corps of Cadets. It is part of their leadership development; the ability to motivate people is a basic trait of all successful leaders. The Army edge is spirit.[5]

Julie reminded me of the replica of a World War II infantry soldier equipped with helmet, cartridge belts, hand grenades, and M-1 Garand rifle that she gave to me when I graduated from the Armor Officer Advanced Course in 1968. On the base of the statue is a quote by General George S. Patton that reads, "It is the spirit of the men who follow and of the man who leads that gains the victory." It was clear to me that inculcating a "Winning Spirit" was not only important at West Point but also contributed to the courage and perseverance essential for leaders to fight and win at the decisive time and place on the battlefield.

Reorganization Week in August was a significant event for the Corps of Cadets as it set the tone for the academic year. The cadets returning from summer training were quickly immersed in basic activities, such as moving into their regular lettered companies; conducting drill and reviews on the Plain; organizing teams for intramural, club, and intercollegiate competition; and picking up books to be ready for classes, which began the following Monday.

One essential component to the Corps of Cadets' effectiveness was the selection of cadet leaders. This included the first captain as well as regimental, battalion, and company commanders. I selected Cadet Shawn L. Daniel to be the first captain for AY 1992–93 due to his excellent performance as the commander of Cadet Field

Training for the yearlings at Camp Buckner. He had prior service as an enlisted soldier, displayed a calm, confident demeanor, possessed high standards of integrity, and was well respected by his peers. Shawn Daniel's story is typical of West Point cadets who remain committed to a lifetime of service to our nation. After graduation, Shawn remained on active duty for 25 years, participating in eight deployments to the Middle East, culminating as Director of Operations for all American and NATO Special Operations Forces in Afghanistan. He continues to serve soldiers today as president and founder of Darby's Warrior Support, a 501(c)3 non-profit organization, providing duck hunting and scholarship opportunities for disabled veterans.

The U.S. Army training doctrine established in *Field Manual (FM) 25-101: Battle Focused Training* defined a Mission Essential Task List (METL) as an unconstrained statement of tasks for accomplishing the mission. The mission essential concept was developed because commanders are unable to train for every task a soldier might be required to perform on the battlefield. Infantry soldiers, for example, must be able to fire and maintain their individual weapon as well as crew-served weapons such as machine guns and light anti-tank weapons. They must also be able to throw hand grenades, perform first aid, and emplace anti-personnel and anti-tank mines. There is not enough time or funding to accommodate all missions in one training cycle. Therefore, training is adjusted as the wartime mission changes.[6] Commanders adopt the METL to plan, execute, and assess training while tailoring leader competencies to execute Army warfighting doctrine.[7] I was convinced that a mission essential task concept like the Army doctrine outlined in *FM 25-101* would enable cadets to better concentrate on their academy responsibilities and simultaneously instill a greater understanding of the same dogma they would press into service as commissioned officers.

On Monday, August 10, 1992, the first day of Reorganization Week, we kicked off a two-day workshop designed to develop the AY 1992–93 METL. The cadet commanders established the conditions and standards for five mission essential tasks: Excellence in Drill; Pride in Achievement; Leadership Through Presence; Winning Spirit; and Discipline.[8]

The METL process provided institutional direction yet empowered cadet leaders to shape their own organizational goals. Regimental, battalion, and company commanders developed tasks from the Corps of Cadets' METL, and commanders at each level of command had the latitude to develop objectives appropriate to their specific needs. The 36 companies included goals such as academic excellence, support of athletic events, barracks maintenance, and community service.

On Tuesday evening in South Auditorium of Thayer Hall, I spoke to the first classmen regarding summer training, the Corps of Cadets' METL, and their responsibilities as leaders for the academic year. The first question came from a young man in the back of the auditorium, who asked if I could still dunk (referring to my time as captain of the 1962–63 Army basketball team). I thought that I might have failed to inspire in them their leadership responsibilities, but the questions achieved greater relevance as the session continued. One cadet asked, "How can we be sure that conducting a spirit mission won't get us in trouble?"

Spontaneous escapades such as displaying posters around campus, planting gravestones, or hanging effigies bearing a message for an opposing team have traditionally been called spirit missions and were conducted by small groups of cadets during the evening hours as a diversion from studies. I welcomed the question because it provided me with the opportunity to articulate "Rules of Engagement." I outlined the importance of wearing athletic uniforms during spirit missions, completing all activities by Taps, (bugle call to announce lights out) and removing any remnants by 10:00 a.m. the next day. Furthermore, I suggested they embrace the Corps of Cadets' mission essential task "Pride in Achievement" by leaving a message with their spirit presentation, such as "Compliments of Company A1." I even offered an example of an appropriate mission—removing one of the revolutionary war cannon barrels from Trophy Point, placing it at another site on campus, and returning it by 10:00 a.m. the following day.

The next morning, our daughter, Sara, who was about to catch the high school bus said, "Dad, you need to see what's on the front porch." When I opened the door, I saw a cannon barrel with a note, "Compliments of the first class." I thought this was a clever way to show me they were listening. At 10:00 a.m., I called Shawn Daniel. He said he had sent 10 cadets to my quarters to remove the cannon barrel, but it was too heavy. However, he submitted a request for assistance from the post engineers. I told Shawn the rules were clear. Cadets placed the cannon barrel on my front porch and cadets must retrieve it. I suggested he ask for help from the Army football team during the noon meal. Shortly after lunch, six big linemen came walking briskly over to our quarters, picked up the cannon barrel, and carried it back to Trophy Point.

General Douglas MacArthur, a 1903 graduate of the Military Academy and former superintendent, was convinced that athletic programs were a key component in cadet development because commissioned officers must rely on teamwork and prompt decision-making on the battlefield.[9] His famous quote, "Upon the fields of friendly strife are sown the seeds that, upon other fields, on other days, will bear the fruits of victory"[10] was prominently displayed at the entrance to Arvin Gymnasium. As superintendent, he directed that all cadets participate in competitive athletics.

While playing basketball as a cadet, I learned the value of toughness, the will to win, teamwork, and discipline—all attributes that I put to good use as a rifle company commander during the Vietnam War. Although I believed strongly in the value of athletic competition, I felt spirit support was essential. I encouraged corps squad athletes to support their individual company's METL and developed incentives for the Corps of Cadets to attend home intercollegiate athletic events. I also made appointments with the head coaches of each intercollegiate athletic team and made it clear that any cadet wearing Army or West Point on their uniform should set the proper example on and off "the fields of friendly strife."

To promote team cohesion, intercollegiate athletes sat together at designated corps squad tables. The Mess Hall protocol required cadets to proceed directly to their tables from accountability formations and remain standing and silent behind their chairs until the brigade adjutant announced, "Take seats." On Wednesday afternoon during Reorganization Week, the first captain stopped by my office to tell me that corps squad athletes were setting a bad example by talking loudly and engaging in boisterous conduct at the mess hall tables. I told Shawn I would check it out and get back to him.

Prior to breakfast the next day, I went through the back door of the Mess Hall in my battle dress uniform—the standard dress for cadets during Reorganization Week. I stood by the kitchen door leading to the corps squad area observing cadets as they walked to their assigned tables. I watched as a first classman told a plebe to throw him one of the half pint milk cartons stacked at the end of the table. The first classman threw the milk carton back and said, "Not that one." Milk cartons went back and forth until "Take seats" was announced. I walked over to the first classman and said, "Get your hat." I took him to the first captain's table, telling Shawn that I had just removed this cadet from corps squad tables and placed him on company tables until graduation day. He would no longer be eating with his teammates and no longer be afforded the extra rations allocated to corps squad athletes. That afternoon, Shawn told me the corps squad athletes got the message. They were standing behind their chairs at the noon meal—no horseplay, no talking, not a sound. They were following Mess Hall protocol in a precise and proper manner—a good way to begin the academic year, reinforcing the mission essential task: "Discipline."

On Friday morning, I received a call from Coach Jack Emmer, the Head Coach of the Army lacrosse team.

"I'm calling about one of my lacrosse players that you confronted at breakfast yesterday and placed on company tables."

"Coach, I remember the incident but didn't know he was a lacrosse player."

"I wonder if there is some other way to handle this situation."

"You do remember the discussion we had in your office about the proper conduct of Corps Squad athletes."

"Yes, I do, but Cadet Midfielder (not real name) is an All-American lacrosse player."

"Well, right now he's an All-American lacrosse player sitting on company tables."

Since lacrosse was a spring sport, I told Coach Emmer I would allow Cadet Midfielder to return to corps squad tables after the Christmas holidays if he maintained the highest standards of cadet decorum, received good grades, and volunteered to support cadet activities in his regular lettered company.

On the first day of second semester, the co-captains of the Army lacrosse team came to see me. They stood at attention in front of my desk and told me Cadet Midfielder had excellent grades and was a superb cadet during first semester. I looked up at these heavy-set lacrosse players and told them the cadet chain of command reports that I received were consistent with their assessment. Then I stood up. Now I was looking down at them and they were looking up at me. I said, "Cadet Midfielder can return to corps squad tables today. But I want to make it perfectly clear that if there is any misconduct by any members of the Army lacrosse team at any time for the rest of the year—and I don't care if it's in Cancun, Mexico—both of you guys are going on company tables. You are dismissed."

There were no more corps squad table incidents. Intercollegiate team captains realized their title was not just honorary and they were responsible for the conduct of their team members on and off the athletic field. The mission essential task, "Leadership Through Presence," had just received positive reinforcement throughout the Corps of Cadets.

While I supported all intercollegiate athletic teams, football brought a special ambiance to academy life. West Point's Michie Stadium is a magnificent venue for the joining of football, autumn foliage, and American history. Attending a Saturday home football game is an unforgettable experience, beginning with the Corps of Cadets' morning review on the Plain followed by tailgating surrounded by the brilliant fall colors of the Hudson Highlands and culminating with the Army football team playing top-ranked division one teams.

The football stadium is named after Captain Dennis Mahan Michie, who was just 28 years old when he was killed leading a patrol during the battle of Santiago in the Spanish American War. Captain Michie was born at West Point on April 10, 1870. His father, Peter Smith Michie, served in the Civil War and was a permanent professor at West Point. Dennis Michie entered the Military Academy with the Class of 1893 and organized football competition against the Naval Academy. He was the coach, player, and manager for an Army team that had 26 other cadets playing games in canvas jackets, white breeches, black socks, and woolen caps. Although Navy won the first game 24-0, Captain Michie was recognized as the founding father of football at West Point.[11]

To reinforce a "Winning Spirit" in football, I encouraged the first classmen branching Artillery to develop a concept for firing the installation 75mm ceremonial howitzers every time Army scored. A touchdown—six rounds; extra point conversion—one or two rounds; field goal—three rounds; and safety—two rounds. The cadets conducted site surveys at various locations around Michie Stadium, including Fort Putnam, and produced a staff study detailing the advantages and disadvantages for each course of action. I approved their recommendation to place the six-gun howitzer battery on the far side of Lusk Reservoir. Each game provided excellent training for these future artillery officers. One day, they ran out of ammunition and another time they parked a howitzer too close to the edge of the water. It was recovered with no damages.

One cadet regiment was scheduled to march into Michie Stadium and remain on the field for the national anthem, reinforcing the mission essential task—Excellence in Drill. This spirit support was well received by the Corps of Cadets and added to the exciting atmosphere of a West Point fall weekend. I coordinated the timing of the regiment marching on the football field before the game with Bob Sutton, the Army head football coach. The "march-on" did not interfere with the team warm-up or any other pregame events, such as the cadet parachute team jumping into Michie Stadium with the game ball.

All claimants for pregame activities were satisfied except for Master Sergeant Dropzone (not real name), the non-commissioned officer in charge (NCOIC) of the cadet parachute team, who heard a rumor that parachuting into Michie Stadium with the game ball would no longer be a part of pregame activities. Without contacting anyone to verify this erroneous information, Master Sergeant Dropzone sent an e-mail to the 4,000 members of the Corps of Cadets asking their opinion of what should take precedence—the cadet parachute team or a regiment of cadets conducting a march-on.

When the master sergeant reported to me in my office, I told him that he had no authority to send an email to the Corps of Cadets; his actions were divisive and irresponsible; he exercised poor judgment; and was guilty of insubordination. He attempted to defend his actions, showed no remorse, and offered no apology. I ended our brief meeting by saying, "You are relieved as NCOIC of the cadet parachute team." He expressed surprise when I informed him that cadet regulations clearly stated that he worked for me. I told him to report to the academy command sergeant major, who promptly processed his reassignment and departure from West Point. The cadet parachute team continued to jump into Michie Stadium with the game ball and the cadet regiment conducted the march-on flawlessly.

The great majority of my time was spent with on-campus cadet activities but in March of each year, the superintendent, dean, commandant, and director of athletics were asked to speak to West Point Society Chapters across the country for the celebration of Founder's Day—March 16, 1802—the day West Point was established by an act of Congress. On one occasion, I was the keynote speaker at Fort Irwin, Nevada—the home of the National Training Center located in the middle of the Mojave Desert. In formal attire, the guests attended a cocktail reception and dinner, and heard brief remarks from the youngest and oldest graduates, followed by my presentation on the state of the academy.

Before my introduction, the master of ceremonies asked all graduates to stand. The colonel then told all those who graduated in the top 10 percent of their class to be seated—expecting me to sit. But I remained standing. He then asked all who graduated in the top 25 percent and then top 50 percent of their class to be seated. I continued to stand. After going to the top 75 percent of the class, I was the only one left standing. Finding himself in an awkward position, the colonel decided that a protocol along the lines of discipline instead of academics would be more appropriate for the commandant of cadets. He again directed the graduates to stand and asked all who had never walked the area to take a seat. (Walking the area was punishment for misconduct violations and was conducted in dress gray uniform with rifle in front of the central area guard room.) The great majority of the graduates sat down—but not me. He then went to less than 25 hours, fully expecting me to sit, but I remained on my feet. Visibly sweating, he then decided to clear up this predicament by jumping to less than 75 hours on the area. I was the only one in the banquet hall still standing. With no credibility left as the commandant of cadets, I was introduced to a standing ovation.

## CHAPTER 19

# Company Tactical Officers and Non-Commissioned Officers

The Tactical Department is the primary leader development organization for the United States Corps of Cadets—a mission dating back to 1817 when Sylvanus Thayer was superintendent. In 1992, successful company commanders with a minimum of eight years of service were selected to be company tactical officers. They were assigned to West Point as senior captains and, prior to assuming their duties, had to complete a rigorous year of study leading to a Master of Arts in Leader Development. They normally departed as majors to attend the Command and General Staff College. Their job was to teach, coach, advise, mentor, train, counsel, and set the standard as role models. They were disciplinarians who ensured fair and impartial application of cadet regulations and counseled cadets on academic, social, and extracurricular activities. They observed each cadet's performance, assessed their progress in becoming leaders of character, and confirmed their qualifications to become commissioned officers.

Beginning in October 1990, tactical non-commissioned officers (TAC NCOs) were assigned to cadet companies. TAC NCOs held the rank of sergeant first class, had 12–14 years of active-duty time, and were seasoned platoon sergeants. They taught cadets about the duties and responsibilities of non-commissioned officers through formal instruction and personal example. They trained cadets in drill, room and barracks standards, self-help maintenance, and personal appearance. They set the example for what is expected of a senior non-commissioned officer and worked directly with the cadet sergeants major, first sergeants, platoon sergeants, and squad leaders. They made an important contribution during the training of new cadets and yearlings at Camp Buckner in such areas as rifle marksmanship, land navigation, and tactical exercises.

When the command sergeant major and I conducted a review of barracks maintenance in 1992, we were alarmed at the high number of items needing repair in cadet rooms. As a result, we turned jurisdiction for barracks maintenance over to the TAC NCOs. Each of the 36 companies received standard toolboxes containing items such as hammers, screwdrivers, saws, and pliers. Every orderly room was supplied with common repair parts, including nails, screws, nuts, bolts, towel racks, lightbulbs, glue, and lubricating oil. We established a procedure for ordering replacement parts patterned after the Army Prescribed Load List (PLL) system. Cadets who volunteered to be members of company repair and maintenance teams were excused from Saturday morning inspection to fix items on the list. Their superb efforts allowed civilian maintenance personnel to focus on areas requiring greater technical expertise, such as plumbing and electrical repairs. The TAC NCOs held monthly maintenance meetings to monitor progress and identify problem areas. The result was a phenomenal decrease in the list of items needing repair and a significant increase in barracks' quality of life.

When I conducted Saturday morning inspections, I was accompanied by the company tactical officer, TAC NCO, and the cadet chain of command from first captain to squad leader. One Saturday morning I entered a yearling room and surmised by the expression on his face that he was thinking, "Why me, Lord?"

I asked, "Do you have any items needing repair?"

"Yes, sir. The top drawer in my wardrobe cabinet is broken."

"What's wrong with it?"

"Sir, I don't know."

I told him to pull out the drawer and lay it on the floor.

"What do you think?"

"Well, sir, it looks to me like the left-side drawer guide is missing."

"What happened to it?"

"Sir, I don't know."

"Well, let's pull out the bottom drawer."

"Sir, it's not broke."

I paused momentarily to stifle my urge to smile. "Now I want you to stay with me on this. Go ahead and pull out the bottom drawer and lay it on the floor."

"What do you see?"

"Sir, there's a drawer guide lying there."

"Go ahead and pick it up."

"How many holes are in the drawer guide."

"Five, sir."

"How many screws do you see lying loose at the bottom of the cabinet?"

"Five, sir."

"What do you need now?"

With a smile on his face he said, "Sir, I need a screwdriver."

Turning to the cadet chain of command I said, "This broken drawer should not have been found by me."

I added that, as commissioned officers, they would be responsible for the maintenance and readiness of far more sophisticated equipment, such as individual weapons, protective masks, trucks, armored personnel carriers, and tanks.

At the beginning of AY 1992–93, I made presentations to the instructors in each academic department on how they could assist in the inculcation of METL tasks and cadet core values. I began by thanking them for volunteering to be officer representatives for intercollegiate athletic teams, for their outstanding contributions as members of the cadet honor education teams, and for their leadership as officers in charge of extracurricular activities. I then emphasized the importance of reinforcing leadership principles, values, and discipline. In one of the sessions, a major told me about a cadet who came to his class with the sleeves of his white undershirt showing below his short-sleeve class shirt. He asked me to address this uniform deficiency with the company tactical officers. When I asked him what he had done about it, he said he took no action because instructors had to maintain a certain rapport with their students. The major promptly became an unwitting training aid to my main teaching point—we are all responsible for developing leaders of character. I told him that he should have counseled the cadet on the importance of pride and self-discipline, sent him back to his room to make the uniform correction and directed he return to class as soon as possible. With such counseling, the major would have established all the rapport he needed with every student in his section.

Because company tactical officers had the responsibility for developing cadet social awareness and proper etiquette, they invited small groups of first classmen to their quarters for dinner. In addition to emphasizing social graces, it was an opportunity for cadets to gain an insight into the lives of officers and their families. One day, the superintendent and his wife hosted a luncheon for a four-star general and his wife from a foreign country on the Poop Deck (second floor balcony in the center of the Cadet Mess Hall). The luncheon guests included the dean and me, our wives, the first captain, and members of the brigade staff. The honored guests sat centered on one side of a long rectangular table opposite General Graves and his wife, Gracie. The brigade adjutant, Cadet Captain Eugenia K. (Gingee) Guilmartin, was seated between me and the visiting general. As soon as we began eating, Cadet Guilmartin turned to me and whispered, "Sir, I have a problem."

"What is it?"

"Sir, the general is eating my salad."

I leaned forward to take a quick look and sure enough, the visiting general was eating from the salad bowl on his right—her salad. Everyone else was eating from the salad bowl to their left.

"What should I do?"

"No problem, you eat my salad, and I won't have one."

"Oh no sir, I couldn't do that."

"Yes, you can because we don't want to embarrass our guests." She ate my salad and the luncheon ended with no one suspecting anything out of the ordinary.

At times, the smallest infraction of uniform violations can have a positive and widespread impact on cadet decorum and accountability. As I was walking up the steps to the front door of the Mess Hall one day, I confronted three cadets coming down the steps wearing short overcoats with gray scarf and dress cap. Two of the cadets were first classmen and one was a second classman. The second classman had tied his scarf in a big knot around his neck like he was going skiing instead of the proper left-over right fold, which should have been tucked into the collar of his short overcoat.

I called out, "Halt. What's wrong with this picture?"

One of the first classman said, "Sir, Cadet Wardrobe (not real name) has his scarf folded wrong."

After reprimanding the Cadet lieutenants for not making the proper correction, I released them to continue to class.

The second classman said, "Excuse me, sir. I am going to be late for class."

"Yes, you're going to be extremely late for class, but I will excuse your tardiness with the dean. Right now, we're going to see the first captain."

"Could I untie my scarf and replace it properly?"

"No."

After a brief visit with the first captain, I took Cadet Wardrobe to see his company tactical officer and discussed his failure to assimilate "Leadership Through Presence." I also told Cadet Wardrobe that I would inspect his room sometime soon. Three weeks later, Cadet Wardrobe asked his classmate, Cadet Corporal Dave Foley, if his dad could please inspect his room. I conducted an inspection the very next day and found his room in excellent condition.

As commandant of cadets, I encouraged creative leadership techniques to change negative behavior or alter counterproductive cultural norms. To set the proper example for this philosophy, I did not award one demerit, punishment tour, or confinement period to any cadet during my tenure as commandant. I expected company tactical officers and TAC NCOs to demand more of upper class leaders as they assimilated their leadership responsibilities. The fourth-class system was established to allow time for plebes to adapt to the West Point way of life—a system that is administered by the upper three classes and supervised by the Tactical Department. Yearlings were learning how to be upper class cadets by observing the leadership techniques of second and first classmen and by making the transition from a follower to a leader. Second classmen were the non-commissioned officers serving throughout the cadet chain of command, from squad leaders, platoon sergeants, and first sergeants to brigade command sergeant major. First classmen were placed in officer positions, from platoon leader through company, battalion, regimental commander, and first captain.

I instructed tactical officers and tactical non-commissioned officers to take this spread in the learning-leadership-accountability mix under consideration when implementing the disciplinary system. Because I found too much reliance on awarding demerits, punishment tours, and confinement for violations of

United States Corps of Cadets (USCC) regulations. I told tactical officers to apply innovative leadership techniques, such as requiring the cadet chain of command to submit weekly progress reports on recalcitrant cadets. This got the attention of the cadet in question and reinforced chain of command responsibilities. I advised tactical officers when dealing with first classmen to implement leadership techniques used by commissioned officers in the regular Army, who regularly counsel officers and NCOs for any lapse in judgment or instances of unsatisfactory performance and save relief or Uniform Code of Military Justice (UCMJ) action for egregious conduct.

Cadet Vigor (not real name), a first classman in the Class of 1994, had been in minor misconduct incidents throughout his cadet career. In the first semester of his senior year, he had exceeded his demerit allowance, triggering a recommendation for his dismissal. Without any knowledge of his record as a cadet, I had observed him as a member of the Army football team walking up and down the sidelines during home games patting his teammates on the back and giving them words of encouragement. It occurred to me that he understood "Consideration of Others" and "Sustaining a Winning Spirit." When he came to my office, I asked him if he wanted to graduate and become a commissioned officer. He looked surprised, thinking that I was going to tell him that he would be dismissed. He said, "Yes, sir, I do—more than anything in the world." I told him that I would give him a second chance under two conditions. "First, no misconduct issues from now until graduation day. Second, I want you to organize cadet spirit support for men's and women's intercollegiate athletic home events beginning with the winter season." Because he didn't have any more indiscipline problems and did an excellent job organizing spirit support, he graduated with the Class of 1994. Eight years later, when I was attending a wedding, I ran into Captain Vigor, who was an Apache helicopter pilot stationed at Fort Rucker, Alabama. He was married and had two children. He thanked me for giving him the opportunity to graduate and I was gratified to see how successful he had become as a commissioned officer.

Company TAC officers and TAC NCOs are the lynchpin to accomplishing the West Point purpose and mission regarding discipline, leadership, military training, physical fitness, and moral-ethical growth. They are held accountable for evaluation and performance counseling of individual cadets. This is an intricate and comprehensive process requiring a daily, hands-on, systemic approach to developing leaders of character.

Furthermore, assignment as a company tactical officer is an essential prerequisite for becoming commandant of cadets at the U.S. Military Academy. Without this foundation, the commandant does not have an appreciation for the cadet leader development and evaluation process and does not have the requisite background for providing guidance to the 36 company tactical officers and 36 company tactical NCOs who ensure that the West Point experience is properly implemented.

With my experience as a company tactical officer for two years and regimental personnel and logistics officer for one year, I knew from day one what my job would be as commandant of cadets. I knew where to be, when to be there, and what to do when I got there. Furthermore, I could anticipate what should happen and issue the right guidance beforehand to ensure optimum results. I had total confidence in every change I made, and I knew how to shape the functional responsibilities of the Tactical Department. I knew what to say at annual briefings to instructors from every academic department and coaches of all intercollegiate athletic teams. And I knew what instruction to give to entities such as the honor committee, intercollegiate team captains, emerging leaders, cadets by year group, OICs of extracurricular activities, members of the company honor education teams, and the cadet cadre for summer training.

## CHAPTER 20

# Mission Essential Task Enhancement

At the beginning of 1993 summer training, I requested a briefing from the first detail New Cadet Barracks commander, Cadet Captain Howard H. Hoege, on the training program for Beast Barracks. When I arrived in the conference room, I found Cadet Lieutenant David C. Foley standing before me. Having never seen my son conduct a briefing, I was quite impressed as Dave made one of the most polished and articulate cadet presentations I received as commandant. Without using notes, he discussed the purpose and mission, goals, objectives, timelines, logistics, and resources with poise and confidence. The ease with which he answered my questions gave me trust and confidence that summer training was going to be immensely successful. Dave's presentation set the example for the "Leadership Through Presence" mission essential task that we found so compelling the previous year and which would become the Class of 1994 top priority for AY 1993–94.

AY 93-94 Mission Essential Task List
1. Leadership through presence.
2. Pride in achievement
3. Cohesion as a combat multiplier.
4. Responsibility through accountability.
5. Sustaining a winning spirit.[1]

Because of his outstanding performance in New Cadet Barracks, I selected Cadet Hoege as the first captain. He was smart, very well respected, and possessed exceptional command presence. After graduation, he was commissioned infantry and spent 14 years on active duty. He obtained a law degree from the University of Virginia (UVA) and deployed with the 101st Airborne Division in support of Operation *Iraqi Freedom*. He later taught at the UVA School of Law, established a leadership consulting business, and became president of the Mariners' Museum and Park in Newport News, Virginia.

We conducted a two-day workshop during Reorganization Week in which the first captain and cadet leaders developed the Corps of Cadets' METL. At mid-semester, Colonel Jim Siket, the brigade tactical officer, and I received briefings by cadet battalion commanders on how well they were accomplishing the METL. The brigade cadet command sergeant major discussed support by cadet non-commissioned officers.

"Leadership Through Presence" had five goals: Setting the example; Developing subordinates; Being positive, professional, and proactive; Establishing the proper bedrock climate; Ensuring support of Corps athletic events.[2]

Two examples of why "Leadership Through Presence" was so important occurred during New Cadet Barracks. First, I noticed that cadet cadre members at PT were making corrections on new cadets but not setting the example of how to properly perform the exercises. I directed that cadet leaders position themselves at the head of the formation and do the push-ups and sit-ups while facing the new cadets for the duration of the PT session. Second, I observed the cadet cadre march new cadets to the classroom for a presentation on the cadet honor code and return to the barracks leaving one second classman behind as the instructor. I changed this shortcoming, requiring that all cadre members attend honor instruction. Six senior cadets in a class of 25 new cadets made a huge difference in the inculcation of a concept so important as honorable living.

"Pride in Achievement" had four goals: Sustaining academic excellence; Volunteering for community service; Enhancing barracks quality of life; Maintaining excellence in drill.[3]

During their second class year, the Class of 1994 donated $8,000 for the relief of victims associated with Hurricane Andrew in Florida and approximately 500 second class cadets volunteered to participate in the spring Special Olympics. This was the genesis for adopting "Volunteering for Community Service" as a METL goal for AY 1993–94. Based upon the increase in the Corps of Cadets' grade point average from 2.70 to 2.85 and the singular accomplishments of the 36 cadet companies, I granted one additional weekend leave for each member of the Corps of Cadets.[4]

I worked closely with the dean to ensure we were "Sustaining academic excellence." When I made presentations to cadets in Thayer Hall, I encouraged them to submit questions or recommendations to me by email. A second classman informed me that she had spent two hours in Thayer Hall one evening completing a survey for a paper being written by a professor for his doctoral studies. Since the dean was a steadfast defender of cadet study time, he agreed that instructor surveys involving cadets should be approved by the commandant. This promptly solved the problem as no instructors came to me for permission to engage cadets in a survey.

In 1993, there were 108 extracurricular activities, such as Rowing Club, Glee Club, Chapel Choir, Cadet Band, and Scoutmaster's Council available for the Corps of Cadets.[5] In my informal assessment of these activities, I found a significant lack of planning. I met with the officers in charge (OICs) of extracurricular activities, directing they submit for my approval their schedule of planned club events for each academic year. The OICs who did not submit a schedule had their club cancelled. OICs who did not submit an after-action report of activities conducted during the academic year had their club cancelled for the following year. As a result, the level of planning and cadet fulfillment of extracurricular activities was markedly energized.

"Cohesion as a Combat Multiplier" had five goals: Teamwork at all levels; Corps/corps squad cohesion; Unity of purpose; Maintaining unit esprit; Reaching out for success.[6]

In 1992, the standard Cadet athletic uniform consisted of a white T-shirt with a black USMA crest on the left front and tight green shorts—the very same uniform I had worn 30 years earlier as a cadet. I asked the staff to design a new uniform consisting of gray T-shirt with the USMA crest and black shorts displaying ARMY in gold letters, like the Corps Squad uniform, which consisted of black shorts with gold ARMY letters and a gray T-shirt with AAA (Army Athletic Association) on the front. We asked male and female cadets for their advice on material and style, settling on a uniform that we issued to the New Cadet Barracks cadre during the summer of 1993. It was a huge hit. From that day on, all cadets in the Corps wore gray T-shirts and black shorts with gold ARMY letters representing the synthesis of "corps/corps squad cohesion."

"Responsibility Through Accountability" had five goals: Individual and unit discipline; Adherence to regulations; Safety and security; Taking ownership of standards; Excellence in personal appearance.[7]

Throughout senior year, members of the first class (roughly 1,000 cadets) attended lectures given by prominent military leaders in the South Auditorium of Thayer Hall. One night, a four-star general from a European country made a presentation on the organization and mission of his nation's armed forces. Unfortunately, he read every word in a tedious monotone. Toward the end of his 45-minute presentation, an abnormal amount of coughing, throat clearing, and murmuring emerged from cadets in the audience, which gained momentum until the speaker concluded his remarks. When the official party left for a VIP reception, I went to the center of the stage, asked the staff and faculty to depart, and directed an apprehensive and subdued group of cadets to "Take seats." After the last faculty member had gone, in a loud voice I said, "Listen." I waited 10 seconds before saying, "Listen again, do you hear that?" There was not one sound—no coughing or throat clearing. I said, "That's the sound of silence. It will be the standard at all future lectures. If you have a cold, go on sick call, obtain medication, or bring cough drops to lectures." I then directed that a memorandum be prepared by the cadet chain of command outlining proper decorum for lectures. This incident prompted immediate reinforcement of "Individual and unit discipline."

While lifting weights in Arvin Gymnasium one day, I noticed a cadet with a hole in his Gym Alpha T-shirt. I told him to come to my office at 8:00 a.m. the next morning with the T-shirt and his cadet company chain of command. I also invited the company tactical officer and TAC NCO as well as Cadet Captain Scott Steele, the cadet regimental commander. After discussing the proper standards for gym uniforms, I told Mr. Steele that sometime in the next two weeks I would be inspecting the 3rd Regiment lockers, where the gym uniforms and footwear are stored, and that I did not expect to see any uniforms with holes, tears, or stains. In about three days, the cadet store ran out of Gym Alpha T-shirts, shorts, socks, and gym shoes. After inspecting lockers from the other regiments, I realized we had a larger problem. We placed sufficient orders of gym uniforms to restock the cadet store and I extended the inspection schedule until the Corps of Cadets had the requisite number of serviceable gym uniforms, socks, and shoes. I was gratified the discovery of one gym shirt with a hole had such a positive impact on the Corps of Cadets' standards for ensuring "Excellence in personal appearance." But I was not happy with the company tactical officers who had not been enforcing gym clothing standards in the past.

"Sustaining a Winning Spirit" had five goals: Balancing spirit with discipline under selected rules of engagement; Rallies and spirit missions conducted at the right time, right place and in the proper manner to accomplish a specific objective; Fall, winter, and spring campaigns; Detailed programs designed to support our Army teams; Internalization is the key.[8]

In support of Army football, I encouraged the 36 company mascots to participate in spirit support during home games. They wore elaborate costumes that depicted their company sobriquet:

> First Regiment: A1-Axman, B1-Barbarian, C1-Chipmunks, D1-Ducks, E1-Vikings, F1-Friars, G1-Greeks, H1-Root Hawgs, and I1-Icemen.
> Second Regiment: A2-Spartan, B2-Bulldogs, C2-Circus, D2-Dragons, E2-Brew Dogs, F2-The Zoo, G2-Gators, H2-Hellions, and I2-Moose.
> Third Regiment: A3-A-boy, B3-Bandit, C3-Fighting Cocks, D3-Devils, E3-Eagles, F3-Cav Trooper, G3-Gophers, H3-Hurricane, and I3-Polar Bear.
> Fourth Regiment: A4-Apaches, B4-Buffaloes, C4-Cowboys, D4-Dukes, E4-Elvis, F4-Frogs, G4-Guppies, H4-Hogs, and I4-Ibeam.[9]

Many older graduates had difficulty accepting this seemingly indecorous convention. An "Old Grad" walked up to me one day at a football game, pointed to the mascots running along the sidelines, and said, "What are all those animals doing down there?" I told him they were mascots like the Duke University Blue Devil and their job was to boost team spirit. With a frown, he looked around, pointed to one of the mascots and said, "Isn't that a chipmunk?" I said, "Yes sir, but it's a fighting chipmunk." The Old Grad walked off with a look of disbelief on his face.

In the 1992 Army–Navy football game at Veterans Stadium in Philadelphia, Cadet First Classman Patmon Malcolm displayed a Winning Spirit when he kicked a field goal from 44 yards with 12 seconds left in the game only to have it nullified when the officials penalized Army 5 yards for delay of game.[10] As we watched from the stadium seats, Cadet Malcolm took five steps to the rear, turned around, and prepared to kick it again—only this time from 49 yards. With poise and confidence, he kicked the second field goal straight through the goal posts with picture-perfect results. The spirit of the Army Football Team and the Corps of Cadets' enthusiastic support for winning is an excellent example of how "Sustaining a Winning Spirit" can be instrumental in achieving victory. In 1992, Army beat Navy in football 25 to 24 and in 1993, Army won 22 to 20.

## CHAPTER 21

# Honor and Respect

In an address to the Corps of Cadets in the Mess Hall on May 12, 1962, General Douglas MacArthur, West Point Class of 1903, said:

> Duty, Honor, Country. Those three hallowed words reverently dictate what you ought to be, what you can be, what you will be. They are your rallying points, to build courage when courage seems to fail, to regain faith when there seems to be little cause for faith, to create hope when hope becomes forlorn.[1]

Honor at West Point is cogently expressed in a passage from the Cadet Prayer authored in 1923 by West Point chaplain Clayton E. Wheat.[2] "Make us to choose the harder right instead of the easier wrong, and never to be content with a half-truth when the whole can be won."[3]

The purpose of the cadet honor code is to foster a commitment to moral-ethical excellence essential to developing leaders of character for the nation, to provide the proper moral-ethical structure and honor system for the Corps of Cadets, and to establish a foundation for a lifetime of honorable living. In the earliest days at the Military Academy, the code of honor was based upon a concept that officers in the Army were honest and trustworthy. Their words were their bond. Initially, the code of honor dealt only with lying and the honor system was an informal procedure conducted on a cadet-to-cadet basis. Sylvanus Thayer expanded the code to include cheating.[4] In 1949, the superintendent, General Maxwell D. Taylor, codified Honor and in 1970 the non-toleration clause was added to the code.[5]

The honor code goes far beyond the walls of the Academy. West Point cadets are expected to be completely trustworthy just as West Point graduates are expected to make a lifelong commitment to honorable living. During the first week of New Cadet Barracks, the West Point Class of 1963 heard an address by a member of the Cadet Honor Committee, who said:

> Honor is not something that can be put on or taken off like your dress coat. It is as much a part of you as your heart and goes with you wherever you may be. When we say that a cadet does not lie, cheat, or steal, we do not mean just at West Point. We mean anywhere, anytime and under any circumstances.[6]

In 1992, the cadet honor code at West Point stated that, "A cadet will not lie, cheat, or steal nor tolerate those who do."[7] During my tenure as commandant, each of the 36 companies had a company honor education team (CHET) comprised of one senior faculty member, three instructors, the cadet company commander, first and second classmen honor representatives, the company tactical officer, and the TAC NCO. Small-group discussions using moral-ethical case studies optimized the time available for cadets to articulate their thoughts, listen to other points of view, and inculcate principles of integrity. In September 1992, the superintendent, dean, and I met with the 83 members of the Cadet Honor Committee as well as the company tactical officers and the academic instructors who served on the CHETs for an annual review of the honor code and system. At the meeting, I directed a comprehensive review of the honor education program to include the subjects taught, the materials and videos used, the number of hours required over the four years, and relevance of subjects to the type of moral-ethical dilemmas faced by cadets and commissioned officers. To prevent curriculum overload, I established one constraint—for every hour of honor instruction added, one hour of instruction in some other military subject would be deleted.

In AY 1991–92, honor instruction consisted of 22 hours over the four-year curriculum. In AY 1992–93, the number of hours increased to 35, and in AY 1993–94, to 45 hours.[8] Although the increase in allotted classroom time signified a boost in commitment, the in-depth analysis in upgrading the reading materials, analyzing videos, and rewriting lesson outlines made an extraordinary contribution to honor education. I discussed honor with first classmen in South Auditorium three times annually, second and third classmen twice, and fourth classmen once. I also met with rising first and second classmen honor representatives along with first class emerging leaders at the Spring Honor Conference.[9]

When General John A. Wickham, Jr., West Point Class of 1950, was the Army chief of staff, he published a pamphlet entitled *Guideposts for a Proud and Ready Army*, which added historical context to the ethical element of leadership and underscored the moral obligation we have as leaders to safeguard the welfare of our soldiers and their families. He stated that:

> Our profession involves deep moral values because we are dealing with matters of life and death—for ourselves, for those who serve shoulder to shoulder with us, for our nation, for our families, and for adversaries and non-combatants. In times of danger, it is the ethical element of leadership which will bond our units together and enable them to withstand the stresses of combat. This is an irrefutable lesson of history. Above all, we must never forget, in the rush of day-to-day activities, that our profession deals with the more profound moral issues, and that the strength of character, in our personal and professional lives, which we and our country seek in time of war must be fostered in times of peace.[10]

Based upon my experience as a rifle company commander during the Vietnam War, respect for others warranted a far greater role in developing leaders of character.

I found that soldiers fought with unsurpassed aggressiveness to prevent their buddies from being killed or wounded. Respect was a key ingredient in the warrior ethos and a lynchpin to the trust and synergy essential in combat operations.

U.S. Army *Field Manual 100-1*, "The Profession of Arms" defines compassion as basic respect for the dignity of everyone—the personification of the Golden Rule: treating others as you would want them to treat you.[11]

In an address to the Corps of Cadets on August 11, 1879, Major General John M. Schofield said, "He who feels the respect which is due to others cannot fail to inspire in them regard for himself...."[12] General Schofield was a member of the Class of 1853 and superintendent of the U.S. Military Academy from 1876 to 1881.

While preparing a briefing for the Board of Visitors in the fall of 1992, I was struck with "Consideration of Others"—one of the 12 leader dimensions used in the formal evaluations each cadet received over the four-year experience. Consideration of Others was defined as "Those actions that indicate a sensitivity to and regard for the feelings and needs of others and an awareness of the impact of one's own behavior on them; being supportive of and fair with others (subordinates, peers, and superiors)."[13]

In the winter of AY 1992–93, we instituted Consideration of Others as a Corps of Cadets' core value by developing a program of instruction, selecting company representatives, and establishing a Consideration of Others Committee. Our intent was to develop a concept that "covers the broad perspective of civility and encompasses harassment, discrimination, prejudice, insensitivity, offensive behavior, verbal abuse and basic thoughtlessness."[14] We wanted to create an environment where "racial, sexual or religious harassment or discrimination is not tolerated."[15]

Cadet Captain Mark Goldschmidt, chairman of the 1992–93 Honor Committee, referred to honor as the "Bedrock, our way of life, a constant, a given, the foundation for everything else we do."[16] With the advent of Consideration of Others, he coined honor as bedrock one and Consideration of Others as bedrock two and promulgated this alliance in his presentations to the Corps of Cadets. In the fall of 1993, the education program for Consideration of Others had gone from zero to a goal of 37 hours of instruction over the four-year curriculum.

One of the preeminent examples of respect and consideration of others was manifested by Joshua Lawrence Chamberlain during the Civil War. Born in Brewer, Maine in 1828, Chamberlain commanded a regiment, a brigade, and a division during the Civil War and was governor of Maine and president of Bowdoin College.[17] When he was appointed a lieutenant colonel of the 20th Maine Regiment, he deployed by train with the regiment from Portland, Maine to Washington, D.C. to await orders.[18]

On July 1, 1863, the 20th Maine was assigned to Colonel Strong Vincent's 3rd Brigade of 5th Corps which began marching toward Gettysburg, Pennsylvania.[19] Colonel Vincent directed that the 20th Maine defend the left flank of the Union line. He added that Confederate forces were expected to attack at any moment and

Chamberlain's position on Little Round Top must be held at all costs.[20] Colonel Vincent's Brigade was attacked by seven Confederate regiments—five from Alabama and two from Texas.[21]

After repelling four assaults, the 20th Maine suffered heavy casualties and was low on ammunition. Chamberlain's company commanders wanted to move off the line. Chamberlain quickly assessed the situation and ordered his companies to fix bayonets and charge down the front of Little Round Top. The Confederate forces coming up the hill were so surprised they turned and ran—never to assault Little Round Top again.[22]

In the Petersburg campaign in June 1864, Chamberlain was seriously wounded and traveled back to his home in Maine to recuperate.[23] After his return, he was promoted to major general and given command of a division.[24] On April 2, 1865, the Union commanders ceased fire all along the line.[25] Subsequently, Lieutenant General Ulysses S. Grant and Lieutenant General Robert E. Lee met at Appomattox Court House to discuss the terms of surrender.[26]

General Grant selected Chamberlain to preside at the surrender of the Army of Northern Virginia with guidance to have a formal but simple ceremony—one that would not belittle the Confederate forces. Early on the morning of April 12, 1865, Union regiments in the Appomattox Courthouse area began lining up on a hillside opposite the Confederate encampment to accept the surrender of General Lee's Army. As far as could be seen in the early mist, regiment after regiment, resplendent in Union blue uniforms, stood at order arms along the ridgeline. At the appointed time, a long column of gray-clad soldiers came marching forward.[27] The members of the vanquished army were not quite sure how they were going to be treated. Soldiers on both sides had been fighting for four years—thousands of their fellow soldiers, friends, and family members had been killed or wounded.[28]

When the Confederate soldiers began crossing the shallow headwaters of the Appomattox River heading toward the first of the Federal units, a Union bugle sounded. Beginning with the 32nd Massachusetts, regiment after regiment came to the position of attention. As the Confederate soldiers closed on the Federal ranks, a second Union bugle sounded. Again, beginning with the 32nd Massachusetts, regiment after regiment came to the rifle salute.[29]

Major General John B. Gordon, whom General Lee had chosen to represent the Confederate forces, led the column on horseback. When he heard the bugles sound, he wheeled to face Chamberlain.[30]

> As he did, his spurs touched the sides of his horse, causing it to rear, and as his horse's head then came down in a bow, the gallant young general dropped his sword point to his boot toe in a graceful salute to the man whom he would call one of the Knightliest soldiers of the Federal army.[31]

As the Confederate soldiers stopped in front of the Federal line, stacking their muskets with bayonets fixed, laying down their cartridge belts, and kissing their tattered battle flags, many had tears flowing down their cheeks. On the Union side—absolute silence. Not a word was spoken, not a whisper, not a sound.[32]

> This last act of esteem is thought to have contributed, in no small fashion, to the beginning of the healing of the wounds from the war between the two sides and is also one of the chief causes for Chamberlain's intense popularity in the North and the South, then and now.[33]

In the summer of 1994, when I was the deputy commanding general of Second Army at Fort Gillem in Atlanta, Georgia, I had the opportunity to visit training conducted by units of the Mississippi Army National Guard at Camp Shelby near Hattiesburg, Mississippi. While walking through the headquarters with Major General Jim Garner, the adjutant general of the State of Mississippi, I looked at prints of famous Confederate generals such as Lee, Longstreet, and Barksdale prominently displayed on the walls. I stopped when I saw one Union general officer—Major General Joshua Lawrence Chamberlain.

I asked, "What's he doing here?"

General Garner replied, "He's a great soldier who has our utmost respect."

This was 129 years after Chamberlain conducted the surrender ceremony at Appomattox Court House.

> The Soldier's heart, the soldier's spirit, the soldier's soul are everything. Unless the soldier's soul sustains him, he cannot be relied on and will fail himself and his country in the end.[34]
>
> General George C. Marshall

## CHAPTER 22

# Deputy Commanding General, Second Army

In June 1994, I was promoted to major general and received orders to be deputy commanding general of Second Army in Atlanta. I was extremely proud of Mark, who was going into his senior year at the Air Force Academy and had been selected as Second Group Honor Chairman—a key position in the cadet wing that required a strong sense of ethical principles and a profound appreciation of the academy's institutional values. He investigated allegations of honor code violations and worked directly with the Wing Honor Committee to resolve individual cases. This was a sensitive and time-consuming process that took him away from his studies, but which made a significant contribution to the Air Force Academy. Dave was on his way to the Infantry Officer Basic Course, Airborne, and Ranger schools at Fort Benning, followed by duty as an infantry platoon leader with the 4th Infantry Division at Fort Carson, Colorado. We decided Sara should stay at O'Neill High School for her senior year, so Julie and Sara moved into a small cottage near West Point while I went to Fort McPherson, Georgia as a geographical bachelor. It was the right decision for Sara as she loved her cheerleading activities, drama club, and senior year social life, which included permission from her father to date cadets (plebes only). When she was selected to represent New York in 1995 as the Cherry Blossom Princess, Julie and I attended the weeklong festival in Washington, D.C.

The Second Army mission was to advise, assist, train, and evaluate reserve component units as well as ensure units selected for overseas deployment met the readiness standards required by combatant commanders. The commanding general, Lieutenant General Samuel E. Ebbesen, was a smart, straightforward leader who possessed an in-depth understanding of the training, readiness, and funding issues inherent in the Army National Guard and Army Reserve. My job was to assess the effectiveness of unit training and advise commanders in accomplishing their assigned missions.

Reserve component units were funded for one weekend a month of individual training and two weeks of annual collective training. In my first visit to an Army

National Guard unit conducting Annual Training (AT), the brigade commander gave me a training highlights briefing but made no mention of mission essential tasks consistent with Army *FM 25-101*. He claimed he had not heard of battle-focused training, which had been standard Army doctrine for four years. After I had advised him to quickly get up to speed, he thanked me for my visit and gave me directions on how to depart the area. He expressed surprise and consternation when I told him I was planning on sticking around to observe training. However, I reminded him of the Second Army mission and subsequently linked up with an infantry company scheduled to conduct patrolling operations.

It didn't take long to determine the company leadership had no training plan and were making things up as they went along. The next morning, they put together a patrol that amounted to a walk down a road. There was no opposing force, no blank ammunition, no pyrotechnics, and no use of patrolling techniques. There was so much missing from a standard training exercise, I hardly knew where to begin, but I sat with the company commander to provide recommendations on improving his training. When I stopped by to provide the brigade commander with my observations, I sensed he was so overwhelmed with the logistical management of a two-week training cycle that he had little time to spend on collective training.

Because of my BFV experience in Germany, I scheduled a visit to a National Guard BFV unit. Shortly after my arrival at the field site, I asked a Bradley driver to take me through the vehicle pre-operational maintenance checks. He explained that he was new and could not tell me what checks were required even though he had driven the BFV from the motor pool to the field site. After looking through the rear compartment of the vehicle, we found the technical manuals still wrapped in plastic from the factory. I told the driver to check the engine oil level—it was below minimum. I directed the battalion commander to ground all BFVs until pre-operational checks had been accomplished. I also conducted a counseling session with him on BFV maintenance.

My summer AT visitation schedule was interrupted by Hurricane Alberto, which dumped up to 27 inches of rain on parts of Georgia from July 4–14, 1994. The Flint and Ocmulgee rivers exceeded 100-year flood levels; damage to highway infrastructure exceeded $130 million; 500,000 people were temporarily left without drinking water; 471,000 acres of farmland were submerged; and there were 31 deaths.[1]

Second Army Headquarters put together a crisis action cell responsible for coordinating active component support to the Federal Emergency Management Agency (FEMA) in coordination with the National Guard and local responders. I was impressed with the rapid and effective assistance provided by the Georgia Army National Guard engineer, aviation, transportation, military police, and medical units. The hurricane damage was devastating but the National Guard soldiers were in the right place at the right time stacking sandbags, providing security, evacuating residents, and bringing in drinking water. They were assisted by reverse osmosis purification units, which drained muddy water from a swollen creek and turned it into potable water in minutes.

In August, I was placed on temporary duty for 90 days as president of the 1994 U.S. Army Sergeant Major Selection Board held in Indianapolis, Indiana. When I returned to Atlanta in November, I learned that Lieutenant General Ebbesen had been reassigned as deputy assistant secretary of defense for military personnel policy in the Pentagon. To fill the vacancy, General Dennis J. Reimer, then commanding general of Forces Command (FORSCOM), assigned me to be acting commander of Second Army. I had known General Reimer since we were cadets in Company A1 at West Point and could not have asked to work for a more distinguished leader.

In January 1995, I made plans to continue the training assessments of reserve component units in the Second Army area of operations. Based upon prior training visits, I was convinced the Army National Guard met or exceeded standards in accomplishing the state disaster relief mission but their ability to accomplish the federal mission needed vast improvement. Mindful of the unsatisfactory performance of the infantry company conducting a patrolling exercise the previous summer, I decided to evaluate training management in reserve component units at the company level.

I used the guidance contained in *Training Circular (TC) 25-30: A Leader's Guide to Company Training Meetings*, which stated that:

> Battle focus is the process of deriving peacetime training requirements from wartime missions. The purpose of developing a battle focus approach to training is to allow commanders to achieve a successful training program by narrowing the focus of the unit's training efforts to a reduced number of vital tasks that are essential to mission accomplishment. Once the commander has developed a battle focus approach to training, the next step is to ensure that the scarce resources of time and training dollars are not wasted.[2]

The unit I selected to evaluate was an infantry company engaged in a Multiple Unit Training Assembly (MUTA-4), amounting to four consecutive four-hour unit training assemblies conducted over Saturday and Sunday. I met with the company commander on Saturday afternoon and asked him a few basic questions about his company training meetings. It was obvious he didn't have a clue about training management. He didn't use a training meeting worksheet with agenda for the last meeting; could not produce training notes; was not aware of who normally attends company training meetings; did not keep a monthly training calendar; and did not have a copy of the training assessment worksheet indicating the status of mission essential tasks categorized by "P"—Partially trained, "T"—Trained, or "U"—Untrained. When I suggested we look at *TC 25-30* for clarification, his first sergeant and company clerk conducted a thorough search but could not find a copy anywhere in the company headquarters.

After returning from this disastrous company-level visit, I attended a Yearly Training Briefing (YTB) for an Army National Guard Brigade Combat Team. YTBs were critical to each state as they provided the means for Second Army to approve funding for annual training. The standard briefing format comprises the following:

1. Unit Mission.
2. Commander's METL assessment by Battle Operating Systems.
3. Higher Headquarters Directives.
4. Commander's guidance to include goals, objectives, and priorities.
5. Commander's strategy to improve or sustain training proficiency.
6. Last year, current year, and upcoming year training calendars.
7. Battalion Command Sergeant Major Soldier Training Assessment.
8. Schools Status, to include Primary Leadership Development Courses.
9. Ammunition, Range, and Training Area allocations.[3]

I was escorted to a seat in the front row of a movie theater with about 50 soldiers seated behind me. The brigade commander made a presentation from the stage using the obsolete "training highlights" format. The presentation made no reference to METL tasks, and the venue did not lend itself to conducting YTB business. I waited patiently until he had completed his remarks then met with him privately in a room at the back of the theater. Since his presentation did not follow standard U.S. Army training doctrine, I informed him that his YTB was disapproved and funding for his brigade for the next fiscal year would be withheld until he conducted a YTB in accordance with *FM 25-101*.

When I returned to Second Army Headquarters, I told my staff to postpone all scheduled YTB approval presentations until state commanders and command sergeants major were prepared to conduct Battle Focused Training briefings in accordance with Appendix F, *FM 25-101*. I also made the decision to withhold all federal training funds for fiscal year 1996 until state YTBs were approved. This caused quite a stir. One state adjutant general challenged my decision. I informed him that he was welcome to submit a letter requesting an exemption from standard training doctrine that had been in effect Army-wide for the past four years and I would be happy to forward his letter to the Commanding General Forces Command, Commanding General Training and Doctrine Command and the director of the Army National Guard. I never received his request for exemption. And from that day forward, there was not one request from state adjutant generals for Second Army to attend a YTB. I was told that rather than comply with this standard training doctrine, they had decided to wait until I departed and appeal to the new Second Army commander, who was scheduled to take command before the end of the fiscal year.

In August, I was assigned as the commanding general of the U.S. Army Military District of Washington (MDW) with headquarters located at Fort McNair in southwest Washington, D.C.

## CHAPTER 23

# Commanding General, U.S. Army Military District of Washington

In 1791, Pierre Charles L'Enfant, the architect of the city of Washington, D.C., designed an arsenal called Greenleaf's Point with seawalls, shops, magazines, and barracks located at the confluence of the Anacostia and Potomac rivers.[1] When President James Madison declared war on Great Britain in 1812, British forces invaded the city, setting fire to buildings and destroying arms at this fledgling fortification. The invading troops, however, suffered a horrific setback when hidden gunpowder exploded, killing 40 British soldiers and injuring 47 others.[2]

In the ensuing years, the post served as the Engineer School, the Army War College, and, during World War II, the Army Ground Force Headquarters commanded by Brigadier General Lesley J. McNair.[3] Sadly, bombs falling short of their targets during the Eighth Air Force bombing of German positions near Saint-Lô, France killed Lieutenant General McNair.[4] After the war, Army leaders changed the name of the post from Greenleaf's Point to Fort Lesley J. McNair in a ceremony attended by General Omar N. Bradley and General J. Lawton Collins, the Army chief of staff.[5]

On August 29, 1995, I took command of the U.S. Army Military District of Washington (MDW) from Major General Fred A. Gorden on the parade field at Fort McNair in a ceremony hosted by General Dennis J. Reimer, the Army chief of staff. Our stately quarters, located at the edge of the Potomac River, had three floors with splendid views, a full basement, and a fenced-in back yard. Mark had just graduated from the Air Force Academy and was in flight school at Columbus Air Force Base, Mississippi. Dave was an infantry platoon leader at Fort Carson, Colorado and Sara was beginning her freshman year at Pepperdine University in Malibu, California.

My mission was to:

- Command the 3rd Infantry Regiment (The Old Guard), the 12th Aviation Battalion, the U.S. Army Band, the 12th Military Police Company, the 911th Engineer Company, and the Joint Personal Property Shipping Office.
- Provide base operations support to Fort McNair, Fort Belvoir, Fort Myer, Cameron Station, Camp AP Hill, Fort Meade, and Fort Richie.

- Conduct official ceremonies at Arlington National Cemetery, the Pentagon, and the White House.
- Direct funeral operations for the incumbent and former presidents of the United States.
- Serve as Chairman of the Armed Forces Inaugural Committee.

With such a diverse command structure and assortment of missions, I was glad that General Reimer had introduced me to re-engineering as a decision-making methodology when he was the commanding general of Forces Command. Re-engineering is defined as "the fundamental rethinking and radical redesign of business processes to achieve dramatic improvements in critical, contemporary measures of performance such as cost, quality, service and speed."[6] Armed with this concept, I approached the problem-solving process by asking four fundamental questions:

1. What is it that we do?
2. Why do we do it?
3. Why do we do it that way?
4. Is there a better way?

While attending a quarterly garrison commander meeting on infrastructure funding, I learned that a new seawall was planned for Fort McNair. According to the post engineers, water from the Potomac River was causing erosion to the old wall. A $40,000 environmental study had been completed with an artist's rendering of walking paths, benches, streetlamps, and landscaping. Since I regularly walked our Labrador Retriever along the water's edge and never came across any evidence of deterioration, I was interested in the rationale for this $8,000,000 proposal. The next day, I met with the installation engineers to examine a stone wall that had been in place for probably 200 years. Because the experts could not show me one place in need of repair, I cancelled the project. That was more than 25 years ago, and the old seawall is still standing.

Walking out of the front door of my quarters at Fort McNair one day, I confronted a backhoe operator who was about to scoop up the concrete walkway leading from my front porch to the sidewalk. I told him to take a break while I called the garrison commander.

"Why are you replacing the concrete sidewalks at Fort McNair?"

"Sir, I am using funds from our infrastructure maintenance budget which will only be available until the end of the fiscal year."

"But it doesn't make sense to dig up a perfectly good concrete sidewalk and replace it with a perfectly good concrete sidewalk."

"The sidewalks have cracks in them."

"All sidewalks have cracks in them."

"We are also constructing wheelchair access ramps for the golf course."

I cancelled the project.

At the end of the Old Guard Quarterly Training Briefing in March 1996 I asked the company commanders if there were any higher headquarters policies or programs troublesome to them. One of the captains described the inordinate amount of time consumed in conducting funerals outside Arlington National Cemetery. The company on support cycle had to furnish casket bearers, bugler, chaplain, NCOIC, and 10-person vans for funerals held in Maryland, Washington, D.C., and Virginia. When I asked the MDW staff to find documentation requiring support of funerals external to ANC, none existed. I terminated the policy for conducting funerals outside ANC.

On a hot July day, I went to a retirement ceremony for a four-star general at Fort Myer. The Old Guard line companies along with the Presidential Salute Battery, the Fife and Drum Corps, and the Commander-in-Chief's Guard were on Summerall Field in their full-dress wool uniforms. I was impressed with the stamina and discipline of these great soldiers as they stood for one hour in the heat and humidity. I knew how they felt because I was standing beside the reviewing stand wearing my full-dress wool uniform. After the ceremony, I followed soldiers from one of the companies to the top floor of a barracks, where they took off their dress coats and began shining their brass in a room without air conditioning. With only three rouge wheels, the soldiers stood in line with sweat pouring down their faces, wearing masks to alleviate breathing in dust from the rouge wheels. I didn't receive one good answer from the NCOs to my question, "What's wrong with this picture?" That afternoon, I told the Old Guard commander I would provide funding for installing air conditioners in soldier locker rooms and I would allocate funds to purchase anodized insignia and buttons for their uniforms. Very quickly, the NCOs requested reconsideration of the anodized brass policy because shining brass was a tradition in the Old Guard.

At a subsequent meeting with company commanders, sergeants major, and first sergeants present, I pulled out two buttons and asked them which one was brass and which one was anodized. Sitting 10 feet away, they couldn't tell the difference. I said, "Anyone sitting in the reviewing stand at an Old Guard ceremony can't tell the difference either." I gave them 60 days to change to anodized buttons and insignia. A few weeks after the transition was complete, the regimental command sergeant major came to see me. He thanked me for abolishing the requirement to shine brass as eight hours were saved each week and set aside for soldier's time.

One of the most fascinating units in the Old Guard is the caisson platoon, which conveys deceased members of the U.S. Armed Forces for funerals at Arlington National Cemetery (ANC). The 3,290-pound caisson is pulled by six large horses. In my first visit to the platoon, I was impressed with the cleanliness of the stable area and the excellent-looking horses with their heads out looking for a neck rub or treat. In one stall, though, I thought it strange to see a horse leaning against the back wall.

"What's wrong with him?"

One of the NCOs said with a smile, "Sir, he doesn't want to go to work."

"Why?"

"Because he has sores on his back from the harness rubbing against his body while he pulls the caisson."

After examining several lesions on the horse's back, I said, "No wonder he doesn't want to go to work. What's being done for him?"

"Sir, we put salve on the lesions, but he's got to continue pulling the caisson to keep up with funeral demands."

"No, he doesn't."

I told the NCOs that this horse and any other sick or injured horses were not pulling a caisson. Instead, they would be sent to the 10-acre farm at Fort Belvoir until completely healthy and cleared for duty by the veterinarian.

"How many horses do you have?"

"Thirty-five, Sir."

"How many do you need?

Dead silence. Apparently, nobody had asked this fundamental question in a long time. I ordered a total caisson platoon analysis, taking into consideration the number of horses required by type—Shire, Percheron, Quarter Horse, Mustang—from acquisition to retirement. The results were not surprising: 65 horses were needed. Over the next several months, a small team of soldiers traveled to rodeos and ranches in Texas, Montana, Wyoming, and Colorado, resulting in the acquisition of 35 more horses. Excited about their steeds participating in funerals and other ceremonies in the nation's capital, many of the ranch owners donated the horses and transported them to Washington free of charge.

Arlington National Cemetery was established in 1864 to honor the remains of Union soldiers who fought and died in the Civil War. After World War I, Great Britain interred an unknown soldier at Westminster Abbey in London. In 1920, France interred an unknown soldier at the Arc de Triomphe in Paris. Legislation sponsored by U.S. Congressman Hamilton Fish of New York authorized the burial of an unknown American Expeditionary Force (AEF) soldier from World War I in ANC. Four of 1,237 AEF soldiers whose remains could not be identified were disinterred from four different French cemeteries, placed in identical caskets, and brought to the town of Châlons-sur-Marne. Sergeant Edward F. Younger, a highly decorated infantryman, selected the unknown soldier by placing a single rose on one of the caskets. The remains were shipped back to the Washington Navy Yard aboard the USS *Olympia* and conveyed to lie in state in the rotunda of the Capitol. For two days, 90,000 people came by to pay their respects. On November 11, 1921, the remains were taken by caisson from the Capitol, down Constitution Avenue, across Memorial Bridge to the cemetery. Huge crowds lined the funeral route. President Harding presided at the interment ceremony, presenting the unknown soldier with the Medal of Honor and the Distinguished Service Cross. Five thousand people attended the funeral service with another 100,000 outside the amphitheater listening through loudspeakers.[7]

In 1931, a 50-ton piece of granite was placed at the tomb site and sculpted with the words, "Here Rests in Honored Glory an American Soldier Known but to God." President Eisenhower hosted a ceremony on May 30, 1958, for the World War II and Korea unknowns who were buried in identical crypts flanking the grave of the World War I unknown and marked with flat, white memorial stones. On May 28, 1984, President Reagan hosted a ceremony for the burial of the Vietnam unknown.[8]

On Memorial Day, American flags are placed at each of the 250,000 headstones located on the 624 acres of this hallowed ground and a wreath-laying ceremony is held to honor the men and women who made the ultimate sacrifice for our nation. During my tenure as commanding general of MDW, I escorted President William J. Clinton for the wreath-laying ceremony at the Tomb of the Unknown Soldier. The Joint Service Honor Guard, consisting of soldiers, Marines, sailors, airmen, and Coast Guardsmen, rendered honors as the band played the national anthem. After the wreath was placed on its stand, the bugler played Taps (signifying honors to servicemembers) and we paused for a moment of silence. Following the chaplain's invocation and my welcome in the amphitheater, I introduced the president for his remarks.

In addition to Memorial Day and Veterans Day activities, I was the host for 103 wreath-laying ceremonies with heads of state, ministers of defense, or chiefs of defense forces from countries throughout the world. This included Eastern European nations and former members of the Union of Soviet Socialist Republics[9] (see Appendix One). After I met and briefed the visiting delegation, the band played the national anthems of both countries, the Old Guard NCO placed the wreath on its stand, and the bugler played Taps. I gave a short presentation on the tomb history, which naturally generated questions about ANC and the tomb sentinels who were on guard 24 hours a day. The Joint Service Honor Guard created a compelling image of U.S. Armed Forces with their rifle and fixed bayonet precision drill. One loud crack was heard when the troops in formation clicked their heels at the command "Attention" and one loud slap as they simultaneously grabbed their rifles for "Present arms." The highest accolade from my three years of escorting foreign dignitaries came from the delegate of an Eastern European nation who said to his associate, "I think we should stick with these guys."

I was fortunate to have as commander of the Old Guard Colonel David H. Huntoon, a brilliant leader who I have known since he was a plebe in my cadet company when I was a tactical officer at West Point. His sound advice, proactive planning, and masterful execution of multiple ceremonial taskings ensured that the U.S. Armed Forces honor guards represented the United States in splendid fashion at every formation. In addition, Dave has made enduring contributions to the U.S. Army as an educator and strategist. He rose to the rank of lieutenant general and was the longest-serving commandant at the Army War College. He was also appointed director of the Army staff and superintendent of the U.S. Military Academy, completing 40 years of service to the U.S. Army and our nation.

As part of the MDW commanding general's diplomacy function, I attended official embassy receptions. This proved to be a great way to develop working relationships with military representatives from all over the world. We reciprocated with invitations for them to attend events such as Memorial Day and Veterans Day ceremonies at ANC, Twilight Tattoos at the Ellipse, and the 1812 Overture at the National Mall. One evening, Julie and I were invited to a grand dinner at the residence of the French ambassador. The cocktail hour was extended because two American couples were late in arriving and the ambassador was not happy. When the chef made one or two nervous appearances, the ambassador decided to proceed to the dining room. Since Julie was seated next to him and fluent in French, she attempted to provide a calming influence. He was extremely upset with the two couples, who never did make it to dinner. In our experience with European protocol, everyone was expected to be on time for social events or notify the host immediately of a late appearance or cancellation. Julie and I remember arriving early for receptions in Germany and waiting in our car until precisely the time on the invitation when all guests left their cars and walked en masse to the residence.

In October 1996, our beagle wandered into the pantry, opened a bag of chocolate chips—a toxic ingredient for dogs—and ate the contents. Unfortunately, the veterinarian could not save her. Since I was despondent over her loss, Julie and Sara drove to Shenandoah Valley and surprised me with the purchase of a six-week-old, fox red, Labrador Retriever puppy. Still thinking about Maggie, I asked Julie if this new dog could be returned. The next morning, when that playful little puppy jumped into my arms and licked my face, I promptly changed my mind about Lady Cassandra—aka Cassie.

State funeral plans for the incumbent and former presidents were updated annually and maintained at MDW headquarters. The documents included a list of honorary pallbearers, speakers for the memorial service, and a Washington National Cathedral seating plan for family, friends, members of congress, the diplomatic corps, and the press. Timelines were specified for vehicles and aircraft transporting the remains with honor guard escorts. Each displacement of the remains constituted a ceremony with band members, casket bearers, chaplain, officer in charge and color guard. Since there were 16 formal ceremonies from the funeral home to the burial site, personnel, vehicles, and aircraft were prepositioned at designated locations. The commanding general of MDW escorted the widow and surviving family members while the MDW staff directed the funeral proceedings from Fort McNair. In case I had to be called upon to conduct a state funeral, I rehearsed my escort duties at a variety of places, including Andrews Air Force Base, the Capitol rotunda, the National Cathedral, and the Constitution Avenue transfer point.

I was thankful I had studied my duties and rehearsed the sequence of events at each venue because on Wednesday, April 3, 1996, the secretary of commerce, the Honorable Ronald H. Brown, was killed in a plane crash in Croatia on a trade mission along with 34 state department and business leaders. The Honorable John P. White, deputy secretary of defense, tasked MDW to conduct the funeral planning. At Dover Air Force Base on Saturday, April 6, I met the president as he walked off Air Force One with the Brown family and escorted Mrs. Brown, her children, and relatives to the reception area for the arrival ceremony. When the C-17 pulled up in front of the hangar, 35 new hearses moved to a location between the aircraft and the reviewing area. When the C-17 ramp was lowered, Army, Marine Corps, Navy, Air Force, and Coast Guard pallbearers entered the aircraft, picked up the transfer cases and placed them in hearses, which departed, one by one, in solemn transit to designated locations. Secretary Brown was transported to a Washington, D.C. funeral home for burial preparation and casket transfer. The next day, his remains were delivered to the U.S. Commerce Department to lie in repose. The funeral on April 10 began with a memorial service at the National Cathedral and ended with burial proceedings at ANC.

When I was chief of staff of the 7th Infantry Division at Fort Ord, California, Colonel David H. (Hack) Hackworth, U.S. Army Retired, a highly decorated veteran from the Vietnam and Korean wars, called on me. I had not seen him for eight years and after a few hours of swapping Wolfhound stories, I arranged for him to make a leadership presentation to the 2nd and 3rd battalions of the 27th Infantry (Wolfhounds). Unfortunately, the senior Army leadership in Washington directed that we withdraw the invitation. Hack had a colorful and sometimes controversial Army career that began with joining the U.S. Merchant Marine at age 14 and later enlisting in the Army with false documents. He was a sergeant with the 27th Infantry Regiment (Wolfhounds) during the Korean War, where he received a battlefield commission and served a second tour with the 40th Infantry Division. He served two tours of duty in Vietnam—first as a battalion commander with the 101st Airborne Division and then as a Vietnamese Army senior military advisor. He was promoted to colonel and turned down attendance at the Army War College. Throughout his career, he received two awards of the Distinguished Service Cross, 10 Silver Stars, and eight Purple Hearts. Disillusioned with the Army leadership, Hack retired and moved to Australia, where he sold real estate, owned a duck farm, and ran a popular restaurant. Upon his return to the United States, he became a *Newsweek* reporter, a writer, and a blogger focusing on troop welfare.[10]

When he came to see me at Fort McNair, I arranged for him to visit MDW subordinate commands with my aide-de-camp and driver. He received a great welcome wherever he went and could not have been happier spending the day with soldiers. In August 1998, I smiled reading Hack's unique parlance when he acknowledged my promotion to lieutenant general on his website:

> Foley is one of our best Soldiers. Thought he was on the way out, but he just got a third star and will soon be the CG, Fifth Army located in San Antonio. I met him as a young Captain right after the action where he policed up the Medal of Honor with the 2/27th Wolfhounds— America's best and the unit I got my battlefield commission in. I was impressed then and have watched him lead by example since. Maybe the Army will get lucky and make him Chief one day. In a word, he's a stud. There is hope when a guy like Foley GETS THREE BIG ONES. He ain't no Perfumed Prince.[11]

As chairman of the Armed Forces Inaugural Committee (AFIC), I knew MDW would be decisively engaged in planning and coordinating military support for the 1997 presidential inauguration. I realized we would have about two months beginning with the presidential election in November to prepare for an event in January significant to millions of people around the world. We promptly took possession of leased office space and commenced the buildup of a joint headquarters that would ultimately comprise 850 soldiers, Marines, sailors, airmen, and Coast Guardsmen.

I met with Senator John Warner to brief him on plans for the swearing-in ceremony at the Capitol on Inauguration Day. In his role as chairman of the Congressional Inaugural Committee, he emphasized the importance of good weather. He said that an observance inside the Capitol with only 2,000 spectators and limited access to the press would not have the same impact as a ceremony on the west face of the Capitol with 100,000 spectators covered by global news media. "Therefore," he said, "the swearing-in ceremony must be done outside." He smiled when I told him that I might have to seek assistance from a higher authority. Fortunately, the weather on Monday, January 20 was cold for the swearing-in ceremony but pleasant for the parade with the sun breaking through the clouds in mid-afternoon. Along with the component commanders and their wives, Julie and I ate box lunches at the Capitol. At about 2:00 p.m. I escorted the president, vice president, and their families to limousines as they came out of the congressional luncheon on the east side of the Capitol. I led the parade with the five component commanders from the Capitol to the White House past the reviewing stand, joined Julie, who was already seated there to watch the parade, and departed in time for the Armed Forces Inaugural Ball.

While we were implementing the Consideration of Others Program at MDW installations, sexual harassment scandals involving drill sergeants and female recruits at Aberdeen Proving Ground and Fort Leonard Wood were generating negative publicity for the Army. Secretary of the Army Togo D. West, Jr. directed that a Senior Review Panel on Sexual Harassment be convened with the specific goal of eradicating sexual harassment in the Army.[12] When he asked me to be the chairman of this panel, I told him it would be difficult with my responsibilities for the presidential inauguration. He was convinced I could do it but, thankfully, General

Ronald H. Griffith, the Army vice chief of staff, persuaded him to appoint me as a panel member but not the chairman.

The morning after we arrived at Fort Leavenworth, Kansas to conduct interviews and sensing sessions, John McLaurin, deputy assistant secretary of the Army for military personnel management and equal opportunity and fellow panel member, brought a *New York Times* article to my attention. It described allegations by a retired female sergeant major accusing sergeant major of the Army (SMA) Gene C. McKinney of sexually assaulting her while on a business trip to Hawaii. I was halfway through the article when it struck me that I was the General Court-Martial Convening Authority (GCMCA) for all soldiers in the National Capital Region, which included SMA McKinney. By listening to soldiers from across the Army discuss sexual harassment, I felt I would be subject to unlawful command influence in violation of the Uniform Code of Military Justice. Accordingly, the secretary of the Army approved my recommendation to excuse me as a member of the panel.[13]

As the first order of GCMCA business for the McKinney case, I initiated brainstorming sessions with my staff judge advocate, Colonel Frankie D. Hoskey. He was an invaluable asset in providing me with sound recommendations and precise legal interpretations—focusing heavily on two enduring principles: due process and a determination of the truth. Because I didn't want to convey even the appearance of unlawful command influence, I asked my chief of staff, Colonel Ralph Tuccillo, to take all calls from general officers and senior officials and explain that I would be out of communication until the McKinney case was resolved. This not only reduced my exposure to unlawful command influence but also protected senior officials from being unwittingly called as a witness.

I also asked Brigadier General Chuck Viale, the commanding general, First Army East, to take my place for wreath-laying ceremonies at ANC. Although I conducted normal business with the MDW staff, I didn't discuss the McKinney case with anyone except Colonel Hoskey and the judge advocate general of the Army. This left me in the unique position of not being able to ask others for their opinion on this high-profile case. I had historically advocated the importance of obtaining the views of others, especially the NCO chain of command, during any decision-making process. While I was comfortable making judgments regarding the judicial proceedings in this case I found that doing so based upon my own sense of fairness and impartiality was a lonely and onerous task.

To achieve a favorable outcome for their client, the defense team, led by Mr. Charles Gittins, adopted a strategy for intimidating the Army through negative publicity. In his initial foray, Mr. Gittins tried to demonstrate that I was racially prejudiced because I was White and Sergeant Major McKinney was Black. This strategy fell apart before it could begin when Gittins discovered that the MDW staff judge advocate, the garrison commander who preferred charges against SMA McKinney, my officer aide-de-camp, my enlisted aide, and my driver were all African

American. And they were all selected by me long before February 5, 1997, when the allegations against SMA McKinney first came to my attention.

Colonel Robert Jarvis, the Article 32 investigating officer, heard eight weeks of testimony from 57 witnesses before making a final recommendation. After carefully reviewing the Article 32 witness statements and associated evidence, I concluded in September 1997 that the case should go to a general court-martial. When I decided to retain the MDW court-martial panel I had selected prior to the allegations against SMA McKinney becoming public, the defense team dropped their long-planned strategy to discredit the members of the court-martial panel as prejudicial to the case.

The last element of the defense team strategy was a motion based upon unlawful command influence in the panel representation. The defense team held that there was a disproportionate number of senior officers (two colonels, three lieutenant colonels, and one major) on the panel and three of the seven officers were women.[14] But there were also six enlisted soldiers with a date of rank senior to SMA McKinney on the panel. The military judge dismissed the motion and ruled that the defense did not make a case on the grounds of improper panel selection. After a trial lasting the better part of one year, McKinney was found guilty of obstruction of justice. On the following Monday, he was sentenced to reduction to the grade of master sergeant and given a reprimand. Shortly afterward, he retired from the Army.

After the results of the Senior Review Panel on Sexual Harassment were made public, General Reimer asked me if the MDW Consideration of Others Program was mature enough to go Army-wide. I told him our program with instructors facilitating small-group discussions in two-hour sessions every 90 days had received very positive feedback and was ready for Army-wide implementation. In a message to General Officers, Subject: "Building a Values Based Army—The Consideration of Others Program," General Reimer said:

> I want to bring your attention to an important commander's tool for building and maintaining a values-based Army—The Consideration of Others Program. The objective of the program is to foster and strengthen the command climate, reinforcing the importance of trust, teamwork, dignity, and respect for others. Modeled on an innovative program developed at the United States Military Academy at West Point, the Consideration of Others Program reinforces Army values through the discussion of human relations issues in small interactive groups which focus on basic leadership and respect principles. The heart of the Consideration of Others Program is the small group sessions. Well organized meetings in small groups are the ideal for discussing, learning, and soliciting feedback within the command.[15]

Major General Thomas J. Plewes, the chief, Army Reserve, introduced Consideration of Others in *U.S. Army Reserve Command Pamphlet 600-4* by saying:

> The Consideration of Others must become a vital and active program in your respective command as a mechanism for promoting and strengthening a climate of dignity and respect for others. For Consideration of Others to be effective, command emphasis is essential. For that reason, your attention and personal involvement in this program is necessary and expected.

> The inculcation of Consideration of Others as a core value in the US Army Reserve is centered on a comprehensive and dynamic process which involves all personnel, military and civilian, assigned throughout the command.[16]

In the fall of 1997, the 12th Aviation Battalion commander notified me of an aviation safety of flight message indicating that Blackhawk helicopters would not be able to fly passengers until a modification was applied to each aircraft. Yet flight crews could continue to operate the aircraft for training purposes. I gave the commander a confused cocker spaniel look as I found it difficult to ascertain why it was safe for the crew to fly in Blackhawks but not passengers. He told me the crew would be able to take immediate action if a mechanical failure occurred in flight. After I grounded all Blackhawk helicopters in the MDW fleet, I received a call from General William D. Crouch, the vice chief of staff, whose flight was cancelled that day. After hearing my rationale, he called the commanding general of the U.S. Army Aviation Center and grounded all Blackhawks Army-wide.

In March 1998, Mr. Jack Metzler, the superintendent at ANC, told me about a Defense Department working group that was examining whether the remains of the Vietnam unknown buried at the Tomb of the Unknown Soldier should be disinterred for DNA testing. First Lieutenant Michael J. Blassie was shot down in his A-37 aircraft over An Loc, Vietnam near the Cambodian border on May 11, 1972. Six months later, a South Vietnamese Army patrol located the crash site and the remains of the pilot, including flight suit remnants, ID card, and a wallet containing a photograph of Blassie's family. The remains were turned over to Army Mortuary Affairs in Saigon and transported to the Army Central Identification Laboratory in Hawaii. Unfortunately, the ID card and wallet were lost in transit. With nothing but bone fragments for identification, the anthropologist team classified the case as unknown and stored the remains under a file labeled "X-26." However, when evidence was provided to the Blassie family that the Vietnam unknown was probably Lieutenant Blassie, Secretary of Defense William Cohen announced that the Vietnam remains would be disinterred and DNA tested.[17]

The Vietnam unknown remains were interred at the Tomb of the Unknown Soldier site with the understanding they would be buried forever. The casket was sealed inside a metal container, enclosed in reinforced concrete, and placed under the marble walkway. Fortunately, the same crew who had performed the interment was available and they were confident the casket could be retrieved. The disinterment ceremony at the tomb was scheduled for May 14, 1998. To prevent premature publicity, we tasked the Fort Myer Military Police with sealing off the area around the tomb during the night of 13/14 May. The disinterment operation began shortly after dark. Once the removal of the marble had been accomplished, the work crew began the difficult process of cutting through the concrete and steel reinforcing bars using saws, steel cutters, hammers, and pickaxes. Because Mr. Charles L. Cragin, the assistant secretary of defense for reserve affairs, and I had been designated as official witnesses, we decided to wait inside the amphitheater behind the tomb until the remains were uncovered. About midnight, Jack Metzler walked in and told us they were having trouble getting to the casket. Since the disinterment ceremony was scheduled to commence in just 10 hours, we walked out to assess the situation. All I could see was a mound of concrete chunks next to the tomb monument. Off to the side was a seasoned member of the crew, who suggested they place a cable from the 20-ton crane through the eyeholes in the corners of the concrete block and jerk hard enough to reveal the seams around the casket. We breathed a sigh of relief when a few hard tugs by the crane revealed the seams. The workers then knew exactly where to use their concrete saws to get through to the casket in an expeditious manner.

Secretary of Defense William S. Cohen presided at the ceremony, which came to closure when the casket was carried off the tomb grounds by a U.S. Armed Forces honor guard to a waiting hearse. The remains were escorted by military police to the U.S. Armed Forces Institute of Pathology. We witnessed the casket inventory conducted by the forensic anthropologist team and departed prior to the mitochondrial DNA testing. The results confirmed that the remains were those of Lieutenant Blassie. He was buried with full military honors in Jefferson National Cemetery, Missouri on July 11, 1998, in the same cemetery as his father.[18] Since DNA testing precludes having any more "unknowns," the slab over the crypt that held the remains of the Vietnam unknown was replaced with a cover dedicated to a full accounting of missing in action servicemembers (MIAs) and inscribed with the words, "Honoring and Keeping Faith with America's Servicemen, 1958–1975."

After a luncheon honoring the Arlington Ladies at the Fort Myer Officer's Club, General Reimer asked me if I would be up for another assignment. I told him I would do whatever he wanted me to do. He asked, "How about Fifth Army?" I told him I would love it.

On May 25, 1998, I escorted President Clinton for Memorial Day activities at ANC—the culmination of three years of attending events with him. After my welcome and introduction of the president, he recognized distinguished guests in the amphitheater audience including Secretary of the Army Togo West, Congressman Ike Skelton, and chairman of the joint chiefs of staff, General Hugh Shelton. Next, he said:

> I would like to begin this Memorial Day service in a somewhat unusual fashion but, I think, an entirely appropriate one. Major General Foley, who just spoke, the commander of the Military District of Washington, is about to move on to higher responsibilities. He is, I believe, now the only person still serving in uniform to have won the Medal of Honor, which he won for repeatedly risking his life for his comrades in Vietnam, and I thank him for his service.[19]

I was beyond surprised at this announcement by the president, but I stood up momentarily to acknowledge his kind words and the standing ovation by the audience.

Since receiving the Medal of Honor at the White House ceremony from President Johnson on May 1, 1968, I have been asked to make remarks at a variety of events, including graduation exercises, Memorial Day and Veterans Day ceremonies, and officer and NCO professional development sessions. Although it has consumed time to prepare remarks and travel to different cities and installations to speak to a variety of audiences, it has been gratifying to pass on my thoughts on leadership to others in the same manner that I listened to speakers as I was coming up through the ranks. Although I appreciate the accolades and gratitude from people about me receiving the Medal of Honor, the award truly represents the magnificent soldiers who were standing tall with me as we assaulted heavily entrenched North Vietnamese Army forces on November 5, 1966.

I have been asked if the Medal of Honor helped me advance throughout my career. When U.S. Army centralized selection boards meet to consider a soldier's qualifications for schools, commands, and promotion, awards and decorations are certainly considered. My philosophy has been straightforward—I paid little attention to where my officers went to college or what awards they have received in the past. Instead, I have focused on what they could do today, tomorrow, and the next day in leading their soldiers and enhancing unit readiness. I am convinced that my superiors have, for the most part, exercised a similar outlook. On the other hand, there have been incidents in the past where Medal of Honor recipients expected special treatment. On one occasion, I received a phone call from the Fort Benning garrison commander requesting my advice about a newly arrived Medal of Honor recipient who complained that he was not being saluted as he wore his award around post and wanted to know when his welcome parade would be scheduled. I took very little time to straighten this soldier out. I see no evidence of such expectations from today's recipients, but I have witnessed disdain from a few leaders with preconceived notions about the self-aggrandizing nature of Medal of Honor recipients. For example, one time a general officer and senior rater of my officer efficiency report said to me, "The blue ribbon you wear is an albatross around your neck." I am convinced that I have earned respect from others not due to past awards but because of who I am and the leadership attributes I possess that can help accomplish the mission and make a difference in leading soldiers.

Major General Robert R. Ivany was named my successor at MDW. The change of command took place on Wednesday, July 15, 1998, at the Fort McNair Parade Field. After a ceremony in the Pentagon on August 5, during which General Reimer promoted me to lieutenant general, Julie and I departed for Texas with our dog, Cassie, and stayed one night with Mark in Columbus, Mississippi to pick up our cat and second car. We arrived about noon on August 10 at 6 Staff Post Road, Fort Sam Houston, where we met Staff Sergeant Carl Lewis, my new enlisted aide.

## CHAPTER 24

# Commanding General, Fifth Army

Fort Sam Houston in San Antonio, Texas was established in the post-Civil War days when westward expansion had a profound impact on the growth of our nation. A quartermaster depot called the Quadrangle was built for the Department of Texas to store supplies for U.S. Army frontier posts.[1] It was a square building covering 8.5 acres, with high walls made of limestone from a San Antonio rock quarry. Constructed in 1878 and designed like a fort, the Quadrangle featured a 90-foot-high combination water and watch tower.[2] On September 1, 1990, the post of San Antonio was formally designated Fort Sam Houston. In March 1916, Brigadier General John J. Pershing's force of 7,000 troops departed on a punitive expedition against Pancho Villa's Mexican forces. They were supported from the Quadrangle with a daily resupply of 60,000 pounds of rations, 230,000 pounds of forage, and 120,000 pounds of fuel. During World War I, General Pershing and his staff occupied the Quadrangle in preparing for the American Expeditionary Force deployment to Europe.[3]

Between the world wars, all supplies were moved to a new warehouse complex while the Quadrangle was renovated to accommodate various unit headquarters. On September 8, 1939, one week after Hitler's invasion of Poland, President Roosevelt issued an emergency proclamation directing expansion of the active Army and National Guard. Fourth Army headquarters was activated at the Quadrangle to organize deploying field army headquarters and shipped almost half of all serving divisions overseas during World War II. This support to unit deployments was continued during the Korean and Vietnam wars. In 1971, Fifth Army headquarters was established in the Quadrangle with the mission of training and deploying Army Reserve and Army National Guard units in 13 states from Texas to Minnesota.[4]

On August 12, 1998, I took command of Fifth Army in a ceremony hosted by General David A. Bramlett, the commanding general of Forces Command.

The Fifth Army commanding general's mission was to:

- Coordinate training, mobilization, and deployment of 1,558 Army National Guard and Army Reserve units with 235,136 officers, non-commissioned officers, and soldiers in states west of the Mississippi River.

- Command Headquarters Fifth Army, the 11 Readiness Groups, the Army National Guard Advisor Force in 21 states, three Regional Training Brigades, 52 Training Detachments, two Exercise Divisions, and three Field Training Groups comprised of 2,532 military and civilian personnel.
- Manage $40 million in Army National Guard and Army Reserve operations and maintenance appropriations.
- Serve as Department of Defense Executive Agent for planning operations involving military support to civil authorities.
- Manage the Fifth Army Civilian Aide to the Secretary of the Army program.
- Serve as Department of Defense Senior Military Representative for military-to-military contact with Mexico.[5]

My principal mission was the evaluation and deployment of U.S. Army Reserve and Army National Guard units to combatant commands around the world. We had a comprehensive certification process, which I delegated to my deputy commanding generals, Major General Warren Edwards and Major General Jim Jackson. They both did a terrific job conducting personnel, training, and logistical assessments of each reserve component unit deploying to an overseas location. In March 2000, the Texas Army National Guard's 49th Armored Division headquarters assumed command of Multinational Division-North and Task Force Eagle located in Bosnia and Herzegovina. Preparation for the deployment was led by Lieutenant General Leon J. LaPorte, commanding general, III Corps, supported by Fifth Army readiness and training groups. The deployment, conducted by Major General Robert L. Halvorson, commander of the 49th Armored Division, consisted of 700 military personnel.

On Saturday, September 5, I flew to Milwaukee, Wisconsin to attend the National Guard Association of the United States (NGAUS) Annual Meeting. I thought this would be a great opportunity to meet Army National Guard (ARNG) leaders and listen to their concerns. On Monday, the keynote speaker, Wisconsin governor Tommy Thompson, made several disparaging and divisive remarks about the active component. He ridiculed the leadership in Washington for their lack of funding support to the ARNG. What was equally disturbing was the thundering applause he received from ARNG senior leaders in the audience. Governor Thompson and the NGAUS speechwriters missed a golden opportunity to reinforce the vision for America's Army that General Reimer as Army chief of staff had promulgated three years earlier. It was a process for achieving total Army integration and maximizing the contributions of the ARNG, the Army Reserve, and the Active Component. It was called "One Team, One Fight, One Future." The key principles were: 1. Readiness is non-negotiable; 2. The Reserve Components are our strongest link to the American people; 3. Since Reserve Components forces constitute 54 percent of America's Army, any operation must be a total Army effort; 4. Total Army leadership is essential; 5. New organizational designs that integrate Active, Army National Guard, and Reserve units will enhance Total Army readiness.[6]

Governor Thompson could have announced that in the six years from 1990 to 1995 the Army had invested an unprecedented $21 billion in modernizing Reserve Component forces.[7] He could have mentioned that in the decade between the collapse of the Berlin Wall, from 1989 to 1998, the Army National Guard had its total strength reduced by only 19.6 percent as compared to active component strength, which was reduced by 37.5 percent.[8]

I left the conference concerned that the Army National Guard manifested unwarranted disdain for the active component and made a commitment to change this mindset in the Fifth Army area of operations. Unfortunately, the agenda for our general officer's conference had been established prior to my arrival and was scheduled for the day after the NGAUS conference. It took place in an auditorium where staff members gave long presentations using PowerPoint slides. There was little time for general officer discussion and no time set aside for social events. At the end of the conference, I held an impromptu after-action review with the general officers to look at ways to make our sessions more meaningful.

From that day forward, we held three conferences annually in downtown San Antonio with no more than 15 attendees—the two Fifth Army deputy commanding generals and a mix of Army National Guard and Army Reserve general officers. The agenda included issues the attendees desired to discuss, including component integration, training, synchronization, and full-time support. Spouses were invited for a separate program with lunch along the San Antonio River Walk, and Julie and I hosted a reception for the generals and their spouses at Quarters 6. The results were precisely what I hoped for. We solved problems, enhanced general officer camaraderie, created greater cognizance of active component, Army National Guard, and Army Reserve issues, and strengthened cross-component cohesion.

As the Department of Defense senior military representative for military-to-military contact with Mexico, my first official duty was to represent the U.S. Army chief of staff at the 151st anniversary of the independence of Mexico from Spain. Julie and I flew to Mexico City with protocol staff, my aide-de-camp, and an interpreter. Our first event was a formal gift presentation to the secretary of defense, General Enrique Cervantes Aguirre and Mrs. Aguirre on behalf of General and Mrs. Reimer. We were part of a contingent that included general officers from neighboring Latin American countries. The itinerary was filled with meetings, receptions, and ceremonies designed to promote the history and capabilities of the Mexican Armed Forces.

The essence of my impressions are included in the following excerpt from an email that I sent to General Reimer on Friday, September 18:

> Julie and I returned from attending the El Grito Independence Day celebration in Mexico City on Wednesday evening. We enjoyed the hospitality, generosity and friendship expressed by our hosts in the Mexican armed forces. Each day was filled with ceremonies and social events to include a trip to Acapulco. I was extremely impressed with the precision and discipline of both the cadets at the opening ceremonies at Heroico Colegio Militar as well as the soldiers participating in the Independence Day parade in Mexico City. In talking to unit commanders,

I sensed an operational tempo issue as they focused on their responsibilities for public security, drug eradication and disaster relief. One infantry colonel battalion commander in the Acapulco region described the average tempo as a cycle of 45 days deployed and 15 days rest and retraining.[9]

In March 2000, we reciprocated by inviting a contingent of eight Mexican general officers and their wives to San Antonio for visits to historical sites and a briefing on the Fifth Army mission, followed by a tour of West Point hosted by the superintendent, Lieutenant General Daniel W. Christman. We also had a tour of the New York Stock Exchange hosted by the chairman and CEO, Richard A. Grasso, and made a final stop at the Pentagon in Washington, D.C., to visit with the secretary of the Army, the Honorable Louis Caldera.

During the period June 17–20, 1999, I hosted a Civilian Aide to the Secretary of the Army (CASA) Conference at Fort Chaffee, Arkansas. CASAs have provided an invaluable service to soldiers, their families, and the U.S. Army by providing advice to the secretary of the Army and by informing the American people about Army policies and programs. Mr. Rich Lamanche wrote an article on April 28, 2009, for the U.S. Army website in which he stated:

> The classic example of a civilian aide was Mr. Louis Stumberg, a San Antonio resident and CASA emeritus for the western US, who has spent more than 30 years battling for military issues in San Antonio and throughout Texas. Chairman of the greater San Antonio Chamber of Commerce, member of the Texas Parks and Wildlife commission, president of the Boy Scouts of San Antonio and a member of the Rotary Club are just a few examples of his community service spanning more than six decades. For close to 15 years Stumberg worked with civic leaders and Congress to build the Brooke Army Medical Center in San Antonio. In April of 1996, the 450-bed-state-of-the-art medical center, along with its famed burn center, opened its doors for Soldiers and family members.[10]

Louis also provided extraordinary support to recruiting in the San Antonio area. He encouraged civilian leaders, including Mayor Peak, U.S. Congressman Gonzalez, university presidents, school board presidents, and superintendents of schools to provide recruiter access to high schools and to authorize Armed Services Vocational Aptitude Testing on campus.

One weekend, Louis asked me to go deer hunting on his property in south Texas. Since I had never been deer hunting, I first went to a pond at the ranch to practice shooting with Louis's son. The only rifle available had a stock too short for my long arms but it would have to do. Early the next morning, Louis and I occupied a deer blind overlooking a grassy plain with clumps of low west Texas mesquite and oak trees. We watched several deer walk through the area and each time I whispered, "Now, Louis?" Invariably, he would shake his head, indicating they were too small. Just as the sun rose above the trees, I saw a magnificent buck about to cross a trail. When he stopped and turned his head in our direction, I was reminded of the Hartford Life Insurance logo. I turned to Louis who said, "Shoot, shoot." I took a few more seconds to get the stock properly seated into my shoulder. Just as he said, "What's wrong," I fired. The buck leaped across the road and disappeared into the bushes. I thought I might have missed but Louis went to check and returned smiling, "You just shot your first deer." The deer had made one final jump and collapsed on the other side of the road. We loaded it on his son's Suburban and headed for San Antonio with the other three hunters. On the way back, Louis took great delight in relating the details of how long it took me to shoot. I said, "Louis, what would you have done if I missed?" He replied, "I would have called the chairman of the joint chiefs of staff and told him we have an Army commander here who can't shoot straight."

In 1987, the Army established a Battle Command Training Program (BCTP) for evaluating all active component and National Guard division commanders and their staff on battlefield decision-making. The BCTP is a computer simulation exercise conducted in tactically deployed command posts. The battle is fought in real time with simulation models for battalion commanders to conduct planning and make decisions using enemy and friendly force dispositions. It is a valued learning experience made special by the advice and counsel of senior mentors—normally retired three- or four-star generals. In November 1999, I attended a meeting for a BCTP conducted with the 35th Infantry Division (ID) of the Kansas Army National Guard. I was acting as corps commander with Lieutenant General (Retired) Dave Grange as the senior mentor. At the meeting, we received a briefing from the 35th ID commanding general, brigade and battalion commanders, and their staff. The battle scenario took place in the eastern corridor of South Korea. Since I had been assigned to Korea twice, I had a good appreciation of the terrain. After listening to the division scheme of maneuver, complete with arrows on a large map indicating armor and mechanized units attacking over mountain pinnacles, I stopped the briefing. When I asked how many in the room had ever been assigned to Korea, none of the officers or NCOs raised their hands.

I called General Tom Schwartz, commander in chief of American forces in Korea, and asked him if he would support a visit from the leadership of the 35th Infantry Division to conduct a reconnaissance of selected terrain, including the Demilitarized Zone (DMZ) in South Korea. General Schwartz provided us with HMMWVs (Humvees), drivers, and access to Republic of Korea units. Air travel, food, and lodging was funded by Fifth Army. The visit began with a detailed intelligence and operations briefing in Seoul from Lieutenant General Dan Petrosky, Eighth Army commanding general. At the Republic of Korea Fifth Corps Headquarters, we received a briefing from Lieutenant General Lee Sang Hee on how he envisioned the defense, delay, and counter-offensive phases in his corps' sector. At the DMZ, we received another briefing from the Republic of Korea 3rd Division commanding general, Major General Lee Song Kyu. We had an opportunity to walk the trenches, tunnel systems, and concrete bunkers in the Korean 3rd Infantry Division sector. The 35th Division commander and his staff spent the final day revising their plans by adopting a more realistic approach to warfighting in Korea. The terrain walk proved to be an invaluable experience, which the leadership of the 35th Infantry Division put to good use in the BCTP conducted at the end of July.

During our time in San Antonio, Julie and I hosted receptions and band concerts for the community at the gazebo across the street from our quarters. We enjoyed attending parades and special events during the annual San Antonio Fiesta, which began in 1891 to honor the heroes of the Alamo and the battle of San Jacinto, and now celebrates San Antonio's many rich and diverse cultures. Many of our family members and friends enjoyed the Riverwalk, the annual Stock Show and Rodeo, as well as college football at the Alamo Bowl. Peter Holt, the majority owner of the San Antonio Spurs and a former Army sergeant who served in Vietnam, gave us his center court tickets on several occasions to watch NBA basketball games. And I was delighted to meet David Robinson, U.S. Naval Academy graduate, NBA All-Star, and Hall of Fame member.

Cassie, our Labrador Retriever, had five puppies, who we enjoyed immensely before they went to their new homes. The pick of the litter was Bruiser, our favorite, who Julie held closely in her arms on the day the new owners came. We initially felt bad about Green Man, the runt of the litter who had an imperfection on his left ear. However, a family from Monterrey, Mexico, fell in love with him and came to pick him up in their private Learjet. As he departed for Mexico, we said, "Now there goes a lucky dog."

We developed a special friendship with Richard M. (Tres) Kleberg III and his wife Olive Anne. A former Navy aircraft carrier pilot, Tres was a fifth-generation Texan and managing partner of SFD Enterprises, a private family investment firm. He served on the board of trustees at Trinity University, the advisory board for The Children's Hospital of San Antonio, and the Chancellor's Advisory Council of the University of Texas. He was also chairman of the Board for the San Antonio Stock Show and Rodeo, as well as Civilian Aide to the Secretary of the Army.[11] Tres was a direct descendant of the family who owned the King Ranch, which encompassed 825,000 acres—almost 1,300 square miles, larger than the state of Rhode Island. The King Ranch was founded in 1853 by Captain Richard King, who purchased this creek-fed oasis in the wild horse desert of south Texas. In 1881, Captain King hired a bright young lawyer named Robert Justus Kleberg to represent him in his business dealings. Robert later married Alice Gertrudis King, Captain King's daughter.[12]

Tres invited Julie and me along with my chief of staff, Colonel Ken Knight, and his wife, Brenda, to spend a weekend at the King Ranch—137 miles south of San Antonio. We stayed at a two-story, 27-room, 37,000 square foot mansion that featured white stucco walls, a red tile roof, arched windows, and a courtyard with three stained-glass windows that are 20 feet high. Over 100 years old, the main house accommodated many celebrity guests, including Will Rogers, the King of Morocco,

King Peter of Romania, and Lord and Lady Halifax from England. Edna Ferber also enjoyed a lengthy stay while she was conducting research for the writing of *Giant*.[13]

What a treat it was to drive through miles of ranch property and view thousands of russet-colored King Ranch-bred Santa Gertrudis cattle. We traveled more than 50 miles on the first day, going from pasture to pasture observing the management of large herds. We stopped at the King Ranch colony, built exclusively for the ranch employees and their families who were of Mexican descent. The village comprised homes, churches, a school through 8th grade, commissary, and sports fields. Children in grades 9 through 12 attended Kingsville High School and were encouraged to further their education with scholarships and grants provided by the King Ranch.

On Friday, May 19, 2000, I hosted the annual Armed Forces Day celebration at Fifth Army headquarters. This patriotic program honored soldiers, sailors, airmen, and Marines stationed in San Antonio. The program was scheduled to begin on the grounds of the Quadrangle at 5:00 p.m. Since San Antonio has thundershowers in the early evening at that time of the year, my chief of staff, Colonel Ken Knight, recommended that we move the ceremony inside. I remember telling Ken that the rain wasn't going to come precisely at 5:00 p.m. At his insistence, I finally agreed to begin the ceremony outside but have the reception inside, which turned out to be a game saver. At 5:00 p.m., I introduced Mayor Peak, who spoke for about five minutes under sunny skies. I was the next speaker and as I turned to face the audience, I saw a huge black cloud moving toward the Quadrangle. I said, "I am looking at a fairly large black cloud headed our way so I would ask everyone to slowly move from your seats to the entrance for the upstairs hallway behind you and we will continue the program inside." Just as we gathered inside, the rain came down in buckets. The hallways had large glass windows overlooking where we had been seated. The mayor added a little levity by yelling out, "Good call, General." In an abbreviated program, I introduced the servicemembers we were honoring, presented their certificates, thanked everyone for coming, and told them to enjoy the reception. Thirty minutes later, we lost power, along with lights and air conditioning. The lesson learned was to listen closely to a chief of staff who was born and raised in south Texas.

As I looked back on 37 years in an Army uniform, culminating with our time in San Antonio, Julie and I decided it was time to retire. Although we had no definite plans, spending more time with children and grandchildren as well as exploring new opportunities for employment were at the top of the list.

On August 11, 2000, Fifth Army Headquarters held a farewell luncheon for us at the Fort Sam Houston Officer's Club—hosted by Ken and Brenda Knight. Two days later, General John W. Hendrix, commanding general of Forces Command, presided over a ceremony in the Quadrangle during which I relinquished command of Fifth Army to Lieutenant General Freddy McFarren and retired from active duty.

I had made a commitment to take at least six months to reflect on future employment and decide where we might live. This self-imposed obligation went by the wayside when I accepted an offer to become the president of Marion Military Institute (MMI), a junior college in Marion, Alabama. Since the board of trustees wanted us to be on campus for the start of the academic year, Julie and I drove to Marion, arriving five days after my retirement.

## CHAPTER 25

# Epilogue

MMI had an excellent early commissioning program, enabling students to become U.S. Army second lieutenants after two years of college. In addition, they had a unique one-year service academy preparatory program that enhanced a student's chances for obtaining an appointment to West Point, the Naval Academy, or the Air Force Academy. After four years, Julie and I moved on, with wonderful memories of the fine young men and women who made our time at MMI so rewarding.

In 1995, I was appointed a member of the Senior Army Decorations Board (SADB) comprised of lieutenant generals and the sergeant major of the Army. The SADB reviews recommendations for the Medal of Honor, the Distinguished Service Cross, and the Presidential Unit Citation. In plenary session, the SADB members vote on each case and submit their recommendations to the secretary of the Army for approval. When I retired in 2000, I was asked to continue serving as advisor and non-voting member. "The primary responsibility of the Medal of Honor Advisor is to provide counsel and support to the SADB and the Secretary of the Army on issues relating to execution of Army policy concerning the Medal of Honor."[1] In the 25 years of reviewing over 300 cases, I came away convinced that the SADB provides an invaluable service to the U.S. Army. It ensures an independent and impartial evaluation based upon the merits of each case, guarantees fair and equitable treatment, and certifies the integrity of the review process.

Since 2008, the U.S. Military Academy has presented the Lieutenant General Robert F. Foley award to a graduating cadet who displayed extraordinary character in overcoming difficult circumstances as a cadet. This annual award is sponsored by the Brian LaViolette Scholarship of Honor Foundation. Brian hoped someday to attend West Point but drowned while swimming near his home in Green Bay, Wisconsin. Brian's father created the Scholarship of Honor in 2003 as a tribute to his son. The award is presented annually to deserving students in the United States, Poland, the Czech Republic, and South Africa. Cadet David M. Kennedy was the first recipient of the Robert F. Foley award. While at West Point, he acquired a neurological disease and had to take a one-year leave of absence. He returned for his senior year and graduated with the Class of 2008. The 2018 award was presented to Cadet Megan A. Bryn, who had three knee surgeries from injuries received as a member of the Army women's volleyball team. Megan graduated late but was selected to receive the Schwarzman Scholarship, a one-year master's program at Tsinghua University in Beijing.

For 11 years, I was director of Army Emergency Relief (AER)—a non-profit 501(c)3 that provided interest-free loans and grants to help families with short-term cash flow problems such as initial rent deposit, medical bills, and auto repairs. My focus was on policy, programs, and strategic planning but I took great pleasure in making exceptions to policy on various cases. For instance, the AER officer at Fort Drum called one day on behalf of a young soldier whose family was experiencing anguish due to their five-year-old son's autism. The behavioral health specialist recommended the family purchase a therapy dog at a cost of $7,000. This was beyond the $2,500 approval authority for AER officers, but the request was approved because it fit perfectly with the AER mission. With the dog's arrival, the boy had a new friend, the dog had a new home, and the family experienced an immediate reduction in stress.

During a presentation that I made to a Command and General Staff College class at Fort Leavenworth, an Air Force major in the audience asked me about obtaining AER assistance for a 12-year-old boy being treated for brain cancer. The boy's mother had been on active duty in the Army for 14 years but resigned to care for her son. Her husband had been on active duty in the Army for 10 years and was a department of the Army civilian on the garrison staff. They had used up their savings and were faced with $4,000 in medical bills. Because the parents were not on active duty or in a retired status, they were not eligible for AER assistance. But a total of 24 years of service between the husband and wife was good enough for me. I made an on-the-spot exception to policy directing that a check be prepared by the Fort Leavenworth AER Section for a $4,000 grant and directed that any additional medical expenses be covered by grants until the young man had recovered. A year later, the boy's cancer was in remission.

During retirement, I continued to speak about leadership and character development to a variety of audiences, including the brigade and battalion pre-command courses at Fort Leavenworth, Kansas, the Sergeants Major Academy at Fort Bliss, and officer and NCO leaders in the 1-27 and 2-27 Wolfhound battalions at Schofield Barracks, Hawaii. In addition, I spoke to senior and junior high school students, including Pueblo West High School in Colorado, Archbishop Neale School in La Plata, Maryland, and Middleton High School Junior ROTC in Tampa, Florida.

After graduation from the Air Force Academy, our oldest son, Mark, was on active duty for 12 years flying the MC130H Combat Talon II with U.S. Air Force Special Operations Command. The MC130H is specially equipped with aerial refueling, infrared-guided missile protection, and terrain avoidance radar capable of operating as low as 250 feet. Mark flew 114 combat sorties during the wars in Iraq and Afghanistan and piloted one of the first aircraft to make a combat assault into Baghdad International Airport during the Iraq War. He flew at night using night vision goggles carrying Army Rangers, Navy Seals, and other Special Operations personnel. His mother once asked me why he didn't have a steady girlfriend. I told her that he hadn't been out of the cockpit long enough to meet anyone. All that changed in the spring of 2005 when he was stationed at Hurlburt Field, Florida. He met Miss Kristen Kline and they were married on December 9, 2006. They live in Santa Rosa Beach, Florida and have a son, Connor, who is a terrific athlete and student. Kristen has a Bachelor of Arts in Psychology from Louisiana State University and Mark has a Master of Arts in Global Security Studies from John Hopkins University. He is a consultant and lobbyist for unmanned aerial systems in the global aerospace sector. He is also a lieutenant colonel in the Air Force Reserve and president of CK Technologies and Foley Strategies.

After graduating from West Point, our son, Dave, became an Airborne Ranger Infantry officer, was a company commander in the 25th Infantry Division, and a company commander in the Old Guard. While he was visiting a friend on Capitol Hill in January 2001, he was introduced to Miss K. Claire White from Brent, Alabama. Dave was much taken with her and several weeks later, Julie was told by Jenny Holmes, the wife of the AER Board of Trustees chairman, that a young lady had asked her if Dave had a steady girlfriend. When Julie passed this news to Dave, he followed up with an email to Claire, attaching an invitation to his company change of command at Schofield Barracks, Hawaii and added, "If you happen to be in the area, please stop by." Claire hopped on a flight to Honolulu and secretly went to the ceremony. She asked one of the officers in the receiving line to hand her business card to Dave. She had written on the back, "Happened to be in the area and thought I'd stop by." Dave and Claire were married in the Marion Military Institute chapel on August 10, 2002. He served two tours of duty in Afghanistan, was a cavalry squadron commander at Fort Hood, a Stryker brigade commander at Joint Base Lewis McChord, and executive officer for General Joseph L. Votel, commanding general of U.S. Central Command. He served as deputy commander (operations) for the 101st Airborne Division at Fort Campbell and was promoted to brigadier general on July 1, 2020. Claire attended MMI, has a Bachelor of Business Administration degree from Samford University and a Juris Doctor from the University of Alabama School of Law. Dave has a master's degree in General Administration from Central Michigan University and a master's degree in Strategic Studies from the U.S. Army War College. They have three sons, Price, Harper, and Gates, who are stellar athletes and excellent students. Dave was deputy director of operations, U.S. Central Command in Tampa, Florida until May of 2022, when he became the deputy commanding general for education at the Combined Arms

Center; Army University provost; and deputy commandant, Command and General Staff College.

Sara attended Pepperdine University in Malibu, California on a full scholarship, graduating in 1999 with a Bachelor of Arts in Political Science. Following his mother's prompting, brother Dave invited Sara to an Old Guard party at Fort Myer in January 2002, where she met Captain William D. Edwards II, West Point Class of 1998. In 2003, William asked me for Sara's hand in marriage. Julie and I liked him from the first day we met him but were curious about his future since he didn't plan to make the Army a career. He told me he hoped to get an MBA and someday become the chief financial officer of a major corporation. We were impressed three weeks later when he was accepted to Harvard Business School. Sara and William were married on July 17, 2004, at the Cathedral of St. Matthew the Apostle in Washington, D.C. and moved to Cambridge, where they both received master's degrees from Harvard—William in Business Administration and Sara in Museum Studies. They have one son, Will, an outstanding student and talented young man who plays guitar, chess, and tennis, and is a member of the rowing team. Our only granddaughter, Caroline, has many interests but loves piano and dance. William is the chief financial officer of a private equity backed company in the building materials sector.

On September 27, 2019, Julie and I celebrated our 50th wedding anniversary with our children, their spouses, and our six grandchildren. The 50 years of fond memories would not have been possible without Julie, the family matriarch, who instilled love and happiness in the Foley family every step of the way.

# Afterword

I thought it might be useful to summarize my thoughts on leadership lessons learned not previously mentioned and will begin with professional reading. I found that the Army school system from the Infantry Officer Basic Course and the Armor Officer Advanced Course to the Command and General Staff College and Naval War College did not adequately cover insights essential to the leadership challenges I faced throughout my career. The technical, tactical, systems integration and strategic dimensions were present in most core curricula but missing were leadership classes on organizational values, diversity, and moral-ethical reasoning. An essential understanding of leadership principles, tenets, and ethics can only be gained through a lifetime of professional reading. Books such as *The Killer Angels* by Michael Shaara, *Once an Eagle* by Anton Myrer, *In the Hands of Providence* by Alice Rains Trulock, *Extraordinary Circumstances* by Cynthia Cooper, and *The Heights of Courage* by Avigdor Kahalani are compelling accounts of leadership styles, organizational trust, cohesion, treating others with respect and dignity, personal courage and perseverance. As a brigade commander in Germany, I established a program for battalion commanders to travel to European battlefields with their officers to learn about the history of warfare during World War II. Lieutenant Colonel Jack Mountcastle, commander of 3rd Battalion, 63rd Armor, set the standard when he organized a trip to Normandy, France tasking his lieutenants to research and brief various phases of the Allied landings during Operation *Overlord* and lead discussions on the tactical, logistical, and enemy situations while they walked the actual terrain. This was not only an historical and informative exercise, but it also served to greatly enhance camaraderie—an ingredient that pays big dividends in combat. A similar professional development trip was put together by Lieutenant Colonel Mike Jackson, the battalion commander of 1st Battalion, 64th Armor, in a trip to Anzio, Italy.

Asking for advice is an easy but much-overlooked technique for gaining knowledge during the decision-making process. From the time I was a new second lieutenant in Hawaii I asked non-commissioned officers for their opinions. Why not? I had less than a year of active-duty time while platoon sergeants had been caring for soldiers for 10–15 years. When I thought I had a bright idea as a company, battalion, or brigade commander, I asked my first sergeant or command sergeant major what they thought. I didn't have to follow their advice, but there were many days when

I threw away that bright idea, saving myself from making a big mistake. I also found that taking a problem to my immediate boss had many advantages. Superiors had more experience, were pleased to assist, and many times offered to clear obstacles and provide resources to achieve a solution. I leveraged this practice at every level of command and encouraged my subordinate leaders to seek advice in solving problems by asking them, "Would you like to know what I think?"

Maintaining the highest standards of integrity is an essential element for success in any organization. I remember the senior mentor for a division tactical exercise asking us hypothetically, "If you lost all the values in your unit but could bring back just one, which would it be?" After a general discussion, he said, "I would bring back trust because with trust you can regain all the rest." Frequently, leaders are faced with moral-ethical dilemmas—some big and some small—but all requiring leaders to do the right thing. When I was a mechanized infantry battalion commander in Germany in 1975–76, I had the distinct pleasure of having outstanding company commanders. One of the supply requirements imposed on them was a monthly 10 percent inventory of government property. The company commanders had to sign their names, indicating they had conducted a physical inventory of each item on the list provided by division headquarters. However, it was impossible to physically account for some items. For example, when a soldier went home on leave, they placed their property, including U.S. government sheets and blankets, in a duffel bag with a padlock in a secure storage area, preventing such items from being inventoried. I created a huge uproar at division headquarters when I directed that my company commanders only sign for items that they could physically account for. I held fast to my position until the bureaucrats finally accepted our modified reports. The lesson learned is leaders ought not sign statements containing incorrect information simply for the sake of convenience even if pressured to do so by higher headquarters. Our signature is our word of honor.

Setting the example is a basic leadership principle. Leaders should lead from the front in good times and bad, in cold, rainy weather, during physical training, during memorial services for the fallen, conducting amphibious operations in a BFV, evaluating tank crew proficiency on the firing range, demanding the highest standards of training safety, recognizing units and individuals who have performed in an exceptional manner, disciplining those who are complicit in wrongful conduct, caring for soldiers and family members who have suffered personal tragedies, conducting after-action reviews to ensure procedures are developed to overcome deficiencies in mission execution, encouraging soldiers to take time off for family and friends, scheduling periodic reviews of strategic planning, including vision, values, goals, objectives, and metrics, establishing times and venues to be a good listener, preventing acceptance of business as usual, facilitating change, taking every opportunity to instill organizational trust, cohesion, and camaraderie, looking for opportunities to re-engineer the process of doing business, intensively managing selection of the right person for the right position, continually asking, "What do you recommend?", and being positive, proactive, and upbeat every day.

Innovation, ingenuity, re-engineering, and visionary thinking can produce major and, at times, surprising organizational benefits. In planning for an exercise at the Hohenfels major training area when I was the commander of 2nd Brigade in Kitzingen, Germany, I received a briefing from my operations officer on his proposal for the scheme of maneuver for each day beginning at 6:00 a.m. and terminating at 6:00 p.m. Our BFVs and Abrams Main Battle Tanks had thermal night sights (equipment that allows soldiers to see targets that radiate heat, such as enemy tank engines)—providing us with a distinct advantage over the enemy in fighting at night. Accordingly, I felt we should train at night. I told him to redo the plan with maneuvers beginning at 6:00 p.m. and ending at 6:00 a.m. During the day, soldiers would rest, perform vehicle maintenance, and conduct troop-leading procedures (mission planning and issuing of orders). We learned that movement at night is slower, units get lost, identifying friend from foe is difficult, maneuvering on icy, muddy roads is treacherous, and fighting while wearing Mission Oriented Protective Posture (MOPP) suits with gas mask and gloves is cumbersome. I found a leader's failure to enforce sleep discipline to be the most alarming lesson learned. After 24 hours of little or no sleep, leaders found it difficult to concentrate and were slow in making decisions; after 48 hours, they felt sick and became irritable; after 72 hours, they became tentative—they lost their courage, the most important attribute a leader must have in combat. When I ascertained that the main culprit preventing company commanders from getting enough sleep was the battalion commanders constantly calling for a situation report, I put a stop to it by directing that company commanders would not be awakened to receive a call unless it was an emergency. In later exercises, company executive officers or first sergeants responded to calls if the commander was asleep, without any loss of combat effectiveness.

Misuse of government property is an issue that can befall leaders. It is sometimes convenient to arrange a personal activity while participating in an official function. There have been cases where leaders invite themselves to speak at a place close to their home or other location they wish to visit and take government transportation or use government funds to travel commercially. It is a question of judgment. "What is motivating you to take the trip?" If the answer is to satisfy a personal agenda at any point on the itinerary, even if government business is being conducted, cancel your trip. When I was the commanding general of Fifth Army in San Antonio, I had to fly frequently to fulfill my responsibilities in states west of the Mississippi River. Because flying in Army aircraft is so expensive, military personnel normally flew commercial air. Over two years in command, I used commercial transportation on all but two occasions. Once I used fixed-wing Army aircraft to fly to a base in Mexico that did not have nearby access to commercial airports. The second time, I used an Army aircraft to fly from San Antonio to Camp Grafton near Devils Lake,

North Dakota. When I was getting ready to retire and depart Fort Sam Houston in the summer of 2000, the Office of the Department of Defense Inspector General (DOD IG) requested information on all the trips I had taken using military aircraft during my command tour. When I told them I had used Army fixed-wing aircraft twice in two years, I received a call from a colonel in the Office of the DOD IG who told me that all other retiring general officers indicated the number of trips they had taken using military aircraft were in double figures and asked if I wished to change my response. I told him that my response stands. I never heard from him again.

It is imperative that leaders periodically communicate their organizational values, policies, and standards verbally and in writing. This is especially true when leaders first take the reins of an organization, and they must be tough enough to follow through with rigid enforcement. All leaders must be good speakers to ensure effective guidance to subordinate organizations as well as presenting the purpose and mission of the U.S. Armed Forces in enhancing community relationships. It's a good idea to take public affairs training, especially concerning responses to news media queries. It is intimidating to have a reporter with live TV coverage unexpectedly place a microphone in your face and begin asking questions ranging from installation environmental pollution to national military strategy. Saying, "No comment" does a disservice to you and the U.S. Army. The news media will edit the film and soundbites to create their story so you might as well tell the Army side in the hope that there will be a balanced report.

When I received an invitation to speak, I habitually asked questions about the venue, purpose, and audience so I could adapt my remarks appropriately. While serving as president of Marion Military Institute, I was invited to speak at Pizitz Middle School in Birmingham on Veterans Day. The program coordinator explained that there would be several veterans going to different classrooms to speak with students. Having done this before, I was comfortable with the format. I arrived at the school 30 minutes early and was met by a young woman who was a mother of one of the students. She told me she was excited to be escorting the keynote speaker for the program. I told her she must have me confused with someone else as I was there to participate in student classroom discussions. She then showed me a copy of the program, which clearly indicated that I was the keynote speaker for the assembly occurring before the students went to their classrooms. She told me the audience would comprise about 2,000 people consisting of the student body, staff and faculty, parents, veterans, and community leaders, including the mayor of Birmingham. We promptly found an office, where I made notes in the margins of the program. Fortunately, I had been preparing remarks several weeks earlier for the college students at MMI, many of whom would be commissioned in the Army the following year. The lesson learned is to always have a "hip-pocket speech," even when the event planner tells you there will be no requirement to speak.

One of the most damaging organizational issues is the existence of low morale caused by incivility, harassment, discrimination, prejudice, insensitivity, offensive behavior, verbal abuse, or thoughtlessness. This can impact on productivity and the synergy defined as "the whole is greater than the sum of its parts," by Stephen Covey in his book, *The 7 Habits of Highly Effective People*. The highest accolade for unit commanders is being told they have an excellent command climate. I have been able to determine the status of morale in an organization in the first few minutes of walking into a unit headquarters simply by gauging soldier reaction to my presence. On a few occasions, I have been totally ignored while in uniform walking down the headquarters hallway. On the other hand, I have entered a unit headquarters, heard the command "Battalion attention" with every soldier standing at attention until I say, "Carry on." The senior soldier then escorted me to the commander's office. It's all a matter of unit pride. But a positive command environment doesn't just magically show up. It is created by the people in the organization reaching out to their fellow soldiers or employees who pursue excellence in all that they do every day. In the final analysis, leaders instill the values, courtesies, consideration, and standards that establish and sustain a positive command climate. Soldiers and civilian employees take pride in the camaraderie of a professional, upbeat organization in which they can feel good about who they are, where they are, and where they are headed in life.

# Acknowledgements

The love and support I received from my father, mother, and older brother, Bill, established the foundation for who I am today. I am also grateful to Coach Mel Wenner at Belmont High School and Coach George Hunter at West Point who taught me basketball skills, good sportsmanship, toughness, and the will to win.

As new cadets, we heard the phrase, "Everything we are and ever hope to be, we owe to our Beast Barracks Squad Leader." This rang true with my squad leader, Bob Strauss, who diligently instilled in me the discipline and perseverance necessary to take on the challenges of being a West Point cadet.

I am thankful to General Edward C. "Shy" Meyer for his support when he was commanding general of the 3rd Infantry Division in Germany and again when he was president of Army Emergency Relief. He was an inspirational leader who will always be revered as an Army chief of staff who possessed great strength of character and a willingness to take on and resolve tough issues facing the U.S. Army.

I have known General Dennis J. Reimer since we were cadets in company A1 at West Point. He leads by example, is admired by all who know him, and is precisely the type of leader we seek to emulate. He served two tours of duty in Vietnam, was deputy chief of staff for operations during Operation *Desert Shield/Desert Storm*, Army vice chief of staff, and commanding general, Forces Command. As the 33rd Army chief of staff, he established strong institutional values and created an environment where soldiers could be all they could be. He and his wife, Mary Jo, are a charismatic and beloved team.

General Eric J. Shinseki and I served together when I was a brigade commander and he was the cavalry squadron commander as well as when he was 3rd Infantry Division operations officer. We were also members together on the Senior Army Decorations Board. His contributions to our nation include service as Army chief of staff and secretary of Veteran's Affairs. In addition, his wife, Patty, was a long-term member with me on the Army Emergency Relief Board of Managers.

I worked for General Robert W. RisCassi when he was the Army deputy chief of staff for operations in the Pentagon and later when he was the commander in chief of United Nations Command in Korea. He also served as Army vice chief of staff. He is an outstanding leader and strategist with an in-depth knowledge of international military and geopolitical issues.

General Thomas A. Schwartz and I served together in Korea, and I worked directly for him in Fifth Army when he was the commanding general of Forces Command. He is a decisive and innovative commander who has tremendous strength of character and profound leadership skills.

I was fortunate to have the advice of the Honorable Malcolm J. (Mack) Howard, USMA Class of 1962, with whom I served in Hawaii, Vietnam, and Fort Belvoir, Virginia. His patriotism and dedication continued as U.S. District Judge in North Carolina. Julie and I have greatly enjoyed our friendship with Mack and his talented wife, Eloise, with whom we spent many memorable gatherings.

My West Point classmate and good friend Lieutenant General Thomas P. Carney and I were roommates at the Armored Officer Advanced Course and served together on the Army Emergency Relief Board of Managers. He was always at the forefront tackling the Army's tough issues in key assignments from division commander to the Army deputy chief of staff of personnel during Operation *Desert Shield/Desert Storm*.

Lieutenant General Horace G. (Pete) Taylor and I first worked together as action officers and branch chiefs in the Pentagon. He is a great friend, an exceptional leader, and a forthright commander who sets the example, has courage of his convictions, and has made a magnificent contribution to the U.S. Army and our nation.

I have known Lieutenant General David H. Huntoon since I was his Company Tactical Officer when he was a plebe at West Point. He is one of the finest leaders I have ever known. While serving as director of the Army staff, he provided me with sound recommendations on complex issues. He was the longest-serving commandant at the Army War College and later was superintendent of the U.S. Military Academy, where he and his wife, Margaret, were a magnificent command team. Today, Dave is a recognized authority in strategic thinking and leadership development.

I could not have asked for a more supportive leader than Lieutenant General Howard D. Graves when he was the superintendent at West Point, and I was his commandant of cadets. His ability to articulate the needs of the Military Academy ensured that infrastructure funding and cadet programs were accomplished in a first-class manner. He and his wife, Gracie, were held in the highest esteem.

Lieutenant General Theodore G. Stroup was the Army deputy chief of staff for personnel before he retired and became the vice president for education with the Association of the United States Army. It was his encouragement that led me to become Director of Army Emergency relief—a position I held for 11 years.

When I was the chief of staff of 7th Infantry Division, Lieutenant General Keith Kellogg was my G3 (Division Operations Officer). His outstanding advice, strength of character and exceptional skills as a crisis manager made him a distinct asset to the U.S. Army and served him well during his time as national security advisor to President Trump and Vice President Pence.

Vice Admiral James B. Stockdale, president of the Naval War College, and Joseph G. Brennan, professor emeritus from Columbia University, developed and taught

Foundations of Moral Obligation—a course that had a profound influence on my education in moral-ethical reasoning. Admiral Stockdale not only emphasized the compelling nature of institutional virtues but his status as a prisoner of war for eight years in Hanoi and a recipient of the Congressional Medal of Honor lent considerable credibility to his emphasis on values-based decision-making.

Major General Fred A. Gorden is an outstanding leader and a dedicated professional soldier. We served together several times, were next-door neighbors at various installations, and longtime friends with him and his wife, Marcia. His advice about my future goals truly made a much-appreciated difference in my Army career.

Brigadier General Gerald E. Galloway Jr., PhD, former dean of the academic board at West Point, gave me outstanding advice when I was commandant of cadets. A brilliant educator and an internationally recognized expert on water resource management, he has made extraordinary contributions to the U.S. Army and our nation.

Brigadier General John W. (Jack) Mountcastle, PhD, was a tank battalion commander in my brigade in Germany, where he and his wife, Susan, were an outstanding command team. As a noted military historian and former chief of military history for the U.S. Army, he provided me with excellent historical perspective and recommendations on sources concerning events leading up to America's involvement in the Vietnam War.

Brigadier General Harold W. (Hal) Nelson, PhD, West Point classmate and former U.S. Army chief of military history was enormously helpful in reviewing my approach to how and why America became involved in the Vietnam War.

Colonel Tom Karr, my West Point classmate, was my artillery battalion commander when I was a brigade commander in Germany and my director of military instruction at West Point when I was commandant of cadets. He set the example with his brilliant performance of duty, sound judgment, and ability to accomplish missions in a first-class manner. Julie and I greatly value the friendship we have with Tom and his wife, Judy.

In preparing to write this memoir, I sought the wise counsel of Jack Jacobs, Colonel, U.S. Army, Retired—an author, teacher, businessman, and fellow Medal of Honor recipient who has a sharp mind and a wonderful sense of humor. He was most helpful in passing on the lessons he learned from writing his excellent book, *If Not Now, When?*

I have been blessed with the mentorship of many outstanding non-commissioned officers, beginning with Sergeant First Class James Burroughs, my first platoon sergeant, who emphasized the significance of caring for soldiers, and First Sergeant Edward L. Fulghum, who taught me about setting the example in combat. I am indebted to SMA Julius W. Gates, SMA Robert E. Hall, SMA Kenneth O. Preston, SMA Raymond F. Chandler, and SMA Daniel A. Dailey for their advice and support.

I am most thankful to my West Point classmate Frank Lennon—writer, publisher, and president of the Rhode Island Aviation Hall of Fame. He reviewed key portions of my manuscript and made excellent suggestions as to style, purpose, audience, and the active voice.

My classmate, Allen Clark, wrote *Wounded Soldier, Healing Warrior*—an inspirational account of his life after losing both legs in a mortar attack while a young captain in Vietnam. I am most grateful for his encouragement and advice on the process of writing and publishing a memoir.

I will always value the close friendship of my 1963 classmates, including John Ahern, Gordon Arbogast, Norm Beatty, Pete Bentson, Rodger Bivens, Bill Boice, Don Byrne, Mike Bowers, Larry Capps, Frank Cardile, Gene Cargile, Ed Carns, Bill Clark, Johnny Counts, John Ellerson, Rudy Ehrenberg, Rich Entlich, Curt Esposito, Bob Farris, Tim Grogan, Bob Handcox, Jerry Harrison, Bruce Heim, Dick Higgins, Marty Ischinger, Dave Jackson, Dick James, Mike Keaveney, Bill Kelly, Dewey LaFond, Al LaVoy, Frank Lennon, Duane Myers, Jack O'Donnell, John Oliver, George Pappas, Jerry Pogorzelski, Steve Popielarski, Buz Rolfe, Lou Sill, Bill Sipos, Paul Stanley, Pat Stevens, Steve Silvasy, Gary Sausser, Rob Vanneman, Mike Vopatek, Jay Westermeier, Sandy White, Bill Whitehead, Danny Willson, Dick Wilson, and Bob Zelley.

Lieutenant Colonel David A. Jones, seminar leader at the U.S. Military Academy Simon Center for the Professional Military Ethic, has been tremendously helpful in responding to my requests for information on cadet professional ethics education. In addition, he has also done a magnificent job as coordinator for the Brian LaViolette Scholarship Foundation annual award to a deserving first class cadet.

Great credit goes to Harry Lane, PhD, my good friend, author, university professor, and Belmont High School classmate, who has received international recognition teaching executive global business courses at Northeastern University. His encouragement and advice have been enormously helpful and very much appreciated.

Although I have been in touch with many soldiers from Alpha Company, 2nd Battalion, 27th Infantry, who were with me during Operation *Attleboro* on November 5, 1966, Chuck Dean and Tom Donovan stand out. They were not only by my side on the battlefield but continue to inspire patriotism within the ranks of Wolfhound veterans. Chuck is past president of the Wolfhound Historical Association and Tom has been treasurer for many years.

Joseph Craig, Director of the Association of the United States Army book program, provided me with excellent advice and assistance through his editorial review of my manuscript in which he focused on substance, style, structure, and formulating a compelling book proposal.

I have nothing but the highest praise for Casemate Publisher Ruth Sheppard and her outstanding team of editors, including Eduard Cojocaru, Declan Ingram, and Felicity Goldsack. The trust and confidence I have in their advice, brilliant insights, and editorial assistance has made all the difference in realizing a smooth and effective publishing process.

Finally, I can't say enough about Julie's unique ability to recognize issues of substance and relevance in reviewing my memoir. Her years of experience correcting papers as a schoolteacher came in handy checking my grammar and word usage. She has also been the ultimate source of family events through her photo albums and personal diaries. In addition, she has spent countless hours patiently listening to my out-loud readings and offering excellent suggestions for improvement.

# Wreath Laying Ceremonies Conducted by Major General Robert F. Foley at the Tomb of the Unknowns (1995–98), prepared by Phil Fowler

1. Minister of Defense Poland (September 6, 1995).
2. President of Albania (September 12, 1995).
3. Vice Chief of the United Kingdom Defense Staff (September 22, 1995).
4. President of Romania (September 25, 1995).
5. President of Mexico (October 10, 1995).
6. Minister of Defense Albania (October 17, 1995).
7. Minister for Defense Sweden (October 17, 1995).
8. Chief of the General Staff of the Polish Armed Forces (October 20, 1995).
9. Secretary of the Army Brazil (October 20, 1995).
10. King of Norway (October 30, 1995).
11. Inspector of the German Army (November 1, 1995).
12. Veterans Day, President Clinton (November 11, 1995).
13. Chief of the Defense Staff Canada (December 7, 1995).
14. Prime Minister of Israel (December 11, 1995).
15. Minister of National Defense Portugal (January 17, 1996).
16. Chief of the South African Army (February 22, 1996).
17. Army Chief of Staff Turkey (March 11, 1996).
18. President of Haiti (March 20, 1996).
19. Chief of the South African National Defense Force (March 21, 1996).
20. President of Italy (April 2, 1996).
21. Chief of the General Staff Czech Republic (April 5, 1996).
22. Prime Minister of Greece (April 8, 1996).
23. Minister of Defense Finland (April 9, 1996).
24. Chief of Japan Ground Self Defense Force (April 9, 1996).
25. Chief of the Defense Staff France (April 11, 1996).
26. President of Greece (May 8, 1996).
27. Deputy Minister of National Defense Greece (May 16, 1996).

28. Minister of National Defense Lithuania (May 22, 1996).
29. Chief of the Defense Forces Malaysia (May 23, 1996).
30. Memorial Day, President Clinton (May 27, 1996).
31. Chief of Staff, Joint Staff Japan Self Defense Force (June 6, 1996).
32. President of Ireland (June 14, 1996).
33. Minister of Defense Austria (June 18, 1996).
34. President of Cyprus (June 18, 1996).
35. President of Uzbekistan (June 26, 1996).
36. President of Poland (July 8, 1996).
37. Prime Minister of Israel (July 9, 1996).
38. Chief of the Defense Staff Italy (July 11, 1996).
39. Minister of Defense Belarus (July 17, 1996).
40. Chief of the General Staff, Romanian Armed Forces (July 19, 1996).
41. Minister of National Defense Poland (August 29, 1996).
42. Minister of Defense Spain (September 3, 1996).
43. Chief of the Army Staff India (September 12, 1996).
44. Minister of Defense Japan (September 18, 1996).
45. Chief of the Hellenic National Defense General Staff (October 1, 1996).
46. Minister of Defense Italy (October 2, 1996).
47. Ambassador of Israel to the United States (October 10, 1996).
48. Minister of Defense Israel (October 15, 1996).
49. Minister of Defense Switzerland (October 16, 1996).
50. Army Chief of Staff Brazil (October 31, 1996).
51. Veterans Day, President Clinton (November 11, 1996).
52. Chief of Defense Staff Netherlands (November 14, 1996).
53. Russian Ambassador to the United States (November 24, 1996).
54. Chief of the Defense Staff United Kingdom (January 23, 1997).
55. Chief of Staff of the French Army (January 28, 1997).
56. Chief of the Armed Forces of the Argentine Republic (February 7, 1997).
57. Chief of Defense of the Republic of Finland (February 24, 1997).
58. Chief of the Joint Staff of the Armed Forces Brazil (February 27, 1997).
59. Prime Minister of Portugal (March 3, 1997).
60. Prime Minister of Canada (March 9, 1997).
61. Inspector General of the Bundeswehr Germany (March 18, 1997).
62. Prime Minister of Japan (March 26, 1997).
63. Minister of National Defense Romania (March 29, 1997).
64. Minister of Defense of Ukraine (May 2, 1997).
65. Chief of the General Staff Ukrainian Armed Forces (May 8, 1997).
66. Commander in Chief of the Royal Thai Army (May 22, 1997).
67. Chief of Defense Belgium (May 23, 1997).
68. Memorial Day, President Clinton (May 26, 1997).

69. Chief of Defense Norway (May 29, 1997).
70. President of Macedonia (June 17, 1997).
71. Chief of Staff of the Republic of Korea Army (June 18, 1997).
72. Prime Minister of Romania (June 20, 1997).
73. President of Marshall Islands (June 23, 1997).
74. Minister for National Defense Greece (June 24, 1997).
75. Prime Minister of Australia (June 28, 1997).
76. Chief of the General Staff Austria (July 3, 1997).
77. Chief of Defence Force Australia (July 17, 1997).
78. President of Azerbaijan (July 31, 1997).
79. Army Chief of Staff Brazil (August 17, 1997).
80. Minister of Defense Japan (August 24, 1997).
81. Prime Minister of Albania (August 30, 1997).
82. President of Israel (October 7, 1997).
83. Minister of National Defence Lithuania (October 15, 1997).
84. Chief of Staff German Army (October 27, 1997).
85. Veterans Day, President Clinton (November 11, 1997).
86. President of Kazakhstan (November 19, 1997).
87. President of the Republic of Mali (November 21, 1997).
88. Prime Minister of Turkey (December 18, 1997).
89. Minister of Defense Moldova (January 29, 1998)
90. Army Chief of Staff Romania (February 4, 1998).
91. Chief of the General Staff, Egyptian Armed Forces (February 19, 1998).
92. Minister of Defense Uzbekistan (February 25, 1998).
93. Chief of Staff, Joint Staff Japan Self-Defense Force (March 5, 1998).
94. Chief of Army Staff Pakistan (March 11, 1998).
95. Prime Minister of Thailand (March 12, 1998).
96. Minister of Defense Georgia (March 24, 1998).
97. Minister of National Defense Romania (March 30, 1998).
98. Minister of Defense Macedonia (April 6, 1998).
99. Chief of the General Staff Slovakia (April 8, 1998).
100. Chief Ground Self-Defense Force Japan (April 9, 1998).
101. Vice Chief of the Defense Force Australia (May 5, 1998).
102. Vice President of Macedonia (April 6, 1998).
103. Army Chief of Staff Poland (May 13, 1998).
104. Memorial Day, President Clinton (May 25, 1998).
105. Chief of General Staff of the Armed Forces of Hungary (June 9, 1998).
106. President of the Republic of Korea (June 9, 1998).
107. Prime Minister of Macedonia (June 30, 1998).
108. Minister of Defense Greece (July 7, 1998).
109. President of Romania (July 14, 1998).

# Official Summary of Assignments

*United States Army*
**Lieutenant General ROBERT F. FOLEY**
**Retired September 2000**

<u>SOURCE OF COMMISSIONED SERVICE</u>    USMA

<u>MILITARY SCHOOLS ATTENDED</u>
Infantry Officer Basic Course
Armor Officer Advanced Course
United States Army Command and General Staff College
United States Naval War College

<u>EDUCATIONAL DEGREES</u>
United States Military Academy—BS Degree—No Major
Fairleigh Dickinson University—MBA Degree—Business Administration

<u>FOREIGN LANGUAGE(S)</u>    None recorded

| <u>PROMOTIONS</u> | <u>DATES OF APPOINTMENT</u> |
|---|---|
| 2LT | 5 Jun 63 |
| 1LT | 5 Dec 64 |
| CPT | 23 Jun 66 |
| MAJ | 19 Jan 70 |
| LTC | 2 Jul 76 |
| COL | 1 Oct 82 |
| BG | 1 Aug 91 |
| MG | 1 Jun 94 |
| LTG | 12 Aug 98 |

## MAJOR DUTY ASSIGNMENTS

| FROM | TO | ASSIGNMENT |
|------|-----|------------|
| Dec 63 | Dec 65 | Platoon Leader later Executive Officer, B Company, 2d Battalion, 27th Infantry Regiment, 25th Infantry Division, United States Army, Hawaii |
| Dec 65 | Aug 66 | Heavy Mortar Platoon Leader, later S-3 (Operations) Air, 2d Battalion, 27th Infantry Regiment, 25th Infantry Division, United States Army, Vietnam |
| Aug 66 | Dec 66 | Commander, A Company, 2d Battalion, 27th Infantry Regiment, 25th Infantry Division, United States Army, Vietnam |
| Dec 66 | Aug 68 | Infantry Instructor, Combat Arms Branch, Combined Arms Division, Department of Engineering and Military Science, United States Army Engineer School, Fort Belvoir, Virginia |
| Sep 68 | Jun 69 | Student, Armor Officer Advanced course, United States Army Armor School, Fort Knox, Kentucky |
| Jun 69 | Jun 72 | Tactical Officer, later S-1 (Personnel) and S-4 (Supply), 3d Regiment, United States Military Academy, West Point, New York |
| Jun 72 | Jun 73 | Aide-de-Camp to the Commanding General, I Corps (Republic of Korea/United States) Group, Eighth United States Army, United States Army, Korea |
| Aug 73 | Jun 74 | Student, United States Army Command and General Staff College, Fort Leavenworth, Kansas |
| Jun 74 | Jan 76 | S-3 (Operations), 1st Battalion, 7th Infantry Brigade, 3d Infantry Division, United States Army Europe and Seventh Army, Germany |
| Jan 76 | Oct 76 | Chief of Staff (REFORGER), 2d Brigade, 3d Infantry Division, United States Army Europe and Seventh Army, Germany |
| Oct 76 | Jun 78 | Commander, 1st Battalion, 4th Infantry Regiment, 3d Infantry Division, United States Army Europe and Seventh Army, Germany |
| Aug 78 | Jun 79 | Student, College of Naval Warfare, United States Naval War College, Newport, Rhode Island |
| Jul 79 | Oct 81 | Staff Officer, Regional Operations Division, later Chief, Europe/Africa/Middle East/Southwest Asia Branch, Office of the Deputy Chief of Staff for Operations and Plans, Washington, DC |

| FROM | TO | ASSIGNMENT |
|------|-----|-----------|
| Oct 81 | Apr 83 | Chief, Assignment Branch later Acting Chief and then Chief, Colonels Division, United States Army Military Personnel Center, Alexandria, Virginia |
| Jun 83 | Sep 83 | Project Manager, Bradley Fighting Vehicle System, with duty in Vilseck, Germany as Chief, Bradley Fielding Team, United States Army Europe and Seventh Army, Germany |
| Sep 83 | Nov 85 | Commander, 2d Brigade, 3d Infantry Division, United States Army Europe, Germany |
| Nov 85 | Nov 86 | Chief, Operations and Contingency Plans Division, Office of the Deputy Chief of Staff for Operations and Plans, United States Army, Washington, DC |
| Jan 87 | Aug 89 | Chief of Staff, 7th Infantry Division, Fort Ord, California |
| Sep 89 | Jun 90 | Deputy for Reserve Forces and Mobilization, Office of the Assistant Secretary of the Army (Manpower and Reserve Affairs), United States Army, Washington, DC |
| Jun 90 | Feb 91 | Executive Officer, Office of the Assistant Secretary of the Army (Manpower and Reserve Affairs), Washington, DC |
| Feb 91 | Jun 92 | Assistant Division Commander, 2d Infantry Division, Eighth United States Army, Korea |
| Jun 92 | Jun 94 | Commandant of Cadets, United States Military Academy, West Point, New York |
| Jun 94 | Jul 95 | Deputy Commanding General, Second United States Army, Fort Gillem, Georgia |
| Aug 95 | Aug 98 | Commanding General, United States Army Military District of Washington, Fort Lesley J. McNair, Washington, DC |
| Aug 98 | Aug 00 | Commanding General, Fifth United States Army, Fort Sam Houston, Texas |

## SUMMARY OF JOINT ASSIGNMENTS

| Assignment | Dates | Grade |
|-----------|-------|-------|
| * Chief, Europe/Africa/Middle East/ South West Asia Branch, Office of the Deputy Chief of Staff for Operations and Plans, Washington, DC | May 80–Oct 81 | Lieutenant Colonel |

| Assignment | Dates | Grade |
|---|---|---|
| * Division Chief, Operations and Contingency Plans Division, Office of the Deputy Chief of Staff for Operations and Plans, United States Army, Washington, DC | Nov 85–Nov 86 | Colonel |

* Joint Equivalent

US DECORATIONS AND BADGES
Medal of Honor
Distinguished Service Medal (with Oak Leaf Cluster)
Defense Superior Service Medal
Legion of Merit (with 5 Oak Leaf Clusters)
Bronze Star Medal
Purple Heart
Meritorious Service Medal (with 4 Oak Leaf Clusters)
Combat Infantryman Badge
Parachutist Badge
Ranger Tab
Army Staff Identification Badge

As of 22 December 2016

# Citations

## Official Medal of Honor citation

The President of the United States of America, authorized by Act of Congress, March 3, 1863, has awarded in the name of The Congress the Medal of Honor to

### CAPTAIN ROBERT F. FOLEY, INFANTRY
### UNITED STATES ARMY

for conspicuous gallantry and intrepidity in action at the risk of his life above and beyond the call of duty:

On 5 November 1966, while serving as Commander, Company A, 2nd Battalion, 27th Infantry, near Quan Dau Tieng, Republic of Vietnam, Captain Foley's company was ordered to extricate another company of the Battalion. Moving through the dense jungle to aid the besieged unit, Company A encountered a strong enemy force occupying well concealed, defensive positions, and the company's leading element quickly sustained several casualties. Captain Foley immediately ran forward to the scene of most intense action to direct the company's efforts. Deploying one platoon on the flank, he led the other two platoons in an attack on the enemy in the face of intense fire. During this action both radio operators accompanying him were wounded. At grave risk to himself he defied the enemy's murderous fire, and helped the wounded operators to a position where they could receive medical care. As he moved forward again one of his machine gun crews was wounded. Seizing the weapon, he charged forward firing the machine gun, shouting orders and rallying his men thus maintaining the momentum of the attack. Under increasingly heavy enemy fire he ordered his assistant to take cover and, alone, Captain Foley continued to advance firing the machine gun until the wounded had been evacuated and the attack in this area could be resumed. When movement on the other flank was halted by the enemy's fanatical defense, Captain Foley moved to personally direct this critical phase of the battle. Leading the renewed effort he was blown off his feet and wounded by an enemy grenade. Despite his painful wounds he refused medical aid and persevered in the forefront of the attack on the enemy redoubt. He led the assault on several enemy gun emplacements and, singlehandedly, destroyed three such positions. His outstanding personal leadership, under intense enemy fire during the fierce battle which lasted for several hours, inspired his men to heroic efforts and was instrumental in the ultimate success of the operation. Captain Foley's magnificent courage, selfless concern for his men and professional skill reflect the utmost credit upon himself and the United States Army.

## 2009 West Point Distinguished Graduate Award

2009 DISTINGUISHED GRADUATE AWARD
LTG (R) ROBERT FRANKLIN FOLEY '63

Throughout his life of service as an Army officer, scholar, and leader, Lieutenant General Robert F. Foley has continuously dedicated himself to the principles of Duty, Honor, and Country.

LTG Foley began his Army career after graduation from West Point in 1963. He advanced quickly through junior officer assignments while honing the skills he learned at West Point. During this phase of his career, he began demonstrating a characteristic of service to others and compassion for the Soldier, themes which would be reinforced throughout his life both in and out of uniform. An early indication of his commitment to these values became most evident when he earned the Medal of Honor in the Vietnam War for conspicuous gallantry on 5 November 1966 while serving as Company Commander of A Company, 2nd Battalion, 27th Infantry, 25th Infantry Division. His professionalism and caring concern for Soldiers are a sterling reflection of the spirit of "Duty, Honor, Country".

When General Sam Walker became Commandant of Cadets in 1969, he specifically asked for then Cpt Foley to be assigned as a Company Tactical Officer for the Corps of Cadets. According to General Walker, Foley stood out as an officer of tremendous courage, not only for his award of the Medal of Honor for actions during the War in Vietnam, but also for the courage of his convictions and character traits that he demonstrated to members of his company and to the Corps at large.

LTG Foley continued to expand his leadership experience during the next phase of his career by holding positions of increased responsibility including Commander, 1st Battalion, 4th Infantry in Aschaffenburg, Germany; Commander, 2nd Brigade, 3rd Infantry Division in Kitzingen, Germany; and Assistant Division Commander, 2nd Infantry Division, Republic of Korea. Between these commands, he continued to contribute to the war fighting capabilities of the Army, serving in various positions in and out of the Pentagon, where he focused his efforts on the readiness of our forces world-wide.

LTG Foley returned to West Point in 1992 as the 63rd Commandant of Cadets. As Commandant, he established a core value "Consideration for Others," now called "Respect," which inspired cadets to be responsible for treating others with respect and dignity. This became an Army-wide program that focused leaders on the kind of trust and cohesion essential to successful mission accomplishment. The program he began at West Point was and remains an integral part of the inculcation of values and cadet leadership development.

In his final assignment on active duty, LTG Foley became Commanding General of Fifth US Army at Fort Sam Houston, Texas. In this assignment, he was responsible for integrated training support and wartime mobilization for Army National Guard and Army Reserve units, as well as disaster relief support to civilian authorities. After completing thirty-seven years of active duty in 2000, he became the President of Marion Military Institute, a junior college in Marion, Alabama. Since 2005, LTG Foley has been Director of Army Emergency Relief, a private, non-profit organization that has provided emergency financial assistance to Soldiers and their families for more than 67 years.

LTG Foley has distinguished himself for nearly fifty years of selfless service to West Point, the US Army, his Soldiers, their families, and the nation. Accordingly, the West Point Association of Graduates takes great pride in presenting the 2009 Distinguished Graduate Award to Lieutenant General Robert F. Foley.

# The Military Order of the World Wars Distinguished Service Award

## MOWW 2010 DISTINGUISHED SERVICE AWARD RECIPIENT
# Lieutenant General Robert F. Foley
### United States Army (Retired)
#### MEDAL OF HONOR 1966

Lieutenant General Robert F. Foley, United States Army (Retired) graduated from the United States Military Academy in 1963. In 2009, the West Point Association of Graduates presented the 2009 Distinguished Graduate Award to Lieutenant General Foley. The remarks from that presentation follow as they are also a good introduction to MOWW's 2010 Distinguished Service Award Recipient.

"Throughout his life of service as an Army officer, scholar, and leader, Lieutenant General Robert F. Foley has continuously dedicated himself to the principles of Duty, Honor, and Country.

LTG Foley began his Army career after graduation from West Point in 1963. He advanced quickly through junior Officer assignments while honing the skills he learned at West Point. During this phase of his career, he began demonstrating a characteristic of service to others and compassion for the Soldier, themes which would be reinforced throughout his life both in and out of uniform. An early indication of his commitment to these values became most evident when he earned the Medal of Honor in the Vietnam War for conspicuous gallantry on November 5, 1966 while serving as Company Commander of A Company, 2nd Battalion, 27th Infantry, 25th Infantry Division. His professionalism and caring concern for Soldiers are a sterling reflection of the spirit of "Duty, Honor, Country."

When General Sam Walker became Commandant of Cadets in 1969, he specifically asked for then-Captain Foley to be assigned as a Company Tactical Officer for the Corps of Cadets. According to General Walker, Foley stood out as an Officer of tremendous courage, not only for his award of the Medal of Honor for actions during the War in Vietnam, but also for the courage of his convictions and character traits that he demonstrated to members of his company and to the Corps at large.

LTG Foley continued to expand his leadership experience during the next phase of his career by holding positions of increased responsibility including Commander, 1st Battalion, 4th Infantry in Aschaffenburg, Germany; Commander, 2nd Brigade, 3rd Infantry Division in Kitzingen, Germany; and Assistant Division Commander, 2nd Infantry Division, Republic of Korea. Between these commands, he continued to contribute to the war fighting capabilities of the Army, serving in various positions in and out of the Pentagon, where he focused his efforts on the readiness of our forces world-wide.

LTG Foley returned to West Point in 1992 as the 63rd Commandant of Cadets. As Commandant, he established a core value "Consideration for Others," now called "Respect," which inspired cadets to be responsible for treating others with respect and dignity. This became an Army-wide program that focused leaders on the kind of trust and cohesion essential to successful mission accomplishment. The program he began at West Point was and remains an integral part of the inculcation of values and cadet leadership development.

In his final assignment on active duty, LTG Foley became Commanding General of Fifth US Army at Fort Sam Houston, Texas. In this assignment, he was responsible for integrated training support and wartime mobilization for Army National Guard and Army Reserve units, as well as disaster relief support to civilian authorities. After completing thirty-seven years of active duty in 2000, he became the President of Marion Military Institute, a junior college in Marion, Alabama. Since 2005, LTG Foley has been Director of Army Emergency Relief, a private, non-profit organization that has provided emergency financial assistance to Soldiers and their families for more than 67 years.

LTG Foley has distinguished himself for nearly fifty years of selfless service to West Point, the US Army, his Soldiers, their families, and the Nation."

General Foley's Awards for peacetime and combat include the Congressional Medal of Honor, two Distinguished Service Medals, Defense Superior Service Medal, six Legions of Merit, five Meritorious Service Medals, the Bronze Star Medal, the Purple Heart, and the Combat Infantryman's Badge. He also wears the Parachutist Badge and the Ranger Tab.

General Foley and his wife, Julie, have two sons and a daughter.

The MOWW is proud and honored to award the Order's highest award, the 2010 Distinguished Service Award to Lieutenant General Foley.

# 2012 Infantry Doughboy Award

## The Doughboy Award

The Doughboy Award is presented annually to recognize an individual for outstanding contributions to the United States Army Infantry. The award is presented on behalf of all Infantrymen past and present. The award is a chrome replica of a helmet worn by American Expeditionary Soldiers during World War I (WWI) and the early days of World War II. The term "Doughboy" originated in Texas where soldiers trained along the Rio Grande in preparation for WWI. The Soldiers became covered in the dusty, white adobe soil and were called "adobes" by mounted troops. Over time this term transitioned to become doughboys. The Doughboy award is the highest honor the Chief of Infantry can bestow on any Infantryman.

2012      Lieutenant General Robert F. Foley
          Command Sergeant Major Tadeusz Gaweda
          The Honorable Les Brownlee

# Endnotes

## Chapter 1

1  Dave Hawkins, "Tension High Tonight for Sell-Out Game". *Belmont Herald*, February 12, 1958.
2  Ernest Dalton, "Foley Nets 44". *Boston Globe*, March 2, 1959.
3  Robert Frost, *Complete Poems of Robert Frost* (New York, NY, Chicago, IL, San Francisco, CA: Holt, Rinehart & Winston, 1916), 131.

## Chapter 2

1  U.S. Corps of Cadets Memorandum of Instruction. "New Cadet Barracks", U.S. Military Academy Library, February 1, 1960.
2  Kendall Banning, *West Point Today* (New York, NY and London: Funk & Wagnalls, 1937), 13.
3  Appendix F to *Training Manual Number 1, New Cadet Training Schedule* (June 11, 1959).
4  U.S. Military Academy, *Behind the Scenes at the Cadet Mess*, Washington Hall pamphlet, 3–4.
5  Superintendent's Lecture to Class of 1963, July 14, 1959.

## Chapter 3

1  Banning, *West Point Today*, 285.
2  Charles W. G. Rich, "Operation Equality, Memorandum for the Superintendent, USMA", March 31, 1950.
3  U.S. Military Academy, "Academic Record of Robert Franklin Foley, Class of 1963, West Point, New York".
4  Director of Cadet Activities, "Bugle Notes" (84th Volume, booklet of information given to new cadets. West Point, 1992), 126.

## Chapter 4

1  U.S. Military Academy, "Academic Record of Robert Franklin Foley".
2  Wikipedia, "LeRoy Ellis", https://en.wikipedia.org/wiki/LeRoy_Ellis.

## Chapter 5

1  Wikipedia, '27th Infantry Regiment (United States)', https://en.wikipedia.org/w/index.php?title=27th _Infantry_Regiment_(United States)&printable=yes.

2    Maura Dolormente, *Historic "Wolfhounds" of Schofield Barracks Mark 50th Year Bringing Japan Orphans to Hawaii*. Honolulu, HI: Peace Bridge, Inc, 2007.

## Chapter 6

1    Ronald H. Spector, *Advice and Support, The Early Years 1941–1960* (Honolulu, HI: University Press of the Pacific, 2005), 5–11.
2    Ibid., 28–32.
3    Dixee R. Bartholomew-Feis, *The OSS and Ho Chi Minh, Unexpected Allies in the War Against Japan* (Lawrence, KS: Kansas University Press, 2006), 2–3.
4    Ibid., 149–154.
5    Ibid., 155.
6    Ibid., 172–173.
7    Ibid., 207–214.
8    Ibid., 302.
9    Ibid., 304.
10   Spector, *Advice and Support*, 78.
11   Ibid., 107.
12   Ibid., 103.
13   Ibid., 115.
14   Ibid., 148.
15   Ibid., 211–219.
16   Ibid., 228–230.
17   Ibid., 254.
18   History.com Editors, "President Eisenhower delivers Cold War 'domino theory' speech". https://www.history.com/this-day-in-history/eisenhower-gives-famous-domino-theory-speech.
19   Graham Allison, *Destined for War* (Boston, MA and New York, NY: Houghton Mifflin Harcourt, 2017), 39.
20   Harry G. Summers Jr., *On Strategy: A Critical Analysis of the Vietnam War* (New York, NY: Random House, 1982), 197.
21   Edwin E. Moïse, *Tonkin Gulf and the Escalation of the Vietnam War* (Chapel Hill, NC and London: University of North Carolina Press, 1996), 2–6.
22   Robert S. McNamara, *In Retrospect: The Tragedy and Lessons of Vietnam* (New York, NY: Vintage Books, 1996), 109.
23   Moïse, *Tonkin Gulf and the Escalation of the Vietnam War*, 73–82.
24   Ibid., 82–86.
25   Ibid., 110–129.
26   San Francisco (UPI), "Pilot found false alarm escalated Vietnam War", *Stars and Stripes*, October 15, 1984, 9.
27   Moïse, *Tonkin Gulf and the Escalation of the Vietnam War*, 207.
28   Ibid., 214.
29   Ibid., 226.
30   Robert S. McNamara, James G. Blight, Robert K. Brigham, Thomas J. Biersteker, and Herbert Schandler, *Argument Without End: In Search of Answers to the Vietnam Tragedy* (New York, NY: Public Affairs, 1999), Preface.
31   Ibid.
32   Ibid., xxii–xxiii.
33   Ibid., 24.

34   Ibid., 167.
35   H. R. McMaster, *Dereliction of Duty: Lyndon Johnson, Robert McNamara, the Joint Chiefs of Staff, and the Lies That Led to Vietnam* (New York, NY: Harper Collins, 1997), 108.
36   Ibid., 62–63.
37   Doris Kearns Goodwin, *Leadership in Turbulent Times* (London: Penguin Random House, 2018), 339.
38   Ibid., 340–341.
39   Ibid., 342.
40   Carl von Clausewitz, *On War* (Princeton, NJ: Princeton University Press, 1976), 75.
41   Ibid., 87–89.
42   Ibid., 193.
43   Donald T. Phillips, *The Founding Fathers on Leadership: Classic Teamwork in Changing Times* (New York, NY: Warner Books, 1997), 116–117.

# Chapter 7

1   YouTube, "25th Infantry Division Arrives in Vietnam", www.youtube.com/watch?V=_Wtj4CqatiA

# Chapter 8

1   Wikipedia, "Central Office for South Vietnam", https://en.wikipedia.org/wiki/Central_Office_for_South_Vietnam.
2   Rod Paschall, "Operation Attleboro – From Calamity to Crushing Victory", https://www.historynet.com/operation-attleboro-from-calamity-to-crushing-victory/?r, 1–7.
3   Ibid.
4   Guy S. Meloy III, "The Battle of Attleboro" 3–5 November 1966, After-Action Report written by Guy S, Meloy III, Major General, U.S. Army Retired, Former Commander, 1st Battalion, 27th Infantry (Wolfhounds) (August 2010), 4–6.
5   Paschall, "Operation Attleboro – From Calamity to Crushing Victory", 13–15.
6   Ibid., 1–7.
7   Meloy, "The Battle of Attleboro", 6.
8   Ibid., 36–41.
9   Ibid.
10   Ibid., 52–64.
11   Ibid., 64.
12   Ibid., 101.
13   Ibid., 100–101.
14   Ibid., 101.
15   Ibid., 105.
16   Ibid., 105–106.
17   Ibid., 127.
18   Ibid., 110.
19   Ibid., 139.
20   Rick Stevens, email, June 24, 2009.
21   Robert Park, email, October 29, 2011.
22   Paschall, "Operation Attleboro – From Calamity to Crushing Victory", 1–7.
23   Meloy, "The Battle of Attleboro", 137.

24 Ibid., 37–40.
25 Charles K. Nulsen Jr., "Operation Attleboro: A flawed battle plan turned a combat training exercise in War Zone C into a bloody battle during the fall of 1966", PTSD Support Services (December 21, 1990). http://www.ptsdsupport.net/operation_attleboro.html.
26 John A. Wickham, Jr., *Guideposts for a Proud and Ready Army* (Washington, D.C.: Department of the Army, 1985), 1.

## Chapter 9

1 Medal of Honor Project 1987, "Above and Beyond the Call of Duty".

## Chapter 11

1 John H. Cushman. "Letter to Major Robert F. Foley, 1st Bn, 27th Inf, 26 February 1975".
1 Foley, Julie T. "Trip to Russia", personal diary (July 12, 1975).
2 William Taubman, *Gorbachev: His Life and Times* (New York, NY: Norton and Company, New York, 2017), 235.
3 Ibid., 239.
4 Ibid., 240.
5 Anne Applebaum, *Red Famine: Stalin's War on Ukraine* (New York, NY: Doubleday, 2017), front flap.

## Chapter 13

1 Wikipedia, "Newport, Rhode Island", https://en.wikipedia.org/wiki/Newport,_Rhode_Island.

## Chapter 14

1 Foley, Robert, "To what extent did Athens and Sparta pursue military strategies consistent with their political objectives during the various phases of the Peloponnesian War?" Foundations of Moral Obligation. Essay response written at Naval War College, August 29, 1978.
2 Ibid.
3 James Bond Stockdale, "The World of Epictetus", *Atlantic Monthly* (1978), 4.
4 Ibid.
5 Ibid., 5.
6 Unit notes, 'On Kant's Foundation on the Metaphysics of Morals', James B. Stockdale and Joseph Brennan. "On Kant's Foundation on the Metaphysics of Morals", Foundations of Moral Obligation Unit Notes accompanying an elective class. Naval War College (1978–79), 3.
7 Ibid., "Mill's Utilitarianism", 1–5.

## Chapter 16

1 Joe Padula, "101st Airborne Remembers Soldiers of Gander Crash" (December 15, 2011). https://www.army.mil/article/70884/101st_airborne_remembers_soldiers_of_gander_crash.

2   Ibid.

3   Dennis Steele, "The Second Longest Day", *Soldier Magazine*, February 1986, 6–12.

4   Ibid.

5   Department of the Army Historical Summary: FY 1986, "Appendix A – Tragedy at Gander, 2", https://history.army.mil/books/DAHSUM/1986/appA.htm.

6   Ibid., 7.


# Chapter 17

1   Wikipedia, "The Hudson River", https://en.wikipedia.org/wiki/Hudson_River.

2   John Grant, James M. Lynch, and Ronald H. Bailey, *West Point: The First 200 Years* (Guilford, CT: The Globe Pequot Press, 2002), 18–27.

3   Director of Cadet Activities, "Bugle Notes", 122–126.

4   The Civil War in the East. "West Point Officers in the Civil War", http://civilwarintheeast.com/west-point-officers-in-the-civil-war/.

5   West Point Association of Graduates, "The Reality is Now: Branch Night for the Class of 2021", https://www.westpointaog.org/west-point-branch-night-class-of-2021.

6   Wikipedia, "List of astronauts educated at US Military Academy", https://en.wikipedia.org/wiki/List_of_astronauts_educated_at_the_United_States_Military_Academy.


# Chapter 18

1   Wikipedia, "René Edward De Russy", https://en.wikipedia.org/wiki/Rene_Edward_De_Russy.

2   Position description, "Commandant of the United States Military Academy".

3   Director of Cadet Activities, "Bugle Notes", 4.

4   Robert F. Foley, "The Com Reports", *Assembly Magazine* (September 1993), 60.

5   Dave R. Palmer, "Superintendent's Letter", *Assembly Magazine*, May 1987.

6   Headquarters, Department of the Army, *Field Manual 25-101: Battle Focused Training* (September 1990), chapter 2, 2.

7   Ibid., 1–10.

8   Robert F. Foley, "The Com Reports", *Assembly Magazine* (November 1992), 67.

9   Joseph E. Dineen, *The Illustrated History of Sports at the US Military Academy* (Norfolk, VA: The Donning Company, 1988), 12.

10  Ibid., 13.

11  Ibid., 19–21.


# Chapter 20

1   Robert F. Foley, "The Com Reports", *Assembly Magazine* (September 1993), 61.

2   Ibid.

3   Ibid.

4   Ibid.

5   Robert F. Foley, "The Com Reports", *Assembly Magazine* (January 1994), 34.

6   Foley, "The Com Reports", *Assembly Magazine* (September 1993), 61.

7   Ibid.

8    Ibid., 62.
9    John Esterbrook, "Companies Well Represented", *Pointer View* (November 1992).
10   Chuck Eisele, 'Malcolm Comes Through in Clutch for Army Win', *Pointer View* (December 11, 1992).

## Chapter 21

1    Director of Cadet Activities, "Bugle Notes", 42–43.
2    *The New York Times*, "Col. Clayton E. Wheat. 88. Chaplain at West Point" (July 13, 1970), https://nyti.ms/1ik9mnd.
3    Director of Cadet Activities, "Bugle Notes", 25.
4    Robert F. Foley, "The Com Reports", *Assembly Magazine* (May 1993), 27.
5    Sherman L. Fleek, USMA Historian, email, July 15, 2020.
6    "Opening Lecture of the Code and System", Loose notes (July 7, 1959).
7    Director of Cadet Activities, "Bugle Notes", 30.
8    Robert F. Foley, "The Com Reports", *Assembly Magazine* (July 1994), 48.
9    Ibid., 4.
10   John A. Wickham, Jr., *Guideposts for a Proud and Ready Army*, 2–4.
11   Headquarters, Department of the Army, *Field Manual 100-1*, "The Profession of Arms" (June 14, 1994), 7–9.
12   'Schofield's Definition of Discipline', Director of Cadet Activities, "Bugle Notes", 237.
13   "Cadet Leadership Development System", *US Military Academy Circular*, 1–101 (July 1994).
14   Robert F. Foley and Denise A. Goudreau, "Consideration of Others", *Military Review* (January–February 1996), 26.
15   Ibid.
16   Ibid., 25.
17   Alice Rains Trulock, *In the Hands of Providence: Joshua L. Chamberlain and the American Civil War* (Chapel Hill, NC and London: University of North Carolina Press, 1992), 26–362.
18   Ibid., 60–64.
19   Ibid.,123–132.
20   Ibid., 132.
21   Ibid., 133–139.
22   Ibid., 147–149.
23   Ibid., 209–227.
24   Ibid., 504.
25   Ibid., 295–296.
26   Ibid., 297–298.
27   Ibid., 303–305.
28   Ibid.
29   Ibid.
30   Ibid., 304–305.
31   Ibid., 305.
32   Ibid., 305–307.
33   Joshua Chamberlain, *Bayonet Forward, My Civil War Reminiscences* (Gettysburg, PA: Stan Clark Military Books, 1994), back cover.
34   Foley and Goudreau, "Consideration of Others", 25.

# Chapter 22

1   Wikipedia, "Tropical Storm Alberto", https://en.wikipedia.org/wiki/Tropical_Storm_ Alberto_(1994).

2   Headquarters, Department of the Army, *Training Circular 25-30: A Leader's Guide to Company Training Meetings* (April 27, 1994), chapter one, 1.

3   Headquarters, Department of the Army, *Field Manual 25-101: Battle Focused Training*, Appendix F (1980) F-1 to F-13.

# Chapter 23

1   Phyllis I. McClellan, *Silent Sentinel on the Potomac: Fort McNair 1791–1991* (Bowie, MD: Heritage Books, 1993), 1–7.

2   Ibid., 10–12.

3   Ibid., 154.

4   Ibid., 157.

5   Ibid., 159.

6   Michael Hammer and James Champy, *Reengineering the Corporation: A Manifestation for Business Revolution* (New York, NY: Harper-Collins Publishers, 1993), 32.

7   Philip Bigler, *In Honored Glory* (Arlington, VA: Vandamere Press, 1987), 61–66.

8   Ibid., 67–73.

9   Phil Fowler, "Wreath Ceremonies During MG Foley's Command", July 1, 1998.

10  Wikipedia, "David Hackworth", https//en.wikipedia.org/wiki/David_Hackworth (April 1, 2018) 1–14.

11  David H. Hackworth, *Hack Note*, David Hackworth blogsite (August 1998).

12  Secretary of the Army Memorandum, "The Secretary of the Army's Senior Review Panel on Sexual Harassment", November 21, 1996.

13  U.S. Army News Release, "Army Secretary Excuses MG Foley from Panel", Army Public Affairs (February 14, 1997).

14  United States v. CSM Gene McKinney, U.S. Army. "Motion to Dismiss Based upon Unlawful Command Influence in the Member Selection Process" (December 24, 1997).

15  Dennis J. Reimer, 'Building a Values Based Army – The Consideration of Others Program', Army chief of staff general officer mailing list email (November 12, 1997).

16  Thomas J. Plewes, "Message from the Chief, Army Reserve", *USARC Pamphlet 600-4*, A-3.

17  Bill Thomas, "Last Soldier buried in Tomb of the Unknowns wasn't unknown", *The Washington Post Magazine* (November 8, 2012).

18  Visible Proofs: Forensic Views of the Body, "Michael Blassie unknown no more" (February 16, 2006), https://www.nim.nih.gov/visibleproofs/galleries/cases/blassie.html.

19  William Clinton, "Remarks at a Memorial Day Ceremony in Arlington, Virginia, May 25, 1998", *Presidential Documents*, Volume 34, Number 22 (June 1, 1998), 959.

# Chapter 24

1   Fort Sam Houston Museum Staff, *The Quadrangle: Hub of Military Activity in Texas*. Fort Sam Houston, TX: Fort Sam Houston Museum, 2007, 3.

2   Ibid., 17.

3   Ibid., 57–58.
4   Ibid., 85–92.
5   Job description, "Commanding General, Fifth United States Army", Fort Sam Houston, Texas, 1–4.
6   Dennis J. Reimer, "One Fight, One Team, One Future", *Total Army Integration* (1998), 1–2.
7   Ibid., 18.
8   Ibid., 8.
9   Robert F. Foley, "El Grito Celebration", email to General Dennis J. Reimer, Army chief of staff (September 18, 1998).
10  Rich Lamance, "CASAs Sustain Army Strong" (April 28, 2009), 1–2, https://www.army.mil/article/20246/casas_sustain_army_strong.
11  Equilar Board Edge, "Richard M. Kleberg, Executive Work History", http://people.equilar.com/bio/richard-kleberg.
12  King Ranch, "King Ranch's Legacy", https://king-ranch.com/about-us/history.
13  Skip Hollandsworth, "The Kings Palace", *Texas Monthly* (February 2016).

# Bibliography

Allison, Graham. *Destined for War*. Boston, MA and New York, NY: Houghton Mifflin Harcourt, 2017.

Appendix F to *Training Manual Number 1, New Cadet Training Schedule*, June 11, 1959.

Applebaum, Anne. *Red Famine: Stalin's War on Ukraine*. New York, NY: Doubleday, 2017.

Army Regulation 1–15. *Civilian Aides to the Secretary of the Army*. January 31, 2017. armypubs.army. mil/.../ARN4402_AR1-15_Web_Final.pdf.

Banning, Kendall. *West Point Today*. New York, NY and London: Funk & Wagnalls, 1937.

Bartholomew-Feis, Dixee. *The OSS and HO Chi Minh, Unexpected Allies in the War Against Japan*. Lawrence, KS: Kansas University Press, 2006.

Bigler, Philip. *In Honored Glory*. Arlington, VA: Vandamere Press, 1987.

"Cadet Leadership Development System", *US Military Academy Circular*, July 1944, 1–101.

Chamberlain, Joshua. *Bayonet Forward, My Civil War Reminiscences*. Gettysburg, PA: Stan Clark Military Books, 1994.

Clausewitz, Carl von. *On War*. Princeton, NJ: Princeton University Press, 1976.

Clinton, William. "Remarks at a Memorial Day Ceremony in Arlington, Virginia, May 25, 1998". *Presidential Documents*, Volume 34, Number 22, June 1, 1998.

Dalton, Ernest. "Foley Nets 44". *Boston Globe*, March 2, 1959.

Department of the Army Historical Summary: FY 1986. "Appendix A – Tragedy at Gander, 2". Accessed June 11, 2022. https://history.army.mil/books/DAHSUM/1986/appA.htm.

Dineen, Joseph E. *The Illustrated History of Sports at the US Military Academy*. Norfolk, VA: The Donning Company, 1988.

Director of Cadet Activities, "Bugle Notes" (84th Volume, booklet of information given to new cadets. West Point, 1992).

Dolormente, Maura. *Historic "Wolfhounds" of Schofield Barracks Mark 50th Year Bringing Japan Orphans to Hawaii*. Honolulu, HI: Peace Bridge, Inc, 2007.

History.com Editors, "President Eisenhower delivers Cold War 'domino theory' speech". Accessed June 12, 2022. https://www.history.com/this-day-in-history/eisenhower-gives-famous-domino-theory-speech.

Eisele, Chuck. "Malcolm Comes Through in Clutch for Army Win". *Pointer View*, December 11, 1992.

Equilar Board Edge. "Richard M. Kleberg, Executive Work History". Accessed June 12, 2022. https://people.equilar.com/bio/richard-kleberg-cullenfrost-bankers-inc/1920872.

Esterbrook, John. "Companies Well Represented". *Pointer View*. November 1992.

Fehrenbach, T. R. *This Kind of War: The Classic Korean War History*. Washington, D.C.: Brassey's, 1963.

Foley, Robert. "To what extent did Athens and Sparta pursue military strategies consistent with their political objectives during the various phases of the Peloponnesian War?" Foundations of Moral Obligation. Essay response written at Naval War College, August 29, 1978.

Foley, Robert. "The Com Reports". *Assembly Magazine*, November 1992.

Foley, Robert. "The Com Reports". *Assembly Magazine*, May 1993.

Foley, Robert. "The Com Reports". *Assembly Magazine*, September 1993.

Foley, Robert. "The Com Reports". *Assembly Magazine*, January 1994.

Foley, Robert. "The Com Reports". *Assembly Magazine*, July 1994.

Foley, Robert and Goudreau, Denise A. "Consideration of Others". *Military Review* (January–February 1996).

Fort Sam Houston Museum Staff. *The Quadrangle: Hub of Military Activity in Texas*. Fort Sam Houston, TX: Fort Sam Houston Museum, 2007.

Frost, Robert. *Complete Poems of Robert Frost*. New York, NY, Chicago, IL, San Francisco, CA: Holt, Rinehart & Winston, 1916.

Goodwin, Doris Kearns. *Leadership: In Turbulent Times*. London: Penguin Random House, 2018.

Grant, John, James M. Lynch, and Ronald H. Bailey. *West Point: The First 200 Years*. Guilford, CT: Guilford Globe Pequot Press, 2002.

Hackworth, David. *Hack Note*. David Hackworth blogsite (August 1998).

Hammer, Michael and James Champy. *Reengineering the Corporation: A Manifestation for Business Revolution*. New York, NY: Harper Collins Publishers, 1993.

Hawkins, Dave. "Tension High Tonight for Sell-Out Game". *Belmont Herald*, February 12, 1958.

Headquarters, Department of the Army. *Field Manual 25-101: Battle Focused Training*. September 1990.

Headquarters, Department of the Army. *Field Manual 100-1*, "The Profession of Arms", June 14, 1994.

Headquarters, Department of the Army. *Training Circular 25-30: A Leader's Guide to Company Training Meetings*, April 27, 1994.

Headquarters, Department of the Army. *Training Manual Number 1 (Appendix F). New Cadet Training Schedule*, June 11, 1959.

Hollandsworth, Skip. "The Kings Palace". *Texas Monthly*, February 2016.

Job description, "Commanding General, Fifth United States Army". Fort Sam Houston, Texas.

King Ranch, "King Ranch's Legacy". Accessed June 12, 2022. https://king-ranch.com/about-us/history.

Lamance, Richard. "CASAs Sustain Army Strong". Accessed June 12, 2022. https://www.army.mil/article/20246/casas_sustain_army_strong.

McLellan, Phyllis I. *Silent Sentinel on the Potomac: Fort McNair 1791–1991*. Bowie, MD: Heritage Books, 1993.

McMaster, H. R. *Dereliction of Duty: Lyndon Johnson, Robert McNamara, the Joint Chiefs of Staff, and the Lies That Led to Vietnam*. New York, NY: Harper Collins, 1997.

McNamara, Robert. *In Retrospect: The Tragedy and Lessons of Vietnam*. New York, NY: Vintage Books, 1996.

McNamara, Robert, James Blight, Robert K. Brigham, Thomas J. Biersteker, and Herbert Schandler. *Argument Without End: In Search of Answers to the Vietnam Tragedy*. New York, NY: Public Affairs, 1999.

Medal of Honor Project 1987, "Above and Beyond the Call of Duty". CD video of the Medal of Honor ceremony.

Meloy III, Guy S. "The Battle of Attleboro" 3–5 November 1966, After-Action Report written by Guy S, Meloy III, Major General, U.S. Army Retired, Former Commander, 1st Battalion, 27th Infantry (Wolfhounds), August 2010.

Moïse, Edwin E. *Tonkin Gulf and the Escalation of the Vietnam War*. Chapel Hill, NC and London: University of North Carolina Press, 1996.

Nulsen Jr., Charles K. "Operation Attleboro: A flawed battle plan turned a combat training exercise in War Zone C into a bloody battle during the fall of 1966". PTSD Support Services, December 21, 1990. Accessed July 25, 2017. http://www.ptsdsupport.net/operation_attleboro.html.

"Opening Lecture of the Code and System". Loose notes, U.S. Military Academy Library, July 7, 1959.

Padula, Joe. "101st Airborne Remembers Soldiers of Gander Crash" (December 15, 2011). Accessed June 12, 2022. https://www.army.mil/article/70884/101st_airborne_remembers_soldiers_of_gander_crash.

Palmer, Dave R. "Superintendent's Letter". *Assembly Magazine*, May 1987.

Paschall, Rod. "Operation Attleboro – From Calamity to Crushing Victory" (June 20, 2011). Accessed June 12, 2022. https://www.historynet.com/operation-attleboro-from-calamity-to-crushing-victory/?r.

Phillips, Donald T. *The Founding Fathers on Leadership: Classic Teamwork in Changing Times*. New York, NY: Warner Books, 1997.

Plewes, Thomas J. "Message from the Chief, Army Reserve". *USARC Pamphlet 600-4*, A-3, August 1, 2000.

Position description, "Commandant of the United States Military Academy".

Reimer, Dennis J. "One Team, One Fight, One Future". *Total Army Integration*, 1998. 25-page pamphlet describing the Army Chief of Staff, General Reimer's intent for America's army to integrate the contributions of the Army National Guard, the U.S. Army Reserve, and the Active Army to ensure total Army readiness.

Rich, Charles W. G. "Operation Equality, Memorandum for the Superintendent, USMA", March 31, 1950.

San Francisco (UPI). "Pilot found false alarm escalated Vietnam War". *Stars and Stripes*, October 15, 1984.

Secretary of the Army Memorandum, "The Secretary of the Army's Senior Review Panel on Sexual Harassment", November 21, 1996.

Spector, Ronald H. *Advice and Support, The Early Years 1941–1960*. Honolulu, HI: University Press of the Pacific, 2005.

Steele, Dennis. "The Second Longest Day". *Soldier Magazine*, February 1986.

Stockdale, James Bond. "The World of Epictetus". *Atlantic Monthly*, 1978.

Stockdale, James B. and Joseph Brennan. "On Kant's Foundation on the Metaphysics of Morals", Foundations of Moral Obligation Unit Notes accompanying an elective class. Naval War College, 1978–79.

Summers Jr., Harry G. *On Strategy: A Critical Analysis of the Vietnam War*. New York, NY: Random House, 1982.

Superintendent's Lecture to the Class of 1963, July 14, 1959. U.S. Military Academy Library.

*The New York Times*, "Col. Clayton E. Wheat. 88. Chaplain at West Point." (July 13, 1970). Accessed January 20, 2021. https://nyti.ms/1ik9mnd.

Taubman, William. *Gorbachev: His Life and Times*. New York, NY: Norton and Company, New York, 2017.

The Civil War in the East. "West Point Officers in the Civil War". Accessed January 18, 2021. https://civilwarintheeast.com/west-point-officers-in-the-civil-war/.

Thomas, Bill. "Last Soldier buried in Tomb of the Unknowns wasn't unknown". *The Washington Post Magazine*, November 8, 2012.

Trulock, Alice Rains. *In the Hands of Providence: Joshua L. Chamberlain and the American Civil War*. Chapel Hill, NC and London: University of North Carolina Press, 1992.

United States v. CSM Gene McKinney, U.S. Army. "Motion to Dismiss Based upon Unlawful Command Influence in the Member Selection Process", December 27, 1997.

U.S. Army News Release. "Army Secretary Excuses MG Foley from Panel", Army Public Affairs, February 14, 1997.

U.S. Corps of Cadets Memorandum of Instruction. "New Cadet Barracks", U.S. Military Academy Library, February 1, 1960.

U.S. Military Academy. "Academic Record of Robert Franklin Foley, Class of 1963, West Point, New York".

U.S. Military Academy. *Behind the Scenes at the Cadet Mess*, Washington Hall pamphlet.

Visible Proofs: Forensic Views of the Body. "Michael Blassie unknown no more" (February 16, 2006). https://www.nlm.nih.gov/visibleproofs/galleries/cases/blassie.html.

Vowell, Michele. "Fatal Gander Crash". *The Fort Campbell Courier*, August 9, 2012.

West Point Association of Graduates. "The Reality is Now: Branch Night for the Class of 2021". https://www.westpointaog.org/west-point-branch-night-class-of-2021.

Wickham, Jr., John A. *Guideposts for a Proud and Ready Army*. Washington, D.C.: Dept of Army, 1985.

Wikipedia. "Central Office for South Vietnam". Accessed June 20, 2020. https://en.wikipedia.org/wiki/Central_Office_for_South_Vietnam

Wikipedia. "David Hackworth". Accessed November 1, 2020. https://en.wikipedia.org/wiki/David_Hackworth.

Wikipedia. "LeRoy Ellis". Accessed June 14, 2022. https://en.wikipedia.org/wiki/LeRoy_Ellis.

Wikipedia. "List of astronauts educated at US Military Academy". Accessed January 18, 2021. https://en.wikipedia.org/wiki/List_of_astronauts_educated_at_the_United_States_Military_Academy.

Wikipedia. "Newport, Rhode Island". Accessed June 14, 2022. https://en.wikipedia.org/wiki/Newport,_Rhode_Island.

Wikipedia. "René Edward De Russy". Accessed January 18, 2021. https://en.wikipedia.org/wiki/René_Edward_De_Russy.

Wikipedia. "The Hudson River". Accessed June 14, 2022. https://en.wikipedia.org/wiki/Hudson_River.

Wikipedia. "Tropical Storm Alberto". Accessed June 14, 2022. https://en.wikipedia.org/wiki/Tropical_Storm_Alberto_(1994).

Wikipedia. "27th Infantry Regiment (United States)". Accessed May 17, 2017. https://en.wikipedia.org/w/index.php?title=27th_Infantry_Regiment_(United States)&printable=yes.

YouTube. "25th Infantry Division Arrives in Vietnam". Accessed June 14, 2022. www.youtube.com/watch?V=_Wtj4CqatiA.

# Index